AUTOMOBILE TECHNICIAN CERTIFICATION TESTS

National Institute for Automotive Service Excellence Exam

ARCO Editorial Board

MACMILLAN • USA

Third Edition

Macmillan General Reference
A Simon & Schuster Macmillan Company
1633 Broadway
New York, NY 10019-6785

An Arco Book

Library of Congress Cataloging-in-Publication Division

Automobile technician certification tests : National Institute for
Automotive Service Excellence exam / ARCO Editorial Board.—3rd ed.
    p. cm.
Rev. ed. of: Automobile mechanic certification tests / David Sharp.
2nd ed. 1985.
ISBN 0-671-87071-8
1. Automobiles—Maintenance and repair—Examinations, questions, etc.
2. Automobile mechanics—Certification—United States.
I. Sharp, David, 1936- Automobile mechanic certification tests.
II. National Institute for Automotive Service Excellence.
III. ARCO Publishing.
TL152.S466   1993   93-34094
629.28'72'076   CIP

Manufactured in the United States of America

10 9 8 7 6 5 4

CONTENTS

THE CAREER PATH
OPEN TO YOU

Automotive repair is a rapidly expanding field with an increasing demand for competent, well trained technicians. This chapter provides essential information about the field in which you will be working, gives facts and figures concerning your chosen specialty, and points up how desirable and interesting your job can be. When you know more about your job, you'll be more inclined to study for it.

NATURE OF THE WORK

Anyone whose car has broken down knows how important the automotive technician is. The ability to make a quick and accurate diagnosis is a valuable skill that requires good reasoning ability and a thorough knowledge of automobiles. In fact, many technicians consider diagnosing "hard to find" problems one of their most challenging and satisfying duties.

When mechanical or electrical troubles occur, technicians first get a description of the symptoms from the owner or, if they work in a dealership, the service advisor who wrote the repair order. The technician may have to test drive the car or use test equipment, such as engine analyzers, volt-ohm meters, and compression gauges, to locate the problem. Once the cause of the problem is found, the technician determines what adjustments or repairs are needed to correct it.

Most automotive technicians perform a variety of repairs, others specialize. For example; *automatic transmission specialists* work only on gear trains, couplings, hydraulic pumps, and other parts of automatic transmissions. Because these are complex mechanisms, their repair requires considerable experience, training, and in-depth knowledge of hydraulics. *Tune-up specialists* work primarily with the ignition and fuel systems. Their job is to ensure efficient engine performance. They often use precision test equipment to locate malfunctions and make repairs.

Automotive *air-conditioning specialists* install, service, and repair air-conditioners and heaters. *Front-end specialists* perform wheel alignments, balance wheels, and repair steering and suspension systems. They frequently use special alignment equipment and wheel-balancing machines. *Brake specialists* adjust brakes, replace brake linings, repair hydraulic cylinders, and make other repairs on brake systems. Many technicians specialize in both brake and front-end service because the two fields are so closely related.

WORKING CONDITIONS

Generally, technicians work indoors. Modern automobile repair shops are well ventilated, lighted, and heated, but older shops may not have these advantages. Technicians frequently work with dirty and greasy parts, and in awkward positions. Many of the automobile parts and tools that they must lift are heavy. Minor cuts and bruises are common, but serious accidents can be avoided by keeping the shop clean and orderly and observing other safety practices.

PLACES OF EMPLOYMENT

Currently there are more than 800,000 persons working as automotive technicians. These technicians are employed by automobile dealers, independent repair shops, service stations, chain stores that have automobile service facilities, and fleet operators. Fleet operators would include; Federal, State, and local governments, taxicab and leasing companies, and other organizations that repair their own automobiles. Some technicians are also employed by automobile manufacturers to make final adjustments and repairs at the end of the assembly line.

The typical automotive repair shops employs from one to five technicians, but some large shops employ more than 100. Generally, automobile dealers employ more technicians than independent shops.

Automobile technicians work in every section of the country. Geographically, employment is distributed about the same as population.

TRAINING, OTHER QUALIFICATIONS, AND ADVANCEMENT

Automotive technicians have traditionally learned the trade on the job. Beginners would start as helpers, lubrication workers, or gasoline station attendants, and gracually acquire skills by working with experienced technicians. Although a beginner could make simple repairs after several months of experience, it would take 3 to 4 years to develop an expertise and earn the trust of the shop owner and customers. To learn a difficult specialty, such as automatic transmission repair, would require an additional year or two of experience.

The complexity of the modern automobile has drastically altered the traditional approach to training technicians. Good mechanical aptitude, although still necessary, is no longer enough to make it in the automotive repair industry. The technician of today must have an in-depth knowledge of electrical and hydraulic theory, understand physics, and have patience and persistence to diagnose and repair complex systems. Automotive technology changes on a daily basis. To succeed you must be willing to continue learning throughout your career. A good place to start is with a degree from an accredited junior college or trade school, upon graduation you are ready to begin your apprenticeship.

Most training authorities recommend a three or four year formal apprenticeship program. Apprenticeship programs are offered through many auto dealers and independent repair shops. These programs include both on-the-job training and classroom instruction. On-the-job training allows you to work with your hands as you establish your skills. Classroom instruction includes courses in related theory such as mathematics and physics and other areas such as shop safety practices and customer relations.

Technicians usually buy their hand tools and beginners are expected to accumulate tools as they gain experience. Experienced technicians invest thousands of dollars in tools, and are continually adding to their inventory. Employers often furnish large power tools, engine analyzers, and other test equipment and machine tools.

Employers sometimes send experienced technicians to factory training centers to learn to repair new models or to receive special training in automatic transmission or air-conditioning repair. Manufacturers also send representatives to local shops to conduct short training sessions. Automobile dealers may select promising beginners to attend factory-sponsored technician training programs.

Experienced technicians who have leadership ability may advance to shop supervisor or service manager. Technicians who like to work with customers may become service advisors. Many technicians eventually open their own repair shops or service stations, about 1 out of 7 automobile technicians is self-employed.

EMPLOYMENT OUTLOOK

Job opportunities for automobile technicians will be plentiful in the years ahead. Replacement needs are high in this large occupation. Thus, in addition to openings created by the growing need for these workers, thousands of jobs will arise each year as experienced technicians retire or change jobs. Employment of automobile technicians is expected to increase about as fast as the average for all occupations through the 1990's.

Persons who enter the occupation can expect steady work because the automobile repair business is not much affected by changes in economic conditions.

EARNINGS

Skilled automobile technicians employed by automobile dealers in 36 cities had estimated average hourly earnings of about two-thirds more than the average for non-supervisory workers in private industry, except those in farming. Salaries are rising due to the increased knowledge and expertise required to service new vehicles.

Many experienced technicians employed by automobile dealers and independent repair shops receive a commission related to the labor cost charged to the customer. Under this method, weekly earnings depend on the amount of work completed by the technician. Employers frequently guarantee commissioned technicians a minimum weekly salary. Skilled technicians usually earn between two and three times as much as inexperienced helpers and trainees.

Most technicians work between 40 and 48 hours a week, but many work even longer hours during busy periods. Technicians paid by the hour frequently receive overtime rates for hours over 40 a week.

Some technicians are members of labor unions. Among the unions organizing these workers are the International Association of Machinists and Aerospace Workers; the International Union, United Automobile, Aerospace and Agricultural Implement Workers of America; the Sheet Metal Workers' International Association; and the International Brotherhood of Teamsters, Chauffeurs, Warehousemen and Helpers of America (Ind.).

RELATED OCCUPATIONS

Automobile technicians repair and service automobiles. Other related occupations that also repair and service motor vehicles include automobile body repairers, customizers, painters, and service advisors as well as truck and bus technicians.

SOURCES OF ADDITIONAL INFORMATION

For more details about work opportunities, contact local employers such as automobile dealers and repair shops; locals of the unions previously mentioned; or the local office of the state employment service. The State employment service also may have information about apprenticeship and other training programs.

For general information about the work of automotive technicians, and apprenticeship training, write to:

Automotive Service Industry Association
444 North Michigan Avenue
Chicago, IL 60611

Automotive Service Councils, Inc.
188 Industrial Drive, Suite 112
Elmhurst, IL 60126

National Automobile Dealers Association
8400 Westpark Drive
McLean, VA 22102

PART ONE

Applying and Studying for Your Certificate

THE CERTIFICATION PROGRAM

The certification of automobile technicians is becoming a widely accepted standard of excellence throughout the automotive industry. In this book you will learn how to achieve recognition and advancement through this program. The instructions and information provided here will prepare you for the certification tests, and start you on your way to success in the automotive repair industry.

Automobile technicians who wish to become certified in an automotive specialty or to obtain certification as a General Automobile Technician can now do so through a series of tests sponsored by the National Institute for Automotive Service Excellence (ASE). Through this certification program the automobile technician can obtain professional recognition and enhance his changes for higher pay and advancement.

This entirely voluntary program may become a standard practice throughout the industry. Certification is now a mandatory prerequisite for obtaining a job in many repair facilities. At the news conference which introduced the program, it was hailed as a likely first step toward federal licensing of all automobile technicians.

The National Institute for Automotive Service Excellence now offers tests in the field of automotive repair, as well as certification programs for medium and heavy truck technicians, automotive body repairmen, and engine machinists. Light Vehicle Compressed Natural Gas certification, a new field, has recently been added to the program. This book is designed to help prepare you to take the automotive technician tests. The program is a series of eight tests, each test concentrates on a specific area of automotive repair. Certification is awarded for each of the individual tests that you pass. After successfully passing all eight exams, you are eligible to become Certified Master Automobile Technician once you meet the experience requirements.

WHY BE CERTIFIED?

The ASE Certification Program was set up to help automobile owners and automobile service employers distinguish and recognize competent, well trained, and experienced technicians. The certification program also provides a means for the technician to enhance his career.

Certification helps prove to your employer and customers that you have the knowledge and skills to diagnose and repair challenging problem vehicles. Certification is a symbol of quality work. Quality craftsmanship attracts customers and employers are proud to display and promote the fact that they hire certified technicians. Your certification proves that you are a professional and proud of your accomplishments. ASE provides the professional recognition that you deserve. Being certified displays your dedication to excellence, opens opportunities for advancement in your profession, and increases your earning potential.

WHAT DO I RECEIVE WHEN I AM CERTIFIED?

ASE certified technicians are recognized by the familiar Blue Seal of Excellencer logo. You will receive a certificate suitable for framing stating that you are a qualified technician. You will also receive badges to wear on your uniform which represent the area in which you are certified. In addition you will receive a wallet card stating your areas of certification, and a plastic card that your employer may use for display.

FOR HOW LONG IS MY CERTIFICATION GOOD?

Your certification is good for five years. At that time, you take a single re-certification test to renew your credentials. The second test will be half as long as the first tests you took, and it will deal primarily with the new developments and current techniques in automobile repair. This assures that certified technicians are up-to-date with the latest automotive repair and service procedures.

WHO MAY TAKE THE CERTIFICATION TESTS?

Anyone may apply for and take the tests. But in order to become certified you must obtain two years of work experience or a substitute for work experience, in the form of education or other training. If you already have the work experience or an appropriate substitute you will become certified immediately upon passing the tests.

WHAT MAY I SUBSTITUTE FOR EXPERIENCE?

You may substitute training in automotive technology for part, or all of the two year experience requirement. The following guidelines will help you see how credit for experience is granted with different types of training.

1. *High School*. Three years of automotive training in high school may be substituted for one year of work experience.
2. *Post High School*. Two full years of training in a public or private trade school, technical institute, college or apprentice program may be substituted for one year of experience.
3. *Course Work*. For short automobile training courses taken after high school, two months of training courses may be substituted for one month of experience.
4. *Completion of Apprenticeship*. Successful completion of a three-or four-year accredited apprenticeship program is acceptable as meeting the full requirement of two years of work experience.

ASE may also recognize other work experience than that as a technician and apply it toward the two year requirement. If you believe you have experience that warrants such credit, provide documentation along with your application, the institute will determine eligibility.

To have training substituted for experience submit the following:

1. A photocopy of a transcript of courses.
2. A statement of training.

3. A certificate showing satisfactory completion of an apprenticeship program.

Documents should show length of training and should be sent along with your registration form and fee payment. It is up to the discretion of ASE what will apply, and how much credit for experience is to be awarded.

WHO SPONSORS THESE TESTS?

Automotive technician certification tests are sponsored by the National Institute for Automotive Service Excellence. ASE is a non-profit corporation whose purpose is to encourage and promote, in the public interest, high standards of automotive service and repair. It is managed by a member Board of Directors, selected from the automotive service industry, government, education, and consumer groups. The Institute encourages the development of effective training programs and conducts research to determine the best methods for training automobile and truck technicians.

In order to take the tests a technician must register in advance and pay the registration and test fees.

ALL ABOUT THE TESTS

The more you know about the exams you will have to face, the better your chances of success. This chapter sets the stage for the exam to come and spotlights the steps toward scoring high. Here you will find everything you need to know about the exam, from when and where it is given and how to apply, to the kind of test you can expect and how you will be scored.

HOW DO I APPLY FOR THE TESTS?

The first thing you should do if you are considering certification is to write for a Registration Booklet. This pamphlet contains up-to-date and detailed information about upcoming tests, and includes an application. The booklet is free for the asking, simply write:

ASE Registration Booklet
P. O. Box 591
Herndon, VA 22070-0591

WHEN ARE THE TESTS GIVEN?

The tests are presently given twice a year, once each spring and again in the fall. In order to participate in the testing program you must send your registration one month in advance of the testing date. Tests are conducted at the same time nation wide, and are usually scheduled on several weekday evenings. Exact times and dates of upcoming tests are listed in the Registration Booklet.

WHAT TESTS ARE GIVEN?

There are eight tests given in the field of automobile technology. You may become certified in one automotive service area by passing the one test given in that area. To become certified as a Certified Master Automobile Technician you must pass all eight tests.

The eight automobile technicians tests are:

1. Engine Repair
2. Automatic Transmission/Transaxle
3. Manual Drive Train and Axles
4. Suspension and Steering
5. Brakes
6. Electrical Systems
7. Heating and Air Conditioning
8. Engine Performance

Since the Engine Performance Test and the Engine Repair Test are closely related, many people take both at the same time. In fact, many of the questions are the same for both tests so there are actually fewer questions to answer when you take them together.

How long are the tests? The tests consist of 40 to 80 multiple-choice questions, and there is a time limit for each exam. Presently, there are 40 questions for each of the Automatic Transmission/Transaxle, Manual Drive Train and Axles, and Suspension and Steering tests. Brakes, Electrical Systems, and Heating and Air Conditioning tests have 50 questions each. Engine Performance and Engine Repair tests each have 80 questions, however, 40 of them are identical so you only have to answer 120 questions when you take both at the same time. Recertification tests are composed of half as many questions as the original test for each specific field, and the two engine tests have 20 repetitive questions.

The tests are given in three sessions, and each session lasts four hours and fifteen minutes. Four separate testes are offered for two of the sessions, the eight recertification tests can be taken during the third session.

No matter which test you take, you must arrive at the start of the test session. Late arrivals will not be admitted because they may disturb those who have begun testing. Of course, if you finnish early, or are not registered for all the tests, you are free to leave early.

How many tests may I take? You may take one or all of the tests that are offered during each session. If you choose to take only one test in a particular session, you will still arrive at the beginning of that test session. You will be allowed to leave when you have completed that test.

The important thing is to pace yourself when you are taking multiple tests. Avoid spending too much time with one exam so you are unable to complete the others. If you are unsure of an answer, mark the choice that you feel is most correct. Try not to leave any blank spaces because questions not answered are considered wrong answers. It is to your advantage to answer as many questions as you possibly can, even if you have to guess, in the allotted time.

WHAT HAPPENS TO THE TEST RESULTS?

ACT Test Administration will notify you of your test results about six to eight weeks after the last test in the series is given. You will receive a confidential report. The report shows your score for each test, as well as highlights any areas of strength or weakness that your answers reveal. If you fail any test you may take it again at a future session without penalty. However, you will be required to register and pay the fee again.

Are the test results confidential? You are the only person who will know how you did on your test. The results will be sent to you by mail. No one else will be given a copy of your test results. No one may obtain test results by phone.

WHERE ARE THE TESTS GIVEN?

The tests are given at various locations throughout the United States, tests are also given in Guam, Puerto Rico, and the Virgin Islands. There are currently over 300 test sites, so there should be a location convenient for you. When you fill out your registration you indicate the city closest to you where you would like to take the test. Shortly before you take the test, you will be sent an admission ticket that will state the exact address of your test site. The tests are usually given in a school, college, or technical institute. In order to take the test in the location of your choice, you should register as early as possible, since applicants are sent to additional centers after a particular test center has been filled up.

What if I am not near a test center? Special test centers can be set up for registrants who are located more than 50 miles from a test center. Whenever 20 or more technicians register as a group, testing facilities can be made available where they are located.

Special testing arrangements are available for technicians with physical disabilities and learning impairments. You may also qualify to have a translator present during the test if English is your second language.

If you are in a remote location, disabled, or require a translator contact ASE by writing to:

ACT Test Administration
P. O. Box 168
Iowa City, IA 52243

All of the information you need to set up, or become part of, a special testing center is included in the ASE Registration Booklet.

EXAM FORECAST

The topics covered in each of the eight automobile technician tests is broken down in easy-to-read outline form. Look over the topics covered to plan your studies. If you feel you are weak in any of the areas listed under the test you wish to take, you should pay special attention to reviewing that subject.

You may pass one of the tests listed below to become certified in a given specialty. To become certified as a Master Automobile Technician you must pass all the tests. Frequently technicians choose to take both the Engine Repair Test and the Engine Performance Test on the same day, since some of the questions are the same for each test. However, you may take only one of the tests if you do not feel ready to take both at once. If you decide to take them together you will be tested on a total of 120 questions during that session, rather than the 160 required when taking each test separately.

TEST A1, ENGINE REPAIR TECHNICIAN (80 Questions)

1. General Engine Diagnosis
2. Cylinder Head and Valve Train Diagnosis and Repair
3. Block Diagnosis and Repair
4. Lubrication and Cooling Systems Diagnosis and Repair
5. Ignition System Diagnosis and Repair
6. Fuel and Exhaust Systems Diagnosis and Repair
7. Battery and Starting System Diagnosis and Repair

TEST A2, AUTOMATIC TRANSMISSION/TRANSAXLE TECHNICIAN (40 Questions)

1. General Transmission/Transaxle Diagnosis
2. Transmission/Transaxle Maintenance and Adjustment
3. In-Vehicle Transmission/Transaxle Repair
4. Off-Vehicle Transmission/Transaxle Repair
    A. Removal, Disassembly, and assembly
    B. Oil Pump and Converter
    C. Gear Train, Shafts, Bushings, and Case
    D. Friction and Reaction Units

TEST A3, MANUAL DRIVE TRAIN AND AXLE TECHNICIAN (40 Questions)

1. Clutch Diagnosis and Repair
2. Transmission Diagnosis and Repair
3. Transaxle Diagnosis and Repair
4. Drive (Half) Shaft and Universal Joint Diagnosis and Repair
5. Rear Axle Diagnosis and Repair
    A. Ring and Pinion Gears
    B. Differential Case Assembly
    C. Limited Slip Differential
    D. Axle Shafts
6. Four-Wheel Drive Component Diagnosis and Repair

TEST A4, SUSPENSION AND STEERING TECHNICIAN (40 Questions)

1. Steering Systems Diagnosis and Repair
   A. Steering Columns and Manual Steering Gears
   B. Power-Assisted Steering Units
   C. Steering Linkage
2. Suspension Systems Diagnosis and Repair
   A. Front Suspensions
   B. Rear Suspensions
   C. Miscellaneous Service
3. Wheel Alignment Diagnosis, Adjustment, and Repair
4. Wheel and Tire Diagnosis and Repair

TEST A5, BRAKE TECHNICIAN (50 Questions)

1. Hydraulic System Diagnosis and Repair
   A. Master Cylinders
   B. Fluids, Lines, and Hoses
   C. Valves and Switches
   D. Bleeding, Flushing, and Leak Testing
2. Drum Brake Diagnosis and Repair
3. Disc Brake Diagnosis and Repair
4. Power Assist Units Diagnosis and Repair
5. Miscellaneous Diagnosis and Repair
6. Anti-Lock Brake Systems Diagnosis and Repair

TEST A6, ELECTRICAL SYSTEMS TECHNICIAN (50 Questions)

1. General Diagnosis and Repair
2. Battery Diagnosis and Repair
3. Starting System Diagnosis and Repair
4. Charging System Diagnosis and Repair
5. Lighting System Diagnosis and Repair
   A. Headlights, Parking Lights, Taillights, Dash Lights, and Courtesy Lights
   B. Stoplights, Turn Signals, Hazard Lights, and Back-Up Lights
6. Gauges, Warning Devices, and Driver Information Systems Diagnosis and Repair
7. Horn and Wiper/Washer Diagnosis and Repair
8. Accessories Diagnosis and Repair
   A. Body
   B. Miscellaneous

TEST A7, HEATING AND AIR CONDITIONING TECHNICIAN (50 Questions)

1. A/C System Diagnosis and Repair
2. Refrigeration System Components Diagnosis and Repair
   A. Compressor and Clutch
   B. Evaporator, Receiver/Drier, Condenser, etc.
3. Heating and Engine Cooling Systems Diagnosis and Repair
4. Operating Systems and Related Controls Diagnosis and Repair
   A. Electrical
   B. Vacuum/Mechanical
   C. Automatic and Semi-Automatic Temperature Controls
5. Refrigerant Recovery, Recycling, and Handling

TEST A8, ENGINE PERFORMANCE TECHNICIAN (80 Questions)

1. General Engine Diagnosis
2. Ignition System Diagnosis and Repair
3. Fuel, Air Induction, and Exhaust Systems Diagnosis and Repair
4. Emission Control Systems Diagnosis and Repair
    A. Positive Crankcase Ventilation
    B. Spark Timing Controls
    C. Idle Speed Controls
    D. Exhaust Gas Recirculation
    E. Exhaust Gas Treatment
    F. Inlet Air Temperature Controls
    G. Intake Manifold Temperature Controls
    H. Fuel Vapor Controls
5. Engine Related Service
6. Engine Electrical Systems Diagnosis and Repair
    A. Battery
    B. Starting System
    C. Charging System

What Forms Do The Questions Take?

The items asked on the technician certification test are in the form of a question or a phrase followed by four options or suggested answers. You will select the one option that you think best answers the question or completes the statement.

Questions can be divided into four general categories, each test will have an assortment of the different types of questions. The questions will fall into these four categories:

1. Incomplete Phrases
2. Complete Questions
3. Two-part Questions
4. Negative Questions

TYPE ONE: INCOMPLETE PHRASE

In this type question you are given an incomplete sentence and asked to choose the word or phrase that best completes it.

Examples:

1. A compression test shows that one cylinder is too low. A cylinder leakage test reveals too much leakage and air can be heard coming out of the tail pipe. Which of these could be the cause?

    (A) Worn or broken piston rings
    (B) A leaking head gasket
    (C) An intake manifold leak
    (D) A burnt exhaust valve

    Answer: **(D)**. Although any of the problems will result in low compression, only an exhaust valve that is burnt or not seating will cause air to escape from the tailpipe during a cylinder leakage test.

2. A technician sets the proper electrode gap on a spark plug most accurately if he uses a?

(A) dial gauge
(B) round wire feeler gauge
(C) square wire feeler gauge
(D) conventional flat feeler gauge

Answer: **(B)**. A wire feeler gauge should be used to set the gap. The gap is correct when a slight pull is required to free the gauge from between the two electrodes.

TYPE TWO: COMPLETE QUESTION

In this type a complete question is asked, and you are to choose the word or phrase that best answers the question.

Examples:

3. After installing an automatic transmission, a technician hears a squealing noise when the unit is in operation. What is the most likely source of this trouble?

(A) Rear bearing
(B) Speedometer pinion
(C) Front pump drive sleeve or pump pinion
(D) Regulator body mating surfaces

Answer: **(C)**. When installing an automatic transmission, the technician will take care to align the torque converter parts with splines and drive members. They must freely fit the stator shaft, turbine shaft and oil pump. Forcing any of these will damage the parts. The source of a squealing noise is in the pump.

4. An engine is found to be missing on one cylinder. Of the following, what is the most likely cause?

(A) A defective sparkplug
(B) A clogged exhaust
(C) An overheated engine
(D) Vapor lock

Answer: **(A)**. All of the options might cause an engine to miss, but if it misses only on one cylinder a defective sparkplug is a likely cause.

TYPE THREE: TWO-PART QUESTIONS

In this type of question you are asked to evaluate the correctness or suitability of two phrases or statements.

Examples:

5. Technician A says that disc brakes are inherently self-adjusting. Technician B says that disc brakes have superior cooling to drum brakes.

Who is right?

(A) A only
(B) B only
(C) Both A and B
(D) Neither A nor B

Answer: **(C)**. Disc brakes are inherently self-adjusting. After each application the pad is pulled away from the disc only far enough to ensure that the brakes do not drag. Thus, the released position of the piston is continuously adjusted as the pad lining wears. The superior cooling of disc brakes is due to the two swept surfaces that allow cooling air to flow over them.

6. To load a battery to test its condition using the vehicle lights which of the following conditions must be met?
I. Engine running
II. Lights on low beam

(A) I only
(B) II only
(C) Both I and II
(D) Neither I nor II

Answer: **(C)**. Battery condition can be checked by measuring and comparing individual cell voltages while the battery is supplying a comparatively light current flow, low beam headlights generally draw about 10 amperes.

TYPE FOUR: NEGATIVE QUESTIONS

In this type question you are asked to select the sentence or phrase that is NOT true, or that is the EXCEPTION to a rule.

Examples:

7. Which of the following items is NOT part of a positive type crankcase ventilation (PCV) system?

(A) A metering valve
(B) An intake breather
(C) A road draft tube
(D) A manifold suction tube

Answer: **(C)**. The PCV system is a crankcase ventilating system that produces the circulation of air through the crankcase clearing it of water vapor, unburned hydrocarbons, and blow-by. The air passes into the intake system and into the combustion chambers. The metering valve, intake breather, and manifold suction tube are all part of this system.

8. The automotive power train includes all of the following EXCEPT the:

(A) clutch
(B) differential
(C) transmission
(D) steering gear

Answer: **(D)**. The power train consists of those items used to conduct power from the pistons to the wheels.

What Type Of Skill Is Tested?

It is likely that you already have the experience and skill to score successfully on the tests. By studying the following examples you will see how questions are designed to tap the areas of knowledge that you possess. Remember the tests are not designed to fool you. Choose the answer that seems most obvious based on your experience in repairing automobiles.

The automotive technician certification test includes questions that tap three areas of skill and knowledge. The three areas are:

1. Basic Technical Knowledge
2. Correction or Repair Knowledge and Skill
3. Testing and Diagnostic Knowledge and Skill.

BASIC TECHNICAL KNOWLEDGE

Basic technical knowledge requires that you be familiar with the various parts and components of a car and how they work. You need to know how each system in the car functions and what task each part of the system performs. You must also know the procedures and precautions to follow when working on the car, as well as, how to remove and replace, clean and inspect, and lubricate and adjust the components of the vehicle systems.

Basic knowledge questions ask: "What a particular part is?" and "How does it work?"

Examples:

1. Pressure in a mechanical fuel pump is maintained by?

   (A) a pump motor
   (B) rotating vanes
   (C) a needle valve
   (D) a spring under the diaphragm

   Answer: **(D)**. A mechanical fuel pump operates through the action of a rocker arm or push rod that pulls or pushes the diaphragm in one direction and then releases it. A spring under the diaphragm then forces the diaphragm in the opposite direction to create pressure.

2. In the fluid coupling of an automatic transmission, the purpose of the guide ring is to:

   (A) control the amount of fluid used
   (B) prevent gear backlash
   (C) reduce oil turbulence
   (D) prevent leakage in the system

   Answer: **(C)**. In a fluid coupling, oil turbulence reduces the torque and limits the effectiveness of the torque converter. The guide ring helps control the direction of oil flow for maximum efficiency.

CORRECTION OR REPAIR KNOWLEDGE AND SKILL

These questions challenge your ability to isolate the source of a problem and determine the best way to repair it. You must be familiar with the procedures and precautions to follow in disassembly, assembly, and reconditioning. You will need to know how to make major inspections and adjustments, as well as how to use shop manuals and precision tools.

Knowledge and skill questions typically ask: "What is the likely source of a problem?" and "How is the problem corrected?"

Examples:

3. A car with automatic transmission moves forward in neutral at high engine speeds. Of the following, what is the most likely cause?

(A) A broken thrust washer
(B) A leaking reaction shaft seal
(C) A faulty clutch check valve ball
(D) A sticking servo restrictor valve

Answer: **(C)**. The clutch check valve ball should prevent the transmission from being engaged when the car is in neutral.

4. When a technician removes a manual transmission, he may use pilot or guide pins to prevent damage to which of the following parts?

(A) The clutch shaft
(B) The pinion bearing
(C) The gear shift linkage
(D) The clutch friction plate

Answer: **(D)**. The clutch friction plate can be damaged easily unless the transmission is pulled straight out. Pilot or guide pins can aid in the removal of the transmission.

TESTING AND DIAGNOSTIC KNOWLEDGE AND SKILL

In order to find what is wrong and determine the effectiveness of repair, you must be able to recognize the existence of a problem, and know how to use testing equipment to diagnose the difficulty. You must be able to determine the effects of a malfunction, and find the specific cause of symptoms.

These questions will generally ask: "How do you find what is wrong?" and "How do you determine the effectiveness of work done?"

Examples:

5. Discharges from which of the following show up as high voltage surges on the oscilloscope?

(A) battery
(B) distributor
(C) ballast resistor
(D) coil high-tension terminal

Answer: **(D)**. The ignition coil acts as a transformer to step up the battery voltage to thousands of volts. The high-voltage surge then produces a spark at the sparkplug gap. This surge from the coil high-tension terminal registers on the oscilloscope.

6. When a technician measures the distance from the right side lower ball joint to a point on the left side of the rear axle, this is done to check the accuracy of?

(A) camber
(B) caster
(C) tracking
(D) toe-in

Answer: **(C)**. During straight ahead operation the rear wheels of the vehicle must duplicate the path of the front wheels. To complete the operation described, a measurement is made from the left-side lower ball joint to a point on the right side of the rear axle. The length of the two diagonal lines should be within one-quarter inch of equal. If not, the frame of the vehicle is bent or the rear axle is off-center.

PART TWO

Basic Technical Knowledge: Skill in Repair Testing and Diagnosis

ANALYSIS OF THE AUTOMOTIVE TECHNICIAN CERTIFICATION TESTS

For each area of certification there are certain things you are expected to know and tasks you should be able to perform. In this section we will give a brief description of what may be included on each examination.

ENGINE REPAIR EXAM ANALYSIS, TEST A1

The examination to become a Certified Engine Repair Technician is composed of 80 questions from seven categories. Here we will detail the seven categories and briefly explain what you need to know to get a passing score on the exam.

1. General Engine Diagnosis

General diagnosis is an important part of engine repair and is generally the largest category of the test. You can expect to see about 18 to 20 questions, over 20 percent, that deal with engine diagnosis. You are expected to be able to:

- Understand and verify a customer complaint, road test the vehicle in question, and determine repairs needed to remedy the problem.
- Visually inspect an engine for fuel, oil, coolant, or other leaks, and determine the necessary repair operations. Listen to engine noises, locate the origin of the noise, and determine the appropriate repair.
- Identify the cause of excessive oil consumption and unusual exhaust color, odor, and sound, then determine the operations required to correct the problem.
- Use a vacuum gauge to isolate internal engine problems, and recommend repairs based on the gauge readings.
- Perform a cylinder power balance test, interpret test results, and recommend repairs.
- Perform a compression test, both wet and dry, and diagnose internal problems based on the test results.
- Perform a cylinder leakage test to establish the exact nature of a compression loss, and determine the necessary repairs.

2. Cylinder Head and Valve Train Diagnosis and Repair

The cylinder head and valve train is perhaps the most complex assembly of an engine, and the leading cause of engine failure. This is generally the second largest category on the examination, you can expect about 16 to 18 cylinder head and valve train questions. You are expected to be able to:

- Properly remove a cylinder head, inspect the head for cracks, surface warpage, and general condition.
- Install a new cylinder head gasket and properly tighten the head bolts to factory specifications.
- Inspect valve springs by checking squareness, tension pressure, and free height.
- Inspect valve spring retainers, keepers, and valve stem grooves to determine usable condition.
- Replace valve guide seals.
- Inspect valve guides for wear, check valve guide height, measure stem-to-guide clearance, and determine needed repairs.
- Inspect valves, grind the valve face to the proper angle and finish, and grind the valve tip.
- Inspect valve seats, restore seating angles, and install or replace seat inserts.
- Check valve-to-seat contact and seat concentricity, service as necessary to restore proper seating.
- Measure valve stem height and spring assembled height, service as required to restore proper height and position.
- Inspect pushrods, rocker arms, rocker arm pivots, and rocker shafts for wear or damage, repair or replace as necessary. Also, check cylinder head oil galleries and correct any restriction or blockage.
- Inspect, test, and replace hydraulic and mechanical valve lifters.
- Adjust valve lash clearance, both hydraulic and mechanical lifters, to specification.
- Inspect and replace as necessary gear, chain, and belt camshaft drives. Check gear wear patterns and measure backlash.
- Inspect and accurately measure OHC camshaft journals and lobes to determine condition.
- Inspect and measure OHC camshaft bearings for damage, out-of-round, and misalignment, repair as necessary.
- Check camshaft timing according to specifications.

3. Block Diagnosis and Repair

Engine Block Diagnosis and Repair also constitutes a large portion of the examination. Approximately twenty percent of the test questions will deal with bottom-end problems. Expect to see about 15 to 17 block related questions. You are expected to be able to:

- Remove and replace oil pans, side covers, front covers, gaskets, and seals.
- Assemble parts using formed-in-place (RTV silicone) gasket sealants.
- Inspect a cylinder block for cracks, oil and coolant passage condition, core and gallery plug condition, and deck surface warpage to determine needed repairs.
- Inspect and repair damaged threaded holes.
- Remove the cylinder wall ridge.
- Inspect cylinder bores and measure for taper and out-of-round to determine condition and needed repairs.
- Bore, hone, deglaze, and clean cylinder bores.

- Inspect and measure camshaft bearings for damage, out-of-round, and misalignment, repair as necessary.
- Inspect the crankshaft for surface cracks, journal damage, oil passage condition, and measure journal wear to determine overall condition and needed repairs.
- Inspect and measure main and connecting rod bearings for damage, clearance, and play to determine required repairs and select proper replacement bearings.
- Identify piston and bearing wear patterns that indicate connecting rod alignment problems. Check connecting rods for bend and twist using an alignment fixture.
- Inspect, measure, and repair or replace pistons, wrist pins, and wrist pin bushings.
- Measure piston ring end gap and side gap and properly install new piston rings.
- Remove the harmonic balancer, inspect, the balancer, crankshaft snout, key, and keyway, reinstall the balancer.
- Inspect the crankshaft flange and flywheel seating surface, repair as necessary.
- Inspect the flywheel for cracks, ring gear wear, and surface condition, repair as necessary. Install the flywheel and measure and correct runout.
- Inspect, remove, and replace the crankshaft pilot bushing or bearing.
- Remove, inspect, measure, and replace auxiliary shafts and bearings.

4. Lubrication and Cooling Systems Diagnosis and Repair

Diagnosing and repairing engine lubrication cooling system problems accounts for about twelve percent of the test. On the exam, expect to see 8 to 10 questions that deal with these two areas of engine repair. You should be able to:

- Perform an oil pressure test and interpret gauge readings to determine needed repairs.
- Disassemble, inspect, repair, and install an oil pump. Includes measuring gear and rotor clearances, servicing pressure relief valves, and inspecting pump drives.
- Inspect the cooling system components and perform a pressure test to determine needed repairs.
- Inspect, install, and adjust drive belts, both V-type and serpentine, and inspect and replace drive pulleys.
- Inspect and replace radiator and heater hoses.
- Remove, inspect, and test a thermostat and housing, replace as necessary and reinstall.
- Test coolant condition. Drain, flush, refill, and bleed the cooling system using the recommended coolant and blending it to the proper concentration.
- Remove, inspect, and replace a water pump.
- Remove, inspect, and replace a radiator, expansion tank, and pressure cap.
- Remove, inspect, and replace a cooling fan, both engine driven and electric. Service a fan clutch and any cooling related electrical sensors, relays, and switches.
- Inspect, test, and repair or replace an auxiliary oil cooler.

5. Ignition System Diagnosis and Repair

Because the ignition system is covered in detail by the Engine Performance Test, only a small portion (less then ten percent) of the Engine Repair Test deals with ignition system service. Expect to see about six to eight ignition related questions on the actual examination. For engine repair, you are expected to be able to:

- Diagnose no-start, hard-start, and misfire problems on engines equipped with both electronic and breaker point ignition systems.
- Inspect, test, and repair or replace ignition primary circuit wiring and components.
- Inspect, test, rebuild, and install a distributor. Includes servicing both mechanical and vacuum advance units.
- Inspect, test, replace, and adjust breaker points and condensers.
- Inspect, test, and repair or replace ignition secondary circuit wiring and components.
- Inspect, test, and replace an ignition coil.
- Check and adjust ignition timing and check timing advance.
- Inspect, test, and replace electronic ignition sensors, pick-ups and other related components.
- Inspect, test, and replace electronic ignition control units.

6. Fuel and Exhaust Systems Diagnosis and Repair

Like ignition systems, the fuel and exhaust systems are covered more in-depth by the Engine Performance Test. Expect to see about six to eight fuel and exhaust related questions on the actual examination. You are expected to be able to:

- Inspect, test and replace fuel pumps and pump controls, and service the fuel filter.
- Inspect and service fuel injection air induction systems. Includes removing and replacing intake manifolds and gaskets, as well as checking and adjusting idle speed and fuel mixture.
- Remove and replace air filter elements and service the filter housing.
- Inspect, remove, and replace exhaust manifolds, heat control valves, catalytic converters, mufflers, pipes, and heat shields.
- Test the operation of the positive crankcase ventilation system.
- Inspect, remove, and replace positive crankcase ventilation valves and related devices.
- Inspect, remove, and replace positive crankcase ventilation filters, hoses, and piping.
- Test turbocharger operation, and repair as necessary.

7. Battery and Starting System Diagnosis and Repair

The Electrical System Test features in-depth coverage of the battery and starting system, so expect only a few questions on this examination. You should be able to:

- Inspect, test, and service a battery.
- Recharge a battery by both the fast-charge and slow-charge method.

- Properly jump start a vehicle using jumper cables and an auxiliary power source or booster battery.
- Inspect, test, replace, and service battery cables and terminal connections.
- Inspect, test, repair, and replace starter solenoids, starter relays, and starter circuit wiring.
- Test, remove, and replace a starter motor.

In the actual ASE examinations, 40 of the questions for this test are identical to ones on the Engine Performance Test. When preparing for the actual examinations, the more review, the better your chances for a high score. Therefore, in our sample exams, we chose not to repeat questions on the two tests. Keep this in mind, and allow yourself a little extra time.

AUTOMATIC TRANSMISSION/TRANSAXLE EXAM ANALYSIS, TEST A2

The Certified Automatic Transmission/Transaxle Technician Examination is composed of 40 questions from four main categories. Here we will detail the categories and briefly explain what you need to know to get a passing score.

1. General Transmission/Transaxle Diagnosis

About 35 percent of the transmission/transaxle test will involve general diagnostic procedures. You are expected to be able to:

- Understand and verify a customer complaint, road test the vehicle in question, and determine repairs needed to remedy the problem.
- Diagnose and isolate noise and vibration problems to determine the appropriate repairs.
- Diagnose fluid related problems and determine needed repairs based on fluid level, usage, and condition.
- Perform a pressure test and recommend repairs based on test results.
- Perform a stall test and determine needed repairs based on test results.
- Test a lock-up torque converter system and recommend needed repairs.
- Diagnose problems in electronic, mechanical, and vacuum control systems to recommend needed repairs.

2. Transmission/Transaxle Maintenance and Adjustment

With only about 4 to 5 questions, maintenance and adjustment is the smallest category of the test. You should be able to:

- Inspect, adjust and replace the linkage for the manual shift valve.
- Inspect, adjust and replace the cables, or linkages for the throttle valve, kickdown, and accelerator.
- Perform a band adjustment according to specification.
- Perform a fluid maintenance service, including replacement of the filter or screen.
- Inspect, adjust, and replace electronic sensors, as well as repair wiring circuits and connectors.

3. In-Vehicle Transmission/Transaxle Repair

Approximately 8 to 10 test questions will deal with in-vehicle repair procedures. You should have the abilities to:

- Inspect, adjust, and replace a vacuum modulator valve, and repair or replace vacuum lines and hoses.
- Remove, disassemble, and repair the governor valve. Repairs include removing and replacing the cover, seals, sleeve, weights, springs, retainers, and gear.

27

- Inspect and replace all external seals and gaskets.
- Inspect, repair, and replace the extension housing.
- Inspect, test, flush, and replace the fluid cooler lines and fittings.
- Remove the speedometer drive assembly and replace the drive gear, driven gear, and repair as necessary.
- Remove and disassemble the valve body. Inspect mating surfaces, bores, valves, springs, retainers, check balls, screens, and spacers. Reassemble the valve body with new gaskets.
- Install the valve body, properly torque the retaining bolts, and make all necessary connections and adjustments.
- Remove the servo, inspect the bore, piston, seals, pin, spring, and retainers. Replace parts as necessary and reinstall the servo.
- Remove the accumulator, inspect the bore, piston, seals, spring, and retainers. Replace parts as necessary and reinstall the accumulator.
- Inspect and replace the parking pawl, shaft, spring, and retainer.
- Inspect, test, adjust, and replace electronic and electrical processors, solenoids, sensors, relays, switches, and wiring harnesses.
- Inspect and replace chassis mounts, and properly align the power train.

4. Off-Vehicle Transmission/Transaxle Repair

Off-vehicle, or unit repair procedures account for about 30 percent of the entire examination. Unit repair can be broken down into four sub-categories, there will be questions from all four areas. You are expected to be able to:

Removal, Disassembly, and assembly
- Remove and replace automatic transmissions and transaxles.
- Disassemble the unit, then clean, inspect, and evaluate the component parts.
- Assemble unit and reinstall it in the vehicle.

Oil Pump and Converter
- Inspect the flexplate, converter attaching bolts, converter pilot, and pump drive surfaces.
- Inspect and flush the converter, measure end play, and test torque converter operation.
- Inspect, measure, and replace the oil pump housing and related parts.

Gear Train, Shafts, Bushings, and Case
- Check end play and preload to determine required service.
- Inspect, measure, select, and replace thrust washers and bearings.
- Inspect and replace shafts.
- Inspect oil sealing rings, ring grooves, and ring sealing surfaces.
- Inspect and replace bushings.
- Inspect and measure planetary gear assemblies, replace parts as necessary.
- Inspect the case castings, bores, and passages; repair or replace bushings, vents, and mating surfaces as required.
- Inspect, repair, and replace transaxle drive chains, sprockets, gears, bearings, and bushings.

- Inspect, measure, adjust, repair, and replace transaxle final drive components.

Friction and Reaction Units
- Inspect the clutch pack assembly and replace parts as needed.
- Measure clutch pack clearance and adjust to specification.
- Perform an air pressure test on the clutch pack and servo assemblies.
- Inspect one-way clutch and sprag assemblies, replace parts as needed.
- Inspect and replace friction bands and drum assemblies.

MANUAL DRIVE TRAIN AND AXLE EXAM ANALYSIS, TEST A3

The Certified Manual Drive Train and Axle Technician examination is composed of 40 questions from six main categories. Here we will detail the categories and briefly explain what you need to know to prepare for your certification.

1. Clutch Diagnosis and Repair

This category will include about 5 or 6 questions and accounts for approximately 15 percent of the entire examination. You are expected to be able to perform the following tasks:

- Diagnose clutch noise, binding, slipping, pulsation, and chatter problems and recommend needed repairs.
- Inspect, adjust, repair, and replace clutch linkages, cables, and automatic adjuster assemblies.
- Inspect, adjust, repair, and replace clutch hydraulic cylinders (slave and master), lines, and hoses.
- Inspect, adjust, and replace the clutch release bearing, actuating lever, and pivot.
- Inspect and replace the clutch pressure plate assembly.
- Inspect and replace the clutch disc assembly.
- Inspect and replace the pilot bearing or bushing.
- Inspect, repair, and replace the flywheel and ring gear.
- Inspect the bell housing and engine block mating surfaces and repair as necessary.
- Measure flywheel runout and crankshaft end play, determine needed repairs.
- Measure bell housing bore-to-crankshaft runout and face squareness, correct as necessary.
- Inspect, replace, and align the power train mounts.

2. Transmission Diagnosis and Repair

About 20 percent of the test (7 to 8 questions) will involve transmission diagnosis and repair. You must be able to perform the following procedures:

- Diagnose transmission noise, hard shifting, jumping out of gear, and fluid leakage problems to recommend needed repairs.
- Inspect, adjust, and replace shift linkages, brackets, pivots, cables, and levers.
- Inspect and replace gaskets and seals, inspect sealing surfaces for damage.
- Remove and replace the transmission assembly.
- Disassemble the transmission and clean component parts.
- Inspect, repair, and replace the shift cover, shift forks and related grommets, levers, shafts, sleeves, detents, interlocks, and springs.
- Inspect and replace input shaft and bearings.

- Inspect and replace main shaft gears, shaft, thrust washers, bearings, and retainers.
- Inspect and replace synchronizer assemblies, includes hubs, sleeves, keys, springs, blocking rings, and sliding collars.
- Inspect and replace counter shaft gears, shaft, thrust washers, bearings, and retainers.
- Inspect and replace the reverse idler gear, shaft, bearings, thrust washers, and retainers.
- Measure and adjust gear end play.
- Inspect, repair, and replace the extension housing and transmission case mating surfaces, bores, vents, and bushings.
- Inspect and replace the speedometer drive gear, driven gear, and retainer.
- Inspect and repair any lubrication devices.

3. Transaxle Diagnosis and Repair

Approximately 22 percent (8 to 10 questions) will be about diagnosing and repairing transaxles. Many of the tasks are similar to those for transmissions, you are expected to be able to:

- Diagnose transaxle noise, hard shifting, jumping out of gear, and fluid leakage problems to recommend needed repairs.
- Inspect, adjust, and replace shift linkages, brackets, pivots, cables, and levers.
- Inspect and replace gaskets and seals, inspect sealing surfaces for damage.
- Remove and replace the transaxle assembly.
- Disassemble the transaxle and clean component parts.
- Inspect, repair, and replace the shift cover, shift forks and related grommets, levers, shafts, sleeves, detents, interlocks, and springs.
- Inspect and replace input shaft and bearings.
- Inspect and replace output shaft gears, shaft, thrust washers, bearings, and retainers.
- Inspect and replace synchronizer assemblies, includes hubs, sleeves, keys, springs, blocking rings, and sliding collars.
- Inspect and replace counter shaft gears, shaft, thrust washers, bearings, and retainers.
- Inspect and replace the reverse idler gear, shaft, bearings, thrust washers, and retainers.
- Inspect, repair, and replace the transaxle case mating surfaces, bores, vents, and bushings.
- Inspect and replace the speedometer drive gear, driven gear, and retainer.
- Diagnose differential assembly noise and vibration problems and recommend needed repairs.
- Remove and replace the differential assembly.
- Inspect, measure, replace, and adjust the differential carrier, spider gears, shaft, side gears, and thrust washers.
- Inspect, remove, and replace differential side bearings.
- Measure shaft end play and preload the assembly by selecting the correct shims or spacers.
- Inspect and repair any lubrication devices.

4. Drive Shaft and Universal Joint Diagnosis and Repair

Problems and repairs for both RWD propeller and FWD half shaft assemblies are included in this section. Expect to see 5 to 6 questions (15 percent) in this category. You should be able to:

- Diagnose noise and vibration problems that relate to drive shafts, universal joints, and constant velocity joints to determine required repairs.
- Inspect, service, and replace drive shafts. Includes RWD slip yokes and universal joints, as well as FWD constant velocity joints and boots.
- Inspect, service, and replace the drive shaft center support bearing.
- Check and correct drive shaft balance.
- Measure drive shaft runout.
- Measure and adjust drive shaft angles to specification.

5. Rear Wheel Drive Axle Diagnosis and Repair

This portion of the examination concerns RWD vehicles only and constitutes about 20 percent of the entire test. There are four sub-categories and you can expect at least one question from each. You are expected to be able to:

A. Ring and Pinion Gears
- Diagnose noise, vibration, and leakage problems and determine needed repairs.
- Inspect, remove, and replace the companion flange and pinion seal, and measure companion flange runout.
- Inspect, remove, and replace the ring gear.
- Measure ring gear runout and repair as required.
- Inspect, remove, and replace the pinion gear. Includes replacing sleeves and bearings, and properly installing a collapsible spacer.
- Measure pinion depth and adjust to specifications.
- Measure pinion bearing preload and adjust to specifications.
- Measure side bearing preload and ring and pinion backlash, adjust to specifications.
- Check ring and pinion gear tooth contact pattern and adjust assembly for proper contact.

B. Differential Case Assembly
- Diagnose noise and vibration problems to determine needed repairs.
- Remove and replace the differential assembly and ring gear.
- Inspect, measure, replace, and adjust the differential spider gears, shaft, side gears, and thrust washers.
- Inspect, remove, and replace differential side bearings.
- Measure differential case runout to determine needed repairs.

C. Limited-Slip Differential
- Diagnose limited-slip differential noise, slippage, and chatter problems to determine needed repairs.
- Perform a fluid maintenance service, flush the differential and refill with the proper lubricant.
- Inspect, remove, replace and adjust a clutch pack.

D. Axle Shafts

- Diagnose rear axle shaft noise, vibration, and leakage problems to determine needed repairs.
- Inspect, remove, and replace rear axle wheel studs.
- Remove and replace rear axle shafts.
- Inspect, remove and replace rear axle shaft seals, bearings, and retainers.
- Measure rear axle flange runout and shaft end play to determine needed repairs.

6. Four-Wheel Drive Component Diagnosis and Repair

This is the smallest category on the test. Expect only 3 to 4 questions that pertain to four-wheel drive (4WD) components. You should be familiar with the techniques to:

- Diagnose 4WD assembly noise, vibration, leakage, steering, and shifting problems to determine needed repairs.
- Inspect transfer case shift mechanisms, bushings, mounts, levers, and brackets, then adjust and repair as required.
- Inspect and service transfer case components and fluid level.
- Inspect, service, and replace front-drive propeller shafts and universal joints.
- Inspect, service, and replace front-drive axle knuckles and driving shafts.
- Inspect, service, and replace front wheel bearings and hub locking mechanisms.
- Check 4WD unit seals and inspect and clear remote vents.

SUSPENSION AND STEERING EXAM ANALYSIS, TEST A4

To be certified as a Suspension and Steering Technician you must success-fully complete a 40 question examination. The questions fall into four main categories. Here we will detail the categories and briefly explain what is expected of you in order to certify.

1. Steering Systems Diagnosis and Repair

There will be about 8 to 10 questions on steering system diagnosis and repair. Each question will fall into one of the three sub-categories that are detailed below:

Steering Columns and Manual Steering Gears
- Diagnose steering column noises, looseness, and binding problems to determine needed repairs. Tilt and telescoping mechanisms may be included.
- Diagnose manual steering gear problems to determine needed repairs. This section does not include rack-and-pinion units. You must be familiar with noise, binding, uneven turning effort, hard turning, and leakage problems.
- Diagnose rack and pinion steering gear problems, such as noise, vibration, looseness, and hard steering, to determine necessary repair methods.
- Inspect, repair, and replace steering shaft flexible couplings and joints, collapsible columns, and steering wheels. Air bag equipped steering wheels are included.
- Remove and replace manual steering gears, except rack and pinion units.
- Adjust manual steering gear worm bearing preload and sector lash (except rack and pinion).
- Remove and replace a rack and pinion steering gear.
- Adjust a rack and pinion steering gear to specification.
- Inspect, remove, and replace rack and pinion steering gear inner tie rod ends and bellows.
- Inspect, remove, and replace rack-and-pinion steering gear mount-ing bushings and brackets.

Power-Assisted Steering Units
- Diagnose power steering gear problems to determine needed repairs. This section does not include rack and pinion units. You must be familiar with noise, binding, uneven turning effort, loose-ness, hard steering, and leakage problems.
- Diagnose power rack and pinion steering gear problems, such as noise, vibration, looseness, hard steering, and fluid leakage, to determine necessary repair methods.
- Inspect power steering fluid level and condition and top-off fluid level according to specifications.

- Inspect power steering drive belts and adjust belt tension and alignment as necessary.
- Remove and replace the power steering pump and inspect the pump mounts.
- Remove and replace power steering pump seals and gaskets.
- Inspect, remove, and replace power steering pump pulleys.
- Pressure test the power steering system and determine needed repairs based on test findings.
- Inspect, remove and replace power steering hoses, fittings, and O-ring seals.
- Remove and replace a non-rack and pinion power steering gear.
- Remove and replace a power rack and pinion steering gear, inspect the mounting bushings and replace as required.
- Adjust Power steering gear worm bearing preload and sector lash (except rack and pinion).
- Inspect, remove and replace power steering gear seals and gaskets (except rack and pinion).
- Adjust power rack and pinion steering gear.
- Inspect, remove and replace power rack and pinion steering gear inner tie rod ends, seals, gaskets, O-rings, and bellows.
- Diagnose, inspect, adjust, remove, and replace electronic controlled steering system components.
- Drain, flush, fill, and bleed the power steering system.
- Diagnose, inspect, adjust, remove, and replace variable assist steering systems.

Steering Linkage
- Inspect and adjust front and rear steering linkage geometry, including attitude and parallelism.
- Inspect, remove, and replace the pitman arm.
- Inspect, remove, and replace the center link.
- Inspect, adjust, remove, and replace the idler arm and mountings.
- Inspect, remove, replace, and adjust tie rods, tie rod clamps, tie rod sleeves, and tie rod ends.
- Inspect, remove, and replace a steering damper.

2. Suspension Systems Diagnosis and Repair

About one third of the examination involves suspension system diagnosis and repair. Questions will be from three sub-categories. To receive a passing grade you should be able to perform the tasks listed below:

Front Suspensions
- Diagnose front suspension noises, body sway, and ride height problems to estimate needed repairs.
- Inspect, remove, and replace upper and lower control arms, bushings, shafts, and rebound bumpers.
- Inspect, adjust, remove, and replace strut rods, radius arms, and bushings.
- Inspect, remove, and replace upper and lower ball joints.
- Inspect, remove, and replace steering knuckle assemblies.
- Inspect, remove, and replace front coil springs and spring insulators.
- Inspect, remove, and replace front leaf springs, spring insulators, shackles, brackets, bushings, and mounts.

- Inspect, remove, and replace front torsion bars, and inspect torsion bar mounts.
- Inspect, remove, and replace a front sway bar (anti-roll bar), bushings, brackets, and links.
- Inspect, remove, and replace front MacPherson strut cartridges and assemblies.
- Inspect, remove, and replace front MacPherson strut upper bearings and mounts.

Rear Suspensions
- Diagnose rear suspension noises, body sway, and ride height problems to estimate needed repairs.
- Inspect, remove, and replace rear coil springs and spring insulators.
- Inspect, remove, and replace rear transverse links, control arms, sway bars (anti-roll bars), bushings, and mounts.
- Inspect, remove, and replace rear leaf springs, spring insulators, shackles, brackets, bushings, and mounts.
- Inspect, remove, and replace rear MacPherson strut cartridges and assemblies.
- Inspect a non-independent rear axle assembly for bending, warpage, and alignment problems.
- Inspect, remove, and replace rear ball joints and tie rod assemblies.

Miscellaneous Service
- Inspect, remove, and replace shock absorbers.
- Inspect, remove, and replace air shock absorbers, air lines, and fittings.
- Diagnose, remove, inspect, service, and replace wheel bearings.
- Diagnose, inspect, adjust, repair, remove, and replace electronically controlled suspension components.

3. Wheel Alignment Diagnosis, Adjustment, and Repair

With 12 to 14 questions, wheel alignment diagnosis and procedures account for a large portion of the examination. In order to guarantee a passing grade, you must able to perform the following tasks:

- Diagnose the cause of vehicle wander, drift, pull, hard steering, bump steer, memory steer, torque steer, and steering return problems to recommend needed repairs.
- Measure vehicle ride height and determine needed repairs.
- Check and adjust (where applicable) front and rear wheel camber.
- Check front and rear wheel camber and determine needed repairs when camber is non-adjustable.
- Check and adjust (where applicable) wheel caster.
- Check wheel caster and determine needed repairs when caster is non-adjustable.
- Check and adjust front wheel toe according to specifications.
- Properly center the steering wheel.
- Check toe-out on turns and determine needed repairs.
- Check the steering axis inclination angle and determine needed repairs.
- Check the included angle and determine needed repairs.
- Check and adjust rear wheel toe according to specifications.
- Check the rear wheel thrust angle and adjust or repair as required.

- Check for front wheel setback and correct as necessary.
- Check front sub-frame alignment and adjust or repair as required.

4. Wheel and Tire Diagnosis and Repair

A small portion, 4 to 6 questions, will deal with tire wear patterns and tire repair. You should be able to:

- Diagnose tire wear patters and estimate required repairs based on you observations.
- Inspect tire condition, check, and correct air pressure.
- Diagnose wheel vibration, shimmy, and noise problems to determine needed repairs.
- Rotate tires according to specifications.
- Measure wheel, tire, axle, and hub runout and recommend needed repairs based on your findings.
- Diagnose and correct tire pull or lead problems.
- Balance wheel and tire assemblies both statically and dynamically.

BRAKE EXAM ANALYSIS, TEST A5

The examination to become a Certified Brake Technician is composed of 50 questions from six main categories. Here we will detail the categories and briefly explain what you need to know to get a passing score.

1. Hydraulic System Diagnosis and Repair

Hydraulic system diagnosis and repair, the largest section of the test, is divided into four sub-categories. Expect a total of about 14 to 16 hydraulic system questions. Here we detail the operations you must be able to perform in each of the four sub-categories:

Master Cylinders
- Diagnose poor stopping and dragging problems caused by master cylinder failures, and determine repair procedures.
- Diagnose poor stopping, dragging, high or low pedal, and hard pedal problems caused by an internal malfunction of a step bore master cylinder.
- Measure and adjust brake pedal push rod length.
- Check master cylinder condition and determine needed repairs by depressing the brake pedal.
- Check master cylinder for secondary cup defects by performing a visual inspection.
- Remove the master cylinder from the vehicle.
- Disassemble the master cylinder, clean and inspect reusable parts, and hone the master cylinder if allowable.
- Reassemble the master cylinder using a rebuild kit.
- Check function of the master cylinder by bench bleeding.
- Reinstall the master cylinder, bleed and check operation of the hydraulic system.

Fluids, Lines, and Hoses
- Diagnose poor stopping, pulling, and dragging caused by problems in the brake fluid, lines, and hoses to recommend needed repairs.
- Inspect brake lines and fittings for leaks, damage, and wear, correct as necessary and tighten loose fittings and supports.
- Inspect flexible brake hoses for leaks, kinks, cracks, bulging, wear, and other damage, repair as necessary and tighten loose fittings and supports.
- Replace brake lines, double flare and ISO types, properly form the new line, and check and tighten fittings and supports.
- Select, handle, store, and install the correct brake fluid for a specific application.

Valves and Switches
- Diagnose poor stopping, pulling, and dragging caused by problems in the hydraulic system valves, and recommend needed repairs.
- Inspect, test, repair, and replace metering, proportioning, pressure differential, and combination valves.

- Inspect. test. repair, replace. and adjust load or height sensing proportioning valves.
- Inspect. test, repair. and replace the brake warning lamp, switch, and wiring.
- Re-set the brake pressure differential valve as required.

Bleeding, Flushing. and Leak Testing
- Properly flush and bleed the hydraulic system using the manual, pressure. surge. and vacuum methods.
- Perform a hydraulic brake system pressure test.

2. Drum Brake Diagnosis and Repair

Questions related specifically to drum brake service constitutes about 12 percent (5 to 7 questions) of the overall test. You are expected to be able to perform the following:

- Diagnose poor stopping, pulling, and dragging caused by drum brake hydraulic system problems, and recommend needed repairs.
- Diagnose poor stopping, pulling, grabbing, dragging, and noise caused by drum brake mechanical problems, and recommend needed repairs.
- Remove, clean, inspect, and measure brake drums. Machine or replace the drums based on your measurements and the factory specifications.
- Machine brake drums following the manufacturer's recommended procedures and specifications.
- Remove, clean and inspect brake shoes, springs, adjusters, pins, levers, clips, and other hardware. Follow proper safety procedures, and determine condition and needed repairs.
- Clean and inspect, following proper safety procedures, the brake backing plates. Repair or replace as required.
- Disassemble, clean, and inspect the wheel cylinders. Hone the cylinder bore (if allowable) and reassemble the cylinder using new cups, boots, seals, and other parts as needed.
- Use the proper lubricant to lube the shoe support pads on the backing plate, adjuster mechanisms, and other parts as required.
- Install new brake shoes and assemble the related hardware.
- Pre-adjust the brake shoes, then reinstall the brake drums, wheel bearings, and other related parts.
- Install the wheels, torque the lug nuts, and make final checks and adjustments.

3. Disc Brake Diagnosis and Repair

Approximately 25 percent (12 to 14 questions) of the test will be about disc brake diagnosis and service. The certified technician is expected to be able to perform the following:

- Diagnose poor stopping, pulling, and dragging caused by disc brake hydraulic system problems, and recommend needed repairs.
- Diagnose poor stopping, pulling, grabbing, dragging, and noise caused by disc brake mechanical problems, and recommend needed repairs.
- Remove a caliper assembly from its mountings, clean the unit, and inspect for leakage and damage to the caliper housing.

- Clean and inspect caliper mountings and slides for excessive wear and damage.
- Remove, clean, and inspect the brake pads and retaining hardware, determine needed repairs based on your observations.
- Disassemble the caliper, clean the components, and inspect for wear, rust, scoring, or other damage to determine condition.
- Reassemble the caliper using new seals, boots, and other worn or damaged parts.
- Clean and inspect the rotor, measure with a dial indicator and micrometer to determine condition, and machine or replace according to the manufacturer's recommendations.
- Remove and replace the rotor, service wheel bearings as required.
- Machine the rotor, if allowable and within tolerance, according to the manufacturer's procedures and specifications.
- Install new brake pads, refit the calipers, install attaching hardware, and bleed the hydraulic system.
- Adjust calipers with integrated parking brakes according to the manufacturer's procedures and specifications.
- Top-off master cylinder using the proper brake fluid and check for leaks.
- Install the wheels, torque the lug nuts, and make final checks and adjustments.

4. Power Assist Units Diagnosis and Repair

With only 3 to 5 questions, power assist unit service is the smallest of the test categories. As a certified brake technician, you are expected to be able to:

- Test brake pedal free travel with and without the engine running to determine power booster operation.
- Use a vacuum gauge to check supply vacuum for a vacuum boosted brake system.
- Inspect a vacuum booster unit for leaks and test the check valve for proper operation, repair, adjust, or replace parts as necessary to restore normal function.
- Inspect and test a hydraulically boosted brake system and accumulator for leaks and proper operation, repair, adjust, or replace parts as necessary to restore normal function.

5. Miscellaneous Diagnosis and Repair

This category includes; wheel bearings, parking brakes, electrical devices, and other miscellaneous brake system components. About 12 percent (5 to 7 questions) on the test will fall into this category. You are expected to be able to perform the following:

- Diagnose wheel bearing noises, shimmy, and vibration problems to determine and execute needed repairs.
- Remove, clean, inspect, and repack or replace wheel bearings. Includes removing and replacing bearing races and seals, and adjusting bearing preload to specifications.
- Check parking brake operation, inspect cables and related parts for wear and damage, and clean, replace, and lubricate parking brake components as required.
- Adjust the parking brake assembly for proper operation.

- Test, repair, and replace parking brake indicator lamps, switches, and wiring.
- Test, adjust, repair, and replace stop lamps, brake light switches, and wiring.

6. Anti-Lock Brake Systems Diagnosis and Repair

Presently, there are only about 4 to 6 anti-lock brake systems (ABS) questions on the certification test. Expect this category to grow in the future as ABS systems become more common place. You should be able to perform the following tasks:

- Follow accepted safety and service precautions while inspecting, testing, and servicing ABS hydraulic, mechanical, and electrical components.
- Determine needed ABS repairs by diagnosing poor stopping, wheel lock-up, pedal feel, pulsation, and noise problems.
- Observe the on-board ABS warning lamps during start-up to determine if repairs or further diagnosis is required.
- Diagnose ABS electronic controls using self-diagnostics or a factory approved scan tool to determine needed repairs.
- Relieve the ABS hydraulic system pressure according to factory procedures.
- Fill the ABS master cylinder reservoir to the proper level using the correct brake fluid and following the manufacturer's procedures.
- Bleed the ABS hydraulic circuits following the recommended manufacturer's procedures.
- Pressure test the ABS high-pressure hydraulic system to determine condition and needed repairs.
- Remove and replace ABS components according to the manufacturer's procedures and specifications.
- Test, service, and adjust ABS speed sensors following the manufacturer's recommended procedures.

ELECTRICAL SYSTEMS EXAM ANALYSIS, TEST A6

Eight main categories are included in the 50 question examination to become certified as an Electrical Systems Technician. To prepare you for taking the exam, we will detail the tasks you are expected to be able to perform. Here we briefly explain what you need to know from each of the categories:

1. General Diagnosis and Repair

This section, the largest of the test areas, deals with electrical theory and the various tools, meters, and gauges used to trouble shoot electrical circuits. Expect to see about 10 questions from this category on the examination. You should be able to perform the following tasks:

- Check continuity in electrical circuits using a test light to determine needed repairs.
- Check applied voltage and voltage drop in electrical circuits using a voltmeter to determine needed repairs.
- Check current flow in electrical circuits and components using a ammeter to determine needed repairs.
- Check continuity and resistance in electrical circuits and components using an ohmmeter to determine needed repairs.
- Check electrical circuits using jumper wires to determine needed repairs.
- Locate shorts, grounds, opens, and high resistance problems in electrical circuits and determine needed repairs.
- Diagnose the cause of abnormal battery drain, locate and correct the problem.
- Inspect, test, and replace fuses, fusible links, and circuit breakers.

2. Battery Diagnosis and Repair

About ten percent of the examination (5 to 6 questions) will be on battery diagnosis and service. You should be able to do the following:

- Perform a battery state-of-charge test to determine battery condition and needed service.
- Perform a battery capacity test (load test, high-rate discharge test) to determine general battery condition and recommend needed service.
- Perform a three-minute charge test on a low-maintenance battery to determine general battery condition and recommend needed service.
- Inspect, clean, top-off, and remove and replace a battery.
- Charge a battery, both slow and fast charge, according to the manufacturer's recommended procedure.
- Properly jump start a vehicle using jumper cables and an auxiliary power source or booster battery.

3. Starting System Diagnosis and Repair

Questions pertaining to the starting system will account for about ten percent of the total examination. You should be familiar with, and be able to perform the following operations:

- Perform a starter current draw test and determine needed repairs.
- Perform a starter circuit voltage drop test and determine needed repairs.
- Inspect, test, repair, and replace switches, connectors, and wiring in the starter control circuit.
- Inspect, test, repair, and replace starter solenoids and relays.
- Test, remove, and replace a starter motor.
- Disassemble a starter motor, clean, inspect, and test components, reassemble the starter using new parts as needed.
- Perform a free-running bench test on a starter motor, determine condition and repair as required.

4. Charging System Diagnosis and Repair

There will be 5 to 7 questions on charging system trouble shooting and service procedures. You should be able to perform the following tasks:

- Diagnose charging system problems that create an under-charge, no-charge, or over-charge condition.
- Inspect, adjust, and replace alternator drive belts, pulleys, and belt driven fan assemblies.
- Perform a charging system output test and determine needed repairs based on test results.
- Perform an alternator output test and determine needed repairs based on test results.
- Perform an alternator oscilloscope test and determine needed repairs based on test patterns.
- Inspect, test, repair or replace a voltage regulator.
- Perform a charging circuit voltage drop test and determine needed repairs.
- Inspect, repair, and replace charging circuit wiring and wire connectors.
- Remove and replace an alternator.
- Disassemble an alternator, clean, inspect, and test components, reassemble the alternator using new parts as needed.

5. Lighting System Diagnosis and Repair

Vehicle lighting system diagnosis and repair techniques make up about 12 percent of the total examination. This section is divided into two sub-categories, there will be several questions from each. You will need to be familiar with the following procedures:

Headlights, Parking Lights, Taillights, Dash Lights, and Courtesy Lights
- Diagnose the cause of brighter than normal, intermittent, dim, or non-operative headlights.
- Inspect, remove, replace, and aim sealed beam headlights and halogen headlight bulbs.
- Inspect, test, repair, and replace headlight switches, dimmer switches, and combination switches, as well as headlight circuit relays, sockets, connectors, and wiring.

- Diagnose the cause of intermittent, slow, or non-operative retractable headlight assemblies.
- Inspect, test, repair, and replace motors, switches, relays, connectors, and wiring of retractable headlight circuits.
- Diagnose the cause of brighter than normal, intermittent, dim, or non-operative parking lights or tail lights.
- Inspect, test, repair, and replace bulbs, switches, relays, sockets, connectors, and wiring of parking light or tail light circuits.
- Diagnose the cause of intermittent, dim, non-operative, or no brightness control of dash light circuits.
- Inspect, test, repair, and replace bulbs, switches, relays, sockets, connectors, printed circuit boards, and wiring of dash light circuits.
- Diagnose the cause of intermittent, dim, or non-operative courtesy lights.
- Inspect, test, repair, and replace bulbs, switches, relays, sockets, connectors, and wiring of courtesy light circuits.

Stoplights, Turn Signals, Hazard Lights, and Back-Up Lights
- Diagnose the cause of intermittent, dim, or non-operative stop lights.
- Inspect, test, repair, and replace bulbs, switches, sockets, connectors, and wiring of stop light circuits.
- Diagnose the cause of no turn signal or hazard lights, lights on but not flashing, and lights on but not flashing at all locations.
- Inspect, test, repair, and replace bulbs, switches, flasher units, sockets, connectors, and wiring of turn signal and hazard light circuits.
- Diagnose the cause of intermittent, dim, or non-operative back-up lights.
- Inspect, test, repair, and replace bulbs, switches, sockets, connectors, and wiring of back-up light circuits.

6. Gauges, Warning Devices, and Driver Information Systems Diagnosis and Repair

Expect to see 6 to 8 questions (14 percent of the test) on diagnosing and repairing gauge, warning light, and driver information systems problems. You are expected to be able to:

- Diagnose the cause of intermittent, high, or low readings on the dash gauges.
- Test, remove, and replace gauge circuit voltage regulators, limiters, and stabilizers.
- Inspect, test, repair, and replace gauges, gauge sending units, printed circuit boards, connectors, and wiring of gauge circuits.
- Diagnose the cause of intermittent, high, or low readings on electronic digital instrument clusters.
- Inspect, test, repair, and replace sensors, sending units, connectors, and wiring of electronic digital instrument clusters.
- Diagnose the cause of constant, intermittent, or non-operation of warning lamps or driver information systems.
- Inspect, test, repair, and replace bulbs, sockets, connectors, wiring, and electronic components of warning lamps or driver information systems.
- Diagnose the cause of constant, intermittent, or non-operation of audible warning devices.

- Inspect, test, repair, and replace switches, timers, electronic components, printed circuits, connectors, and wiring of audible warning device circuits.

7. Horn and Wiper/Washer Diagnosis and Repair

With only 3 to 4 questions, this is the smallest category of the Electrical Systems Examination. You should be able to perform the following tasks:

- Diagnose the cause of constant, intermittent, or non-operation of horns.
- Inspect, test, repair, and replace horns, as well as the relays, switches, connectors, and wiring of the horn circuit.
- Diagnose the cause of constant, intermittent, poor speed control, no parking, or non-operation of the windshield wipers.
- Inspect, test, repair, and replace intermittent wiper speed controls.
- Inspect, test, repair, and replace wiper motors, resistors, switches, relays, connectors, and wiring of the wiper circuit.
- Diagnose the cause of constant, intermittent, or non-operation of windshield washers.
- Inspect, test, repair, and replace washer motors, pump assemblies, switches, relays, connectors, and wiring of the washer circuit.

8. Accessories Diagnosis and Repair

There will be approximately 8 to 10 questions on accessory diagnosis and repair. The questions are divided into two sub-categories. You should be familiar with the techniques to:

Body
- Diagnose the cause of slow, intermittent, or non-operation of power windows.
- Inspect, test, repair, and replace motors, regulators, switches, relays, connectors, and wiring of power window circuits.
- Diagnose the cause of slow, intermittent, or non-operation of power seats.
- Inspect, test, repair, and replace motors, gear boxes, cables, slave units, switches, relays, solenoids, connectors, and wiring of power seat circuits.
- Diagnose the cause of poor, intermittent, or non-operation of the rear window defroster.
- Inspect, test, repair, and replace switches, relays, heating grids, connectors, and wiring of rear window defroster circuits.
- Diagnose the cause of poor, intermittent, or non-operation of electric door, trunk, and hatch locks.
- Inspect, test, repair, and replace switches, relays, actuators, motors, connectors, and wiring of electric door, trunk, and hatch lock circuits.
- Diagnose the cause of poor, intermittent, or non-operation of keyless entry systems.
- Inspect, test, repair, and replace components, connectors, and wiring of keyless entry system circuits.
- Diagnose the cause of slow, intermittent, or non-operation of electric sunroofs and convertible tops.
- Inspect, test, repair, and replace switches, relays, motors, connectors, and wiring of electric sunroof and convertible top circuits.
- Diagnose the cause of poor, intermittent, or non-operation of electrically operated and heated mirrors.

- Inspect, test, repair, and replace switches, relays, motors, heating grids, connectors, and wiring of electrically operated and heated mirror circuits.

Miscellaneous

- Diagnose the cause of static, intermittent, or no reception of the radio.
- Inspect, test, repair, and replace speakers, antennas, leads, grounds, connectors, and wiring of the sound system circuits.
- Inspect, test, repair, and replace switches, motors, connectors, and wiring of the power antenna circuits.
- Inspect, test, repair, and replace radio noise suppression components.
- Trim the radio antenna for optimum reception.
- Inspect, test, repair, and replace the case, integral fuse, connectors, and wiring of the cigar lighter circuits.
- Inspect, test, repair, and replace the clock, connectors, and wiring of the clock circuits.
- Diagnose the cause of unregulated, intermittent, or non-operation of cruise control systems.
- Inspect, test, adjust, and repair or replace speedometer cables, regulator, servo, hoses, switches, relays, electronic control units, speed sensors, connectors, and wiring of the cruise control circuits.
- Diagnose the cause of poor, intermittent, or non-operation of a vehicle anti-theft system.
- Inspect, test, repair, and replace the components, connectors, and wiring of the vehicle anti-theft system circuits.
- Diagnose the cause of the supplemental restraint (airbag) warning lamp staying on or flashing.
- Inspect, test, repair, and replace the airbag, module, inflator, sensors, connectors, and wiring of the supplemental restraint circuits.

HEATING AND AIR CONDITIONING EXAM ANALYSIS, TEST A7

The examination to become a Certified Heating and Air Conditioning Technician is composed of 50 questions from five categories. Here we briefly detail the categories and give you an idea of what you need to know to get a passing score.

1. A/C System Diagnosis and Repair

Approximately 25 percent (11 to 13 questions) of the examination involves air conditioning system diagnosis and repair procedures. You should be able to perform the following tasks:

- Diagnose the cause of unusual noise from the air conditioner and determine the needed repairs.
- Identify the type of air conditioning system, conduct a performance test, and determine needed repairs.
- Diagnose air conditioning system problems by viewing refrigerant flow past a sight glass and determine needed repairs.
- Diagnose air conditioning system problems using a manifold gauge set and determine needed repairs.
- Diagnose air conditioning system problems using visual, touch, and smell procedures to determine needed repairs.
- Perform a leak test on the air conditioning system to determine needed repairs.
- Identify and recover air conditioning system refrigerant.
- Evacuate the air conditioning system.
- Clean air conditioning system components and hoses.
- Charge the air conditioning system with refrigerant.
- Check compressor oil level, identify type of oil used, and top-off level as necessary.

2. Refrigeration System Components Diagnosis and Repair

Air conditioner system component diagnosis and repair procedures account for approximately 22 percent of the examination. This topic is divided into two sub-categories with about 5 to 6 questions each. You should be able to:

Compressor and Clutch
- Diagnose system problems that cause pressure protection devices to interrupt operation and determine needed repairs.
- Inspect, remove, and replace pressure protection devices.
- Inspect, adjust, and replace compressor drive belts and pulleys.
- Inspect, test, service, and remove and replace compressor clutch components and assemblies.
- Check compressor oil level, identify type of oil used, and top-off level as necessary.

47

- Inspect, test, service, and remove and replace the air conditioner compressor.
- Inspect, repair, and remove and replace the air conditioner compressor mountings.

Evaporator, Receiver/Drier, Condenser, etc.
- Inspect, repair, remove, and replace air conditioning system mufflers, lines, hoses, fittings, and seals.
- Inspect the condenser for air flow restrictions, clean and straighten fins.
- Inspect, test, remove, and replace the condenser and mountings.
- Inspect, remove, and replace the receiver drier.
- Inspect, remove, and replace the accumulator drier in orifice tube systems.
- Inspect, test, remove, and replace the expansion valve.
- Inspect, test, remove, and replace the orifice tube.
- Inspect, test, and clean or remove, and replace the evaporator.
- Inspect, clean, and repair or replace the evaporator housing and water drain.
- Inspect, test, and replace the evaporator pressure control systems and devices.
- Identify, inspect, and replace air conditioning system service valves.
- Inspect and replace air conditioning system high pressure relief devices.

3. Heating and Engine Cooling Systems Diagnosis and Repair

Expect to see about 5 to 7 questions about the vehicle heating and engine cooling systems on the examination. You are expected to be able to perform the following tasks:

- Diagnose the cause of temperature control problems in the heater and ventilation systems to determine needed repairs.
- Diagnose the cause of window fogging problems and determine needed repairs.
- Perform engine cooling system tests to determine needed repairs.
- Inspect and replace cooling system and heater hoses and belts.
- Inspect, test, remove, and replace the radiator, pressure cap, coolant recovery system, and water pump.
- Inspect, test, remove, and replace the thermostat, by-pass, and housing.
- Determine coolant condition and drain, flush and refill the cooling system using the proper coolant and recovery techniques.
- Inspect, test, remove, and replace both mechanical and electrical cooling fans, fan clutch, and fan shrouds.
- Inspect, test, remove, and replace the heater control valve, includes manual, vacuum, and electric valves.
- Inspect, flush, remove, and replace the heater core.

4. Operating Systems and Related Controls Diagnosis and Repair

The largest portion of the examination covers diagnosing and repairing operating systems and controls. This topic accounts for about one third of the total questions, and is divided into three sub-categories. Following is a list of tasks you should be able to perform in each of the sub-categories:

Electrical
- Diagnose the cause of failures in the electrical controls of the heating, air conditioning, and ventilation systems to determine needed repairs.
- Inspect, test, repair, and replace blower motors, relays, resistors, switches, modules, wiring, and protection devices.
- Inspect, test, repair, and replace the compressor clutch, relays, modules, resistors, sensors, switches, diodes, and wiring in the clutch control circuits.
- Inspect, test, adjust, repair, and replace air conditioner related engine idle control devices.
- Inspect, test, repair, and replace load sensitive air conditioner compressor cut-off systems and devices.
- Inspect, test, repair, and replace the fan, motor, relays, modules, sensors, switches, and wiring in the engine cooling circuit.
- Inspect, test, adjust, repair, and replace electric actuator motors, relays, modules, sensors, switches, wiring, and protection devices.

Vacuum/Mechanical
- Diagnose the cause of failures in the vacuum and mechanical controls of the heating, air conditioning, and ventilation systems to determine needed repairs.
- Inspect, test, service, and replace system control panel assemblies.
- Inspect, test, adjust, and replace system control cables and linkages.
- Inspect, test, and replace vacuum control switches and hoses.
- Inspect, test, adjust, and replace system vacuum motors.
- Locate, identify, inspect, test, and replace system vacuum reservoirs, check valves, and restrictors.
- Inspect, test, and repair or replace vent ducts, blend doors, distribution hoses, and outlets.

Automatic and Semi-Automatic Temperature Controls
- Diagnose temperature control system problems and determine needed repairs.
- Diagnose blower system problems and determine needed repairs.
- Diagnose air distribution system problems and determine needed repairs.
- Diagnose compressor clutch control system problems and determine needed repairs.
- Inspect, test, adjust, and replace climate control temperature sensor systems.
- Inspect, test, adjust, and replace vacuum and electric blend door power servo systems.
- Inspect, test, and replace low coolant temperature blower control systems.
- Inspect, test, and replace heater valve and controls.
- Inspect, test, and replace vacuum and electric motors, solenoids, and controls.
- Inspect, test, and replace the Automatic Temperature Control (ATC) panel.
- Inspect, test, adjust, and replace the ATC microprocessor.
- Check and adjust the calibration of the ATC system.

5. Refrigerant Recovery, Recycling, and Handling

Approximately ten percent (5 questions) of the examination is directed toward proper use and handling of refrigerants. You are expected to know the proper procedures for the following:

- Maintaining and verifying the correct operation of certified equipment.
- Identifying and recovering air conditioning system refrigerant.
- Recycling refrigerant.
- Labeling and storing refrigerant.
- Testing recycled refrigerant for non-condensable gases.

ENGINE PERFORMANCE EXAM ANALYSIS, TEST A8

To become a Certified Engine Performance Technician you must successfully pass an 80 question examination. Questions that are likely to appear on the test can be divided into six categories. Here we will detail the categories and briefly explain what you need to know to get a passing score.

1. General Engine Diagnosis

About one quarter of the examination (18 to 20 questions) involve general diagnostic procedures. You should be able top perform the following:

- Understand and verify a customer complaint, road test the vehicle in question, and determine repairs needed to remedy the problem
- Visually inspect an engine for fuel, oil, coolant, or other leaks, and determine the necessary repair operations. Listen to engine noises, locate the origin of the noise, and determine the appropriate repair.
- Identify the cause of excessive oil consumption and unusual exhaust color, odor, and sound, then determine the operations required to correct the problem.
- Use a vacuum gauge to isolate internal engine problems, and recommend repairs based on the gauge readings.
- Perform a cylinder power balance test, interpret test results, and recommend repairs.
- Perform a compression test, both wet and dry, and diagnose internal problems based on the test results.
- Perform a cylinder leakage test to establish the exact nature of a compression loss, and determine the necessary repairs.
- Use an oscilloscope or engine analyzer to diagnose mechanical, electrical, and fuel problems and determine needed repairs.
- Inspect and calibrate an exhaust gas analyzer, inspect the vehicle exhaust system, and obtain exhaust emission readings.
- Use an exhaust gas analyzer to diagnose mechanical, electrical, and fuel problems and determine needed repairs.
- Access on-board self-diagnostic codes and determine needed repairs.
- Inspect, test, adjust, and replace sensors, actuators, and circuits of electronic computer controlled engine management systems.

2. Ignition System Diagnosis and Repair

Ignition system diagnosis and repair procedures account for about 20 percent of the examination. Expect to see 15 to 17 questions in this category. You should be able to perform the following:

- Diagnose no-start, hard-start, misfire, driveability, spark knock, power loss, and poor mileage problems on engines equipped with breaker point ignition systems and determine needed repairs.

- Diagnose no-start, hard-start, misfire driveability, spark knock, power loss, and poor mileage problems on engines equipped with electronic ignition systems and determine needed repairs.
- Inspect, test, and repair or replace ignition primary circuit wiring and components.
- Inspect, test, rebuild, and install a distributor. Includes servicing both mechanical and vacuum advance units.
- Inspect, test, replace, and adjust breaker points and condensers.
- Inspect, test, and repair or replace ignition secondary circuit wiring and components.
- Inspect, test, and replace an ignition coil.
- Check and adjust ignition timing and check timing advance.
- Inspect, test, and replace electronic ignition wiring harnesses and connectors.
- Inspect, test, and replace electronic ignition sensors, pick-ups and other related components.
- Inspect, test, and replace electronic ignition control units.

Fuel, Air Induction, and Exhaust Systems Diagnosis and Repair

You can expect slightly over 25 percent of the test questions to be about fuel, air, and exhaust system diagnosis and repair. You should be able to perform the following tasks:

- Diagnose hot or cold no-start, hard-start, incorrect idle speed, poor idle, flooding, hesitation, surging, engine misfire, power loss, stalling, poor mileage, and dieseling problems on vehicles equipped with fuel injection systems and determine needed repairs.
- Inspect the fuel tank, tank filter, fuel cap, inspect and replace fuel lines, hoses, and fittings, and check fuel for contaminants and quality.
- Inspect, test, and replace both mechanical and electric fuel pumps and pump controls, and service the fuel filter.
- Inspect, test, and repair or replace fuel pressure regulation system and components of a fuel injection system.
- Inspect, test, and repair or replace fuel injection cold enrichment systems.
- Inspect, test, and repair or replace fuel injection acceleration enrichment components and systems.
- Inspect, test, and repair or replace fuel injection deceleration fuel reduction or shut-off components and systems.
- Remove, clean, inspect, and repair or replace the fuel injection throttle body. Includes adjusting related linkages.
- Remove, clean, test, inspect, and replace the fuel injectors.
- Remove, inspect, and replace air filter elements and service the filter housing.
- Inspect, clean, and replace throttle body mounting plates, fuel injection air induction systems, replace intake manifolds, and gaskets.
- Inspect, test, clean, adjust, and replace components of fuel injection closed-loop fuel control system.
- Remove, clean, test, inspect, and repair or replace vacuum and electrical components and connections of fuel injection systems.
- Inspect, remove, and replace exhaust manifolds, heat control valves, catalytic converters, mufflers, pipes, and heat shields.
- Test turbocharger or supercharger operation, and repair as necessary.

- Remove, clean, inspect, and repair or replace turbocharger or supercharger system components.
- Identify the cause of turbocharger or supercharger failure and determine needed repairs.

4. Emission Control Systems Diagnosis and Repair

Diagnosing and repairing problems in the emission control system is a large portion of the examination. Expect about 18 to 20 questions divided into eight sub-categories. Following is a list of operations you should be familiar with in each sub-category:

Positive Crankcase Ventilation
- Test the operation of the Positive Crankcase Ventilation (PCV) system.
- Inspect, service, and replace PCV valve, filter, breather, orifice, tubes, and hoses.

Spark Timing Controls
- Test the operation of spark timing control systems.
- Inspect, test, repair, and replace electrical and electronic components and circuits of the spark timing control system.
- Inspect, test, repair, and replace thermal, vacuum, and mechanical components of the spark timing control system.

Idle and Deceleration Speed Controls
- Test the operation of idle speed control systems.
- Inspect, test, adjust, and replace sensors, vacuum valves, motors, wiring, and hoses of idle speed control systems.
- Test the operation of deceleration control systems.
- Inspect, test, adjust, and replace electrical components and circuits, and vacuum components and hoses of deceleration control systems.

Exhaust Gas Recirculation
- Test the operation of exhaust gas recirculation (EGR) systems.
- Inspect, test, repair, and replace valves, valve manifolds, and exhaust passages of EGR systems.
- Inspect, test, repair, and replace vacuum and pressure controls, filters, and hoses of EGR systems.
- Inspect, test, repair, and replace electrical and electronic sensors, controls, and wiring of EGR systems.

Exhaust Gas Treatment
- Test the operation of pump-type air injection systems.
- Inspect, test, service, and replace pressure relief valves, filters, pulleys, and drive belts of pump-type air injection systems.
- Inspect, test, and replace vacuum-operated air control valves and vacuum hoses of pump-type air injection systems.
- Inspect, test, and replace electric and electronic components and circuits of pump-type air injection systems.
- Inspect, service, and replace hoses, check valves, air manifolds, and nozzles of pump-type air injection systems.
- Test the operation of pulse-type air injection systems.
- Inspect, test, and replace pulse air valves, filters, silencers, and hoses of pulse-type air injection systems.
- Inspect, test, service, and replace converter catalyst or converter assembly of catalytic converter systems.

Inlet Air Temperature Controls
- Test the operation of inlet air temperature control systems.
- Inspect, test, and replace sensors, diaphragms, and hoses of inlet air temperature control systems.
- Inspect, test, and replace heat stove shroud, hot air pipe, and damper of inlet air temperature control systems.

Intake Manifold Temperature Controls
- Test the operation of electrical, vacuum and coolant-type intake manifold temperature control systems.
- Inspect, test, and repair or replace components of electrical, vacuum and coolant-type intake manifold temperature control systems.
- Inspect, service, and replace manifold temperature control (heat riser) valves.

Fuel Vapor Controls
- Test the operation of fuel vapor control systems.
- Inspect and replace fuel tank cap, liquid vapor separator, liquid check valve, lines, and hoses of the fuel vapor control system.
- Inspect, service, and replace canisters, filters, and purge lines of the fuel vapor control system.
- Inspect, test, and replace thermal, vacuum, and electrical controls of the fuel vapor control system.

5. Engine Related Service

Because engine related service is covered in detail by the Engine Repair Examination, only 2 to 3 questions from this category appear on this test. You should be able to perform the following operations:

- Adjust valve lash clearance, both hydraulic and mechanical lifters, to specification.
- Verify correct valve timing and determine needed repairs.
- Verify engine operating temperature and determine needed repairs.
- Perform a cooling system pressure test, check coolant condition, inspect and test the radiator, test the pressure cap, and inspect the coolant recovery tank and hoses to determine needed cooling system repairs and service.
- Inspect, test, and replace the coolant thermostat, by-pass, and housing.
- Inspect, test, and replace both mechanical and electrical cooling fans, fan clutch, fan shroud, ducting, and fan control devices.

6. Engine Electrical Systems Diagnosis and Repair

Engine electrical system service is covered in detail on the Electrical Systems Examination, so there are only several electrical system related questions on this test. Expect to see one question from each of the sub-categories listed below.

Battery
- Inspect, service, and replace, the battery, battery cables, terminal clamps, and hold-down devices.
- Perform a battery capacity test (load test, high-rate discharge test) to determine general battery condition and recommend needed service.
- Slow and fast charge both conventional and maintenance-free batteries.

Starting System

- Perform a starter current draw test and determine needed repairs.
- Perform a starter circuit voltage drop test and determine needed repairs.
- Inspect, test, and replace components and wiring in the starter control circuit.
- Inspect, test, and replace starter relays and solenoids.

Charging System

- Diagnose charging system problems that create an under-charge, no-charge, or over-charge condition.
- Inspect, adjust, and replace alternator drive belts, pulleys, and belt driven fan assemblies.
- Inspect and repair or replace charging circuit connectors and wiring.

PART THREE

Eight Sample Exams for Review and Practice

SAMPLE EXAMS FOR REVIEW AND PRACTICE

The following sample examinations are designed to give you valuable practice for the actual tests. Follow the instructions and take these examinations as if they were the real thing. After you have scored yourself, go back and check, those questions that you got wrong. Determine which areas are most difficult for you, then concentrate your study on those areas. With this preparation you will ready for anything on which you are likely to be tested.

On the pages that follow you will find a complete Sample Examination for each of the eight areas in which you may become certified.

Each test has been professionally constructed to closely simulate the actual certification tests. All of the tests have the same number of questions you may expect. Great care was exercised to prepare questions having just the difficulty level you will encounter on the certification exams.

Although copies of past exams are not released, we were able to piece together a fairly complete picture of the forthcoming examinations.

A principal source of information was our analysis of official announcements going back several years. We have also drawn on the experience of technicians who actually certified by taking the ASE examinations.

Critical comparison of these announcements, and experiences revealed the testing trend; foretold the important subjects, and those that are likely to recur. As a result, the sample examinations presented here should closely resemble the actual tests you will take to obtain your certification.

To best prepare yourself, establish a time limit for your sample examinations. The actual tests are divided into two four hour and fifteen minute sessions. Pace yourself and try not to over do it. ASE suggests you limit yourself to no more than 210 questions per session.

Just as for the actual examinations, there is a separate Answer Booklet. The Answer Booklet has spaces to record your answers for all of the tests. Use a number 2 pencil to darken the space that best answers the question. You can simply remove, or photocopy the answer pages and keep them next to the questions as you work through the tests.

After you complete the sample examinations, check and correct your answers. Answers for all the questions in each test appear at the end of this book. Avoid looking at these answers while you take the exam, they are to be compared with your own answers after the time limit is up.

ANSWER BOOKLET

ENGINE REPAIR, TEST A1

1 Ⓐ Ⓑ Ⓒ Ⓓ	21 Ⓐ Ⓑ Ⓒ Ⓓ	41 Ⓐ Ⓑ Ⓒ Ⓓ	61 Ⓐ Ⓑ Ⓒ Ⓓ
2 Ⓐ Ⓑ Ⓒ Ⓓ	22 Ⓐ Ⓑ Ⓒ Ⓓ	42 Ⓐ Ⓑ Ⓒ Ⓓ	62 Ⓐ Ⓑ Ⓒ Ⓓ
3 Ⓐ Ⓑ Ⓒ Ⓓ	23 Ⓐ Ⓑ Ⓒ Ⓓ	43 Ⓐ Ⓑ Ⓒ Ⓓ	63 Ⓐ Ⓑ Ⓒ Ⓓ
4 Ⓐ Ⓑ Ⓒ Ⓓ	24 Ⓐ Ⓑ Ⓒ Ⓓ	44 Ⓐ Ⓑ Ⓒ Ⓓ	64 Ⓐ Ⓑ Ⓒ Ⓓ
5 Ⓐ Ⓑ Ⓒ Ⓓ	25 Ⓐ Ⓑ Ⓒ Ⓓ	45 Ⓐ Ⓑ Ⓒ Ⓓ	65 Ⓐ Ⓑ Ⓒ Ⓓ
6 Ⓐ Ⓑ Ⓒ Ⓓ	26 Ⓐ Ⓑ Ⓒ Ⓓ	46 Ⓐ Ⓑ Ⓒ Ⓓ	66 Ⓐ Ⓑ Ⓒ Ⓓ
7 Ⓐ Ⓑ Ⓒ Ⓓ	27 Ⓐ Ⓑ Ⓒ Ⓓ	47 Ⓐ Ⓑ Ⓒ Ⓓ	67 Ⓐ Ⓑ Ⓒ Ⓓ
8 Ⓐ Ⓑ Ⓒ Ⓓ	28 Ⓐ Ⓑ Ⓒ Ⓓ	48 Ⓐ Ⓑ Ⓒ Ⓓ	68 Ⓐ Ⓑ Ⓒ Ⓓ
9 Ⓐ Ⓑ Ⓒ Ⓓ	29 Ⓐ Ⓑ Ⓒ Ⓓ	49 Ⓐ Ⓑ Ⓒ Ⓓ	69 Ⓐ Ⓑ Ⓒ Ⓓ
10 Ⓐ Ⓑ Ⓒ Ⓓ	30 Ⓐ Ⓑ Ⓒ Ⓓ	50 Ⓐ Ⓑ Ⓒ Ⓓ	70 Ⓐ Ⓑ Ⓒ Ⓓ
11 Ⓐ Ⓑ Ⓒ Ⓓ	31 Ⓐ Ⓑ Ⓒ Ⓓ	51 Ⓐ Ⓑ Ⓒ Ⓓ	71 Ⓐ Ⓑ Ⓒ Ⓓ
12 Ⓐ Ⓑ Ⓒ Ⓓ	32 Ⓐ Ⓑ Ⓒ Ⓓ	52 Ⓐ Ⓑ Ⓒ Ⓓ	72 Ⓐ Ⓑ Ⓒ Ⓓ
13 Ⓐ Ⓑ Ⓒ Ⓓ	33 Ⓐ Ⓑ Ⓒ Ⓓ	53 Ⓐ Ⓑ Ⓒ Ⓓ	73 Ⓐ Ⓑ Ⓒ Ⓓ
14 Ⓐ Ⓑ Ⓒ Ⓓ	34 Ⓐ Ⓑ Ⓒ Ⓓ	54 Ⓐ Ⓑ Ⓒ Ⓓ	74 Ⓐ Ⓑ Ⓒ Ⓓ
15 Ⓐ Ⓑ Ⓒ Ⓓ	35 Ⓐ Ⓑ Ⓒ Ⓓ	55 Ⓐ Ⓑ Ⓒ Ⓓ	75 Ⓐ Ⓑ Ⓒ Ⓓ
16 Ⓐ Ⓑ Ⓒ Ⓓ	36 Ⓐ Ⓑ Ⓒ Ⓓ	56 Ⓐ Ⓑ Ⓒ Ⓓ	76 Ⓐ Ⓑ Ⓒ Ⓓ
17 Ⓐ Ⓑ Ⓒ Ⓓ	37 Ⓐ Ⓑ Ⓒ Ⓓ	57 Ⓐ Ⓑ Ⓒ Ⓓ	77 Ⓐ Ⓑ Ⓒ Ⓓ
18 Ⓐ Ⓑ Ⓒ Ⓓ	38 Ⓐ Ⓑ Ⓒ Ⓓ	58 Ⓐ Ⓑ Ⓒ Ⓓ	78 Ⓐ Ⓑ Ⓒ Ⓓ
19 Ⓐ Ⓑ Ⓒ Ⓓ	39 Ⓐ Ⓑ Ⓒ Ⓓ	59 Ⓐ Ⓑ Ⓒ Ⓓ	79 Ⓐ Ⓑ Ⓒ Ⓓ
20 Ⓐ Ⓑ Ⓒ Ⓓ	40 Ⓐ Ⓑ Ⓒ Ⓓ	60 Ⓐ Ⓑ Ⓒ Ⓓ	80 Ⓐ Ⓑ Ⓒ Ⓓ

AUTOMATIC TRANSMISSION/TRANSAXLE, TEST A2

1 Ⓐ Ⓑ Ⓒ Ⓓ	9 Ⓐ Ⓑ Ⓒ Ⓓ	17 Ⓐ Ⓑ Ⓒ Ⓓ	25 Ⓐ Ⓑ Ⓒ Ⓓ	33 Ⓐ Ⓑ Ⓒ Ⓓ
2 Ⓐ Ⓑ Ⓒ Ⓓ	10 Ⓐ Ⓑ Ⓒ Ⓓ	18 Ⓐ Ⓑ Ⓒ Ⓓ	26 Ⓐ Ⓑ Ⓒ Ⓓ	34 Ⓐ Ⓑ Ⓒ Ⓓ
3 Ⓐ Ⓑ Ⓒ Ⓓ	11 Ⓐ Ⓑ Ⓒ Ⓓ	19 Ⓐ Ⓑ Ⓒ Ⓓ	27 Ⓐ Ⓑ Ⓒ Ⓓ	35 Ⓐ Ⓑ Ⓒ Ⓓ
4 Ⓐ Ⓑ Ⓒ Ⓓ	12 Ⓐ Ⓑ Ⓒ Ⓓ	20 Ⓐ Ⓑ Ⓒ Ⓓ	28 Ⓐ Ⓑ Ⓒ Ⓓ	36 Ⓐ Ⓑ Ⓒ Ⓓ
5 Ⓐ Ⓑ Ⓒ Ⓓ	13 Ⓐ Ⓑ Ⓒ Ⓓ	21 Ⓐ Ⓑ Ⓒ Ⓓ	29 Ⓐ Ⓑ Ⓒ Ⓓ	37 Ⓐ Ⓑ Ⓒ Ⓓ
6 Ⓐ Ⓑ Ⓒ Ⓓ	14 Ⓐ Ⓑ Ⓒ Ⓓ	22 Ⓐ Ⓑ Ⓒ Ⓓ	30 Ⓐ Ⓑ Ⓒ Ⓓ	38 Ⓐ Ⓑ Ⓒ Ⓓ
7 Ⓐ Ⓑ Ⓒ Ⓓ	15 Ⓐ Ⓑ Ⓒ Ⓓ	23 Ⓐ Ⓑ Ⓒ Ⓓ	31 Ⓐ Ⓑ Ⓒ Ⓓ	39 Ⓐ Ⓑ Ⓒ Ⓓ
8 Ⓐ Ⓑ Ⓒ Ⓓ	16 Ⓐ Ⓑ Ⓒ Ⓓ	24 Ⓐ Ⓑ Ⓒ Ⓓ	32 Ⓐ Ⓑ Ⓒ Ⓓ	40 Ⓐ Ⓑ Ⓒ Ⓓ

MANUAL DRIVE TRAIN AND AXLE, TEST A3

1 Ⓐ Ⓑ Ⓒ Ⓓ	9 Ⓐ Ⓑ Ⓒ Ⓓ	17 Ⓐ Ⓑ Ⓒ Ⓓ	25 Ⓐ Ⓑ Ⓒ Ⓓ	33 Ⓐ Ⓑ Ⓒ Ⓓ
2 Ⓐ Ⓑ Ⓒ Ⓓ	10 Ⓐ Ⓑ Ⓒ Ⓓ	18 Ⓐ Ⓑ Ⓒ Ⓓ	26 Ⓐ Ⓑ Ⓒ Ⓓ	34 Ⓐ Ⓑ Ⓒ Ⓓ
3 Ⓐ Ⓑ Ⓒ Ⓓ	11 Ⓐ Ⓑ Ⓒ Ⓓ	19 Ⓐ Ⓑ Ⓒ Ⓓ	27 Ⓐ Ⓑ Ⓒ Ⓓ	35 Ⓐ Ⓑ Ⓒ Ⓓ
4 Ⓐ Ⓑ Ⓒ Ⓓ	12 Ⓐ Ⓑ Ⓒ Ⓓ	20 Ⓐ Ⓑ Ⓒ Ⓓ	28 Ⓐ Ⓑ Ⓒ Ⓓ	36 Ⓐ Ⓑ Ⓒ Ⓓ
5 Ⓐ Ⓑ Ⓒ Ⓓ	13 Ⓐ Ⓑ Ⓒ Ⓓ	21 Ⓐ Ⓑ Ⓒ Ⓓ	29 Ⓐ Ⓑ Ⓒ Ⓓ	37 Ⓐ Ⓑ Ⓒ Ⓓ
6 Ⓐ Ⓑ Ⓒ Ⓓ	14 Ⓐ Ⓑ Ⓒ Ⓓ	22 Ⓐ Ⓑ Ⓒ Ⓓ	30 Ⓐ Ⓑ Ⓒ Ⓓ	38 Ⓐ Ⓑ Ⓒ Ⓓ
7 Ⓐ Ⓑ Ⓒ Ⓓ	15 Ⓐ Ⓑ Ⓒ Ⓓ	23 Ⓐ Ⓑ Ⓒ Ⓓ	31 Ⓐ Ⓑ Ⓒ Ⓓ	39 Ⓐ Ⓑ Ⓒ Ⓓ
8 Ⓐ Ⓑ Ⓒ Ⓓ	16 Ⓐ Ⓑ Ⓒ Ⓓ	24 Ⓐ Ⓑ Ⓒ Ⓓ	32 Ⓐ Ⓑ Ⓒ Ⓓ	40 Ⓐ Ⓑ Ⓒ Ⓓ

SUSPENSION AND STEERING, TEST A4

1 Ⓐ Ⓑ Ⓒ Ⓓ	9 Ⓐ Ⓑ Ⓒ Ⓓ	17 Ⓐ Ⓑ Ⓒ Ⓓ	25 Ⓐ Ⓑ Ⓒ Ⓓ	33 Ⓐ Ⓑ Ⓒ Ⓓ
2 Ⓐ Ⓑ Ⓒ Ⓓ	10 Ⓐ Ⓑ Ⓒ Ⓓ	18 Ⓐ Ⓑ Ⓒ Ⓓ	26 Ⓐ Ⓑ Ⓒ Ⓓ	34 Ⓐ Ⓑ Ⓒ Ⓓ
3 Ⓐ Ⓑ Ⓒ Ⓓ	11 Ⓐ Ⓑ Ⓒ Ⓓ	19 Ⓐ Ⓑ Ⓒ Ⓓ	27 Ⓐ Ⓑ Ⓒ Ⓓ	35 Ⓐ Ⓑ Ⓒ Ⓓ
4 Ⓐ Ⓑ Ⓒ Ⓓ	12 Ⓐ Ⓑ Ⓒ Ⓓ	20 Ⓐ Ⓑ Ⓒ Ⓓ	28 Ⓐ Ⓑ Ⓒ Ⓓ	36 Ⓐ Ⓑ Ⓒ Ⓓ
5 Ⓐ Ⓑ Ⓒ Ⓓ	13 Ⓐ Ⓑ Ⓒ Ⓓ	21 Ⓐ Ⓑ Ⓒ Ⓓ	29 Ⓐ Ⓑ Ⓒ Ⓓ	37 Ⓐ Ⓑ Ⓒ Ⓓ
6 Ⓐ Ⓑ Ⓒ Ⓓ	14 Ⓐ Ⓑ Ⓒ Ⓓ	22 Ⓐ Ⓑ Ⓒ Ⓓ	30 Ⓐ Ⓑ Ⓒ Ⓓ	38 Ⓐ Ⓑ Ⓒ Ⓓ
7 Ⓐ Ⓑ Ⓒ Ⓓ	15 Ⓐ Ⓑ Ⓒ Ⓓ	23 Ⓐ Ⓑ Ⓒ Ⓓ	31 Ⓐ Ⓑ Ⓒ Ⓓ	39 Ⓐ Ⓑ Ⓒ Ⓓ
8 Ⓐ Ⓑ Ⓒ Ⓓ	16 Ⓐ Ⓑ Ⓒ Ⓓ	24 Ⓐ Ⓑ Ⓒ Ⓓ	32 Ⓐ Ⓑ Ⓒ Ⓓ	40 Ⓐ Ⓑ Ⓒ Ⓓ

BRAKES, TEST A5

1 (A)(B)(C)(D)	11 (A)(B)(C)(D)	21 (A)(B)(C)(D)	31 (A)(B)(C)(D)	41 (A)(B)(C)(D)
2 (A)(B)(C)(D)	12 (A)(B)(C)(D)	22 (A)(B)(C)(D)	32 (A)(B)(C)(D)	42 (A)(B)(C)(D)
3 (A)(B)(C)(D)	13 (A)(B)(C)(D)	23 (A)(B)(C)(D)	33 (A)(B)(C)(D)	43 (A)(B)(C)(D)
4 (A)(B)(C)(D)	14 (A)(B)(C)(D)	24 (A)(B)(C)(D)	34 (A)(B)(C)(D)	44 (A)(B)(C)(D)
5 (A)(B)(C)(D)	15 (A)(B)(C)(D)	25 (A)(B)(C)(D)	35 (A)(B)(C)(D)	45 (A)(B)(C)(D)
6 (A)(B)(C)(D)	16 (A)(B)(C)(D)	26 (A)(B)(C)(D)	36 (A)(B)(C)(D)	46 (A)(B)(C)(D)
7 (A)(B)(C)(D)	17 (A)(B)(C)(D)	27 (A)(B)(C)(D)	37 (A)(B)(C)(D)	47 (A)(B)(C)(D)
8 (A)(B)(C)(D)	18 (A)(B)(C)(D)	28 (A)(B)(C)(D)	38 (A)(B)(C)(D)	48 (A)(B)(C)(D)
9 (A)(B)(C)(D)	19 (A)(B)(C)(D)	29 (A)(B)(C)(D)	39 (A)(B)(C)(D)	49 (A)(B)(C)(D)
10 (A)(B)(C)(D)	20 (A)(B)(C)(D)	30 (A)(B)(C)(D)	40 (A)(B)(C)(D)	50 (A)(B)(C)(D)

ELECTRICAL SYSTEMS, TEST A6

1 (A)(B)(C)(D)	11 (A)(B)(C)(D)	21 (A)(B)(C)(D)	31 (A)(B)(C)(D)	41 (A)(B)(C)(D)
2 (A)(B)(C)(D)	12 (A)(B)(C)(D)	22 (A)(B)(C)(D)	32 (A)(B)(C)(D)	42 (A)(B)(C)(D)
3 (A)(B)(C)(D)	13 (A)(B)(C)(D)	23 (A)(B)(C)(D)	33 (A)(B)(C)(D)	43 (A)(B)(C)(D)
4 (A)(B)(C)(D)	14 (A)(B)(C)(D)	24 (A)(B)(C)(D)	34 (A)(B)(C)(D)	44 (A)(B)(C)(D)
5 (A)(B)(C)(D)	15 (A)(B)(C)(D)	25 (A)(B)(C)(D)	35 (A)(B)(C)(D)	45 (A)(B)(C)(D)
6 (A)(B)(C)(D)	16 (A)(B)(C)(D)	26 (A)(B)(C)(D)	36 (A)(B)(C)(D)	46 (A)(B)(C)(D)
7 (A)(B)(C)(D)	17 (A)(B)(C)(D)	27 (A)(B)(C)(D)	37 (A)(B)(C)(D)	47 (A)(B)(C)(D)
8 (A)(B)(C)(D)	18 (A)(B)(C)(D)	28 (A)(B)(C)(D)	38 (A)(B)(C)(D)	48 (A)(B)(C)(D)
9 (A)(B)(C)(D)	19 (A)(B)(C)(D)	29 (A)(B)(C)(D)	39 (A)(B)(C)(D)	49 (A)(B)(C)(D)
10 (A)(B)(C)(D)	20 (A)(B)(C)(D)	30 (A)(B)(C)(D)	40 (A)(B)(C)(D)	50 (A)(B)(C)(D)

HEATING AND AIR CONDITIONING, TEST A7

1 (A)(B)(C)(D)	11 (A)(B)(C)(D)	21 (A)(B)(C)(D)	31 (A)(B)(C)(D)	41 (A)(B)(C)(D)
2 (A)(B)(C)(D)	12 (A)(B)(C)(D)	22 (A)(B)(C)(D)	32 (A)(B)(C)(D)	42 (A)(B)(C)(D)
3 (A)(B)(C)(D)	13 (A)(B)(C)(D)	23 (A)(B)(C)(D)	33 (A)(B)(C)(D)	43 (A)(B)(C)(D)
4 (A)(B)(C)(D)	14 (A)(B)(C)(D)	24 (A)(B)(C)(D)	34 (A)(B)(C)(D)	44 (A)(B)(C)(D)
5 (A)(B)(C)(D)	15 (A)(B)(C)(D)	25 (A)(B)(C)(D)	35 (A)(B)(C)(D)	45 (A)(B)(C)(D)
6 (A)(B)(C)(D)	16 (A)(B)(C)(D)	26 (A)(B)(C)(D)	36 (A)(B)(C)(D)	46 (A)(B)(C)(D)
7 (A)(B)(C)(D)	17 (A)(B)(C)(D)	27 (A)(B)(C)(D)	37 (A)(B)(C)(D)	47 (A)(B)(C)(D)
8 (A)(B)(C)(D)	18 (A)(B)(C)(D)	28 (A)(B)(C)(D)	38 (A)(B)(C)(D)	48 (A)(B)(C)(D)
9 (A)(B)(C)(D)	19 (A)(B)(C)(D)	29 (A)(B)(C)(D)	39 (A)(B)(C)(D)	49 (A)(B)(C)(D)
10 (A)(B)(C)(D)	20 (A)(B)(C)(D)	30 (A)(B)(C)(D)	40 (A)(B)(C)(D)	50 (A)(B)(C)(D)

ENGINE PERFORMANCE, TEST A8

1 Ⓐ Ⓑ Ⓒ Ⓓ	21 Ⓐ Ⓑ Ⓒ Ⓓ	41 Ⓐ Ⓑ Ⓒ Ⓓ	61 Ⓐ Ⓑ Ⓒ Ⓓ
2 Ⓐ Ⓑ Ⓒ Ⓓ	22 Ⓐ Ⓑ Ⓒ Ⓓ	42 Ⓐ Ⓑ Ⓒ Ⓓ	62 Ⓐ Ⓑ Ⓒ Ⓓ
3 Ⓐ Ⓑ Ⓒ Ⓓ	23 Ⓐ Ⓑ Ⓒ Ⓓ	43 Ⓐ Ⓑ Ⓒ Ⓓ	63 Ⓐ Ⓑ Ⓒ Ⓓ
4 Ⓐ Ⓑ Ⓒ Ⓓ	24 Ⓐ Ⓑ Ⓒ Ⓓ	44 Ⓐ Ⓑ Ⓒ Ⓓ	64 Ⓐ Ⓑ Ⓒ Ⓓ
5 Ⓐ Ⓑ Ⓒ Ⓓ	25 Ⓐ Ⓑ Ⓒ Ⓓ	45 Ⓐ Ⓑ Ⓒ Ⓓ	65 Ⓐ Ⓑ Ⓒ Ⓓ
6 Ⓐ Ⓑ Ⓒ Ⓓ	26 Ⓐ Ⓑ Ⓒ Ⓓ	46 Ⓐ Ⓑ Ⓒ Ⓓ	66 Ⓐ Ⓑ Ⓒ Ⓓ
7 Ⓐ Ⓑ Ⓒ Ⓓ	27 Ⓐ Ⓑ Ⓒ Ⓓ	47 Ⓐ Ⓑ Ⓒ Ⓓ	67 Ⓐ Ⓑ Ⓒ Ⓓ
8 Ⓐ Ⓑ Ⓒ Ⓓ	28 Ⓐ Ⓑ Ⓒ Ⓓ	48 Ⓐ Ⓑ Ⓒ Ⓓ	68 Ⓐ Ⓑ Ⓒ Ⓓ
9 Ⓐ Ⓑ Ⓒ Ⓓ	29 Ⓐ Ⓑ Ⓒ Ⓓ	49 Ⓐ Ⓑ Ⓒ Ⓓ	69 Ⓐ Ⓑ Ⓒ Ⓓ
10 Ⓐ Ⓑ Ⓒ Ⓓ	30 Ⓐ Ⓑ Ⓒ Ⓓ	50 Ⓐ Ⓑ Ⓒ Ⓓ	70 Ⓐ Ⓑ Ⓒ Ⓓ
11 Ⓐ Ⓑ Ⓒ Ⓓ	31 Ⓐ Ⓑ Ⓒ Ⓓ	51 Ⓐ Ⓑ Ⓒ Ⓓ	71 Ⓐ Ⓑ Ⓒ Ⓓ
12 Ⓐ Ⓑ Ⓒ Ⓓ	32 Ⓐ Ⓑ Ⓒ Ⓓ	52 Ⓐ Ⓑ Ⓒ Ⓓ	72 Ⓐ Ⓑ Ⓒ Ⓓ
13 Ⓐ Ⓑ Ⓒ Ⓓ	33 Ⓐ Ⓑ Ⓒ Ⓓ	53 Ⓐ Ⓑ Ⓒ Ⓓ	73 Ⓐ Ⓑ Ⓒ Ⓓ
14 Ⓐ Ⓑ Ⓒ Ⓓ	34 Ⓐ Ⓑ Ⓒ Ⓓ	54 Ⓐ Ⓑ Ⓒ Ⓓ	74 Ⓐ Ⓑ Ⓒ Ⓓ
15 Ⓐ Ⓑ Ⓒ Ⓓ	35 Ⓐ Ⓑ Ⓒ Ⓓ	55 Ⓐ Ⓑ Ⓒ Ⓓ	75 Ⓐ Ⓑ Ⓒ Ⓓ
16 Ⓐ Ⓑ Ⓒ Ⓓ	36 Ⓐ Ⓑ Ⓒ Ⓓ	56 Ⓐ Ⓑ Ⓒ Ⓓ	76 Ⓐ Ⓑ Ⓒ Ⓓ
17 Ⓐ Ⓑ Ⓒ Ⓓ	37 Ⓐ Ⓑ Ⓒ Ⓓ	57 Ⓐ Ⓑ Ⓒ Ⓓ	77 Ⓐ Ⓑ Ⓒ Ⓓ
18 Ⓐ Ⓑ Ⓒ Ⓓ	38 Ⓐ Ⓑ Ⓒ Ⓓ	58 Ⓐ Ⓑ Ⓒ Ⓓ	78 Ⓐ Ⓑ Ⓒ Ⓓ
19 Ⓐ Ⓑ Ⓒ Ⓓ	39 Ⓐ Ⓑ Ⓒ Ⓓ	59 Ⓐ Ⓑ Ⓒ Ⓓ	79 Ⓐ Ⓑ Ⓒ Ⓓ
20 Ⓐ Ⓑ Ⓒ Ⓓ	40 Ⓐ Ⓑ Ⓒ Ⓓ	60 Ⓐ Ⓑ Ⓒ Ⓓ	80 Ⓐ Ⓑ Ⓒ Ⓓ

SAMPLE EXAM, ENGINE REPAIR TECHNICIAN

TEST A1, 80 Questions

DIRECTIONS: Each question has four suggested answers, lettered A, B, C, and D. Decide which one is the best answer, locate the question number on the answer sheet, and with a soft pencil darken the area that corresponds to the answer you have selected.

1. If the intake manifold of a gasoline engine is warped to the extent that it leaks, the engine will most likely:

   (A) Have a rough idle
   (B) Have higher compression in that cylinder
   (C) Have a high steady vacuum reading
   (D) Have an oil leak

2. The "cylinder balance test" can be used to locate all of the following EXCEPT?

   (A) Worn piston rings
   (B) Defective sparkplug
   (C) A leaky exhaust manifold
   (D) A valve which does not open properly

3. A valve job was done on a customer's car. Several days after picking up the car, the customer returns complaining of a misfire. A compression test is performed and the engine shows low compression on three cylinders, after removing the cylinder head the technician finds three burned valves. Which is the most likely cause of the burnt valves?

   (A) Insufficient margin after grinding
   (B) Improper valve adjustment
   (C) Defective parts
   (D) Excessive guide clearance

4. A technician inspecting engine crankshaft bearings and camshaft bearings in a high mileage engine should expect to find:

   (A) Crankshaft and camshaft bearings showing equal wear
   (B) Crankshaft bearings showing more wear than the camshaft bearings
   (C) Camshaft bearings showing more wear than the crankshaft bearings
   (D) Crankshaft bearings may or may not be more worn than the camshaft bearings

63

5. An engine has a hollow-metallic knock when it is started cold, the noise diminishes and eventually goes away as the engine warms up to operating temperature.

Technician A says the noise could result from low oil pressure caused by worn main bearings.

Technician B says the noise could be piston slap caused by too much piston to cylinder wall clearance.

Who is right?

(A) A only
(B) B only
(C) Both A and B
(D) Neither A nor B

6. The first sign of excessive intake valve guide clearance on an OHV engine is usually:

(A) Excessive oil consumption
(B) Increased manifold vacuum
(C) Fluffy black deposits on sparkplug
(D) Lowered cylinder compression pressure

Figure A1-1.

7. In Figure A1-1 the technician is checking?

(A) Bearing clearance
(B) Piston clearance
(C) Piston ring end gap
(D) Cylinder taper

8. Two measurements are taken near the top of a cylinder bore, one perpendicular to and the other in line with the crankshaft. These two measurements are taken in order to determine:

(A) Cylinder out-of-round
(B) Cylinder taper
(C) Cylinder warpage
(D) Cylinder ridge

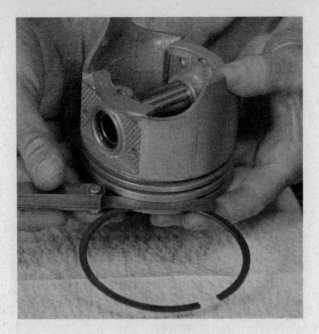

Figure A1-2.

9. The technician in Figure A1-2 is checking:

    (A) Piston clearance
    (B) Piston ring end gap
    (C) Piston ring side gap
    (D) Piston ring groove taper

10. Of the following valve problems, which is most likely caused by metal fatigue when spring tension is too high?

    (A) Valve face burning
    (B) Cracked piston
    (C) Excessive deposits
    (D) Radial cracks in the valve head

11. When installing a piston assembly, the notch on the head of the piston should face toward:

    (A) The rear of the engine
    (B) The major thrust side
    (C) The front of the engine
    (D) The minor thrust side

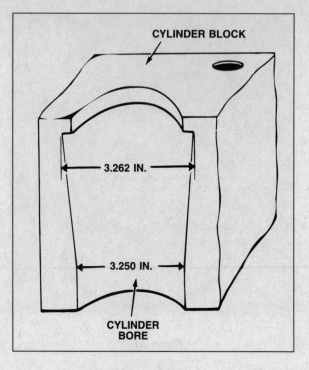

CYLINDER BLOCK

3.262 IN.

3.250 IN.

CYLINDER BORE

Figure A1-3.

12. The cylinder in Figure A1-3 shows that the cylinder is:

(A) 0.012 inch out-of-round
(B) 0.006 inch out-of-round
(C) 0.012 inch ridge wear
(D) 0.012 inch taper

13. A cooling system pressure tester is connected to the radiator and pumped up to the proper pressure. The engine is started and after a while the pressure begins to rise. What could be the cause of the problem?

(A) The thermostat is bad
(B) The bypass hose is blocked
(C) The tester is being used incorrectly
(D) The head gasket is leaking

14. Intake and exhaust valves in an OHC gasoline engine are held closed by which of the following?

(A) The camshaft
(B) Torsion springs
(C) Compression pressure
(D) Compression springs

15. An engine is found to be missing on one cylinder. Of the following, what is the most likely cause?

(A) Vapor lock
(B) A clogged exhaust
(C) An overheated engine
(D) A defective sparkplug

16. Correct valve timing of a gasoline engine involves the proper opening and closing of valves with reference to the:

    (A) Position of the piston
    (B) Setting of the distributor
    (C) Carburetor mixing jets
    (D) Cylinder compression ratio

17. While performing a leakage test on cylinder number 2 of a 4 cylinder engine air escapes from the number three sparkplug hole.

    Technician A says that a leaking head gasket could be the problem.

    Technician B says that the number 2 intake valve not seating could be the problem.

    Who is right?
    (A) A only
    (B) B only
    (C) Both A and B
    (D) Neither A nor B

18. A cylinder compression test (dry) is performed, results are fairly even compression, but lower than specification. A second wet type test is performed and readings are higher on all cylinders. These results indicate:

    (A) Poor valve seating
    (B) Worn valve guides
    (C) Worn piston rings
    (D) Leaking head gasket

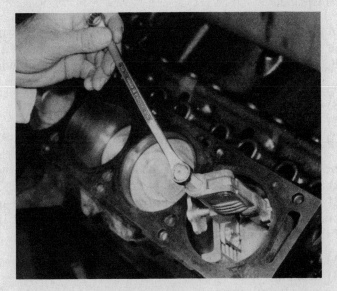

Figure A1-4.

19. The tool being used in Figure A1-4 is a:

    (A) Cylinder hone
    (B) Deglazing tool
    (C) Ridge reamer
    (D) Boring bar

42532

20. The main function of a flywheel is:

    (A) To provide a mounting for the clutch assembly
    (B) To insure proper engine timing
    (C) To smooth out the power impulses from the pistons
    (D) To support the starter gearing arrangement

21. A vacuum gauge is connected to an engine. The gauge rapidly vibrates between 14 and 18 in-Hg at idle, when engine speed is increased the gauge stops vibrating and stabilizes. These readings are most likely caused by:

    (A) Weak piston rings
    (B) Incorrect fuel mixture
    (C) Worn valve guides
    (D) Weak valve springs

22. After the cylinder head of an engine has been removed, a wet oily condition is noticed on the block between two adjacent cylinders. What is the most likely cause of this condition?

    (A) Worn valve guides
    (B) A scored cylinder wall
    (C) A ruptured pump diaphragm
    (D) A blown cylinder head gasket

23. Before a technician grinds a valve seat, the valve guides must be:

    (A) Replaced
    (B) Reamed
    (C) Knurled
    (D) Cleaned

24. An engine is being tested with a vacuum gauge. It is noticed that the needle on the vacuum gauge drifts slowly back and forth at idle. This result generally indicates which of the following?

    (A) Late valve timing
    (B) Poor air-fuel mixture
    (C) A blown cylinder head gasket
    (D) An air leak in the intake manifold

25. The cylinder head of an OHV gasoline engine is removed. All the exhaust valves are covered by dry, dark deposits, The intake valves have a minimal amount of dry carbon build-up, and the combustion chambers are also dry. What is the most likely cause of this condition?

    (A) Too-rich mixture
    (B) Leaking valves
    (C) A faulty oil pump
    (D) A misfiring distributor cap

26. A typical camshaft for an OHV V-8 engine will have:

    (A) 4 lobes
    (B) 8 lobes
    (C) 12 lobes
    (D) 16 lobes

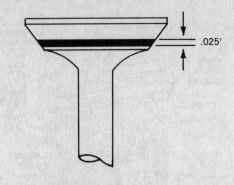

Figure A1-5.

27. After grinding the valve you note that the valve seat contacts the valve face as shown in Figure A1-5. The proper procedure to correct seat contact would be to:

    (A) Grind the seat with a 45° stone and narrow it with a 60° stone
    (B) Grind the seat with a 45° stone and narrow it with a 30° stone
    (C) Grind the seat with a 44° stone to get an interference angle
    (D) Grind the seat with a 30° stone and throat it with a 60° stone

28. An engine has poor power balance, acceptable leakage, but low compression on all cylinders.

    Technician A says the problem could be ignition related and too low a cranking speed during compression testing.

    Technician B says the problem could worn camshaft lobes or an intake manifold vacuum leak.

    Who is right?

    (A) A only
    (B) B only
    (C) Both A and B
    (D) Neither A nor B

29. One of the best ways to check the concentricity of the valve guide and valve seat is by the use of:

    (A) A dial bore gauge
    (B) A dial indicator
    (C) An inside micrometer
    (D) A bevel protractor

30. In servicing a worn and badly tapered gasoline engine cylinder that has quite a "step" at the bottom of the ring travel, it is best to:

    (A) Start the honing in the unworn area below the ring travel
    (B) Start the honing in the center of the ring travel
    (C) Start the honing in the unworn area above the ring travel
    (D) Just fit an oversized piston to the top part of the cylinder

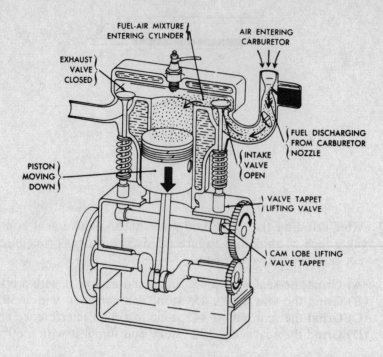

Figure A1-6.

31. Figure A1-6 shows which of the following strokes in a four-stroke gasoline engine?

    (A) Power
    (B) Exhaust
    (C) Intake
    (D) Compression

32. Cam ground pistons are used to:

    (A) Reduce reciprocating weight
    (B) Improve drainage of excess oil
    (C) Improve engine balance
    (D) Allow for piston expansion

33. Which of the following is the proper procedure for performing a cylinder balance test?

    (A) Run the engine at idle, short the sparkplugs one at a time, and note any rpm drop
    (B) Run the engine at 1500 rpm, short the sparkplugs two at a time, and note any rpm drop
    (C) Run the engine at idle speed, shorting all but two sparkplugs, and note any rpm drop
    (D) Run the engine at 1500 rpm, short the sparkplugs one at a time, and note any rpm drop

34. A compression test was performed on a four cylinder engine with the following results: Cylinder #1 = 140 psi, cylinder #2 = 127 psi, cylinder #3 = 115 psi, cylinder #4 = 135 psi.

Technician A says low compression in cylinders #2 and #3 indicates that the cylinder head gasket is leaking between these two cylinders.

Technician B says the compression test is not conclusive enough to determine the problem. Uneven readings may be caused by burnt, sticking, or improperly adjusted valves or carbon deposits on the valve faces.

Who is right?

(A) A only
(B) B only
(C) Both A and B
(D) Neither A nor B

35. Before installing pistons into freshly honed cylinder bores, the cylinders should be cleaned using:

(A) Solvent and a soft brush
(B) Hot soapy water and a rag
(C) Water soluble oil and a rag
(D) Carbon tetrachloride and compressed air

36. A dry compression test is performed on a six-cylinder gasoline engine with the following results; 152 psi readings were recorded for cylinders #1, #2, #4, and #6, only 128 psi was recorded for cylinders #3 and #5. Upon squirting engine oil into the cylinder and rechecking pressures again, it was found that cylinder #5 came up to 147 psi., but only 132 psi developed in cylinder #3. Which of the following would be logical assumption from these test?

(A) The valves on cylinder #5 do not seat properly
(B) The piston rings or cylinder are worn in cylinder #3
(C) The piston rings are worn in cylinder #5
(D) Carbon deposits are causing high readings for cylinders #1, #2, #4, and #6

37. A compression test reveals that compression is low only in two adjacent cylinders. What is the most likely cause?

(A) Faulty rings
(B) Burned valves
(C) Incorrect cam timing
(D) Head gasket leakage

38. Adjusting valve clearance too tight can cause:

(A) The valves to overheat
(B) Late valve timing
(C) High oil consumption
(D) Excessive valve train noise

39. All of the following methods are used for detecting cracks in a cast iron cylinder block or head EXCEPT?

(A) Dye penetrant
(B) Pressure testing
(C) Magnetic particle testing
(D) The sheradizing method

Figure A1-7.

40. The wear pattern on the piston shown in Figure A1-7 indicates which of the following?

    (A) A collapsed piston shirt
    (B) A bent connecting rod
    (C) Engine overheating
    (D) Normal operating conditions

41. Connecting rods are often checked for alignments by using a rod aligner. The mandrel used with this fixture should be mounted, depending on the jig used, so that the angle it makes with the face plate is most nearly:

    (A) 15 or 20 degrees
    (B) 30 or 60 degrees
    (C) 90 or 180 degrees
    (D) 120 or 240 degrees

42. Upon dismantling a gasoline engine, it is found that the piston rings are stuck in the grooves and are not free to rotate. Of the following, what is the most likely cause of this condition?

    (A) Operating the engine with spark setting in an advanced position
    (B) Maintaining the thermostat at too low an engine temperature
    (C) Using the wrong type of sparkplugs in the engine
    (D) Using dirty or contaminated lubricating oil

43. A connecting rod bearing loose in its bore will often result in:

    (A) An engine knock
    (B) Low oil pressure
    (C) Detonation
    (D) Increased blow-by

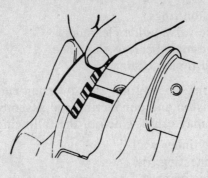

Figure A1-8.

44. The technician in Figure A1-8 is checking:

(A) Crankshaft out of round
(B) Main bearing clearance
(C) Crankshaft thrust clearance
(D) Main bearing diameter

45. Before new main bearings are installed in an engine, it is always necessary to:

(A) Replace or recondition the crankshaft
(B) Grind the crankshaft journals
(C) Check the crankshaft balance
(D) Inspect the crankshaft journals

46. What will cause a diagonal wear pattern to develop on the thrust surface of a piston?

(A) Bent connecting rod
(B) Too much piston pin clearance
(C) Out-of-round cylinder bore
(D) Collapsed piston skirt

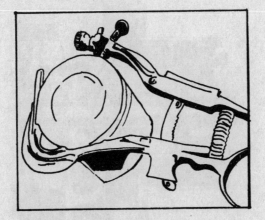

Figure A1-9.

47. The tool shown in Figure A1-9 is used to:

(A) Remove and install piston rings
(B) Clean piston ring grooves
(C) Counterbore piston ring grooves
(D) Measure piston diameter

48. Which of the following may be a cause of low oil pressure?

    (A) Worn piston rings
    (B) Excessive valve guide clearance
    (C) Excessive main bearing clearance
    (D) Stretched timing chain

49. In dismantling an engine, the cylinder ridge must be removed before the piston and connecting rod assembly are removed. Failure to do so may cause which of the following problems?

    (A) Scored cylinder wall
    (B) Bent connecting rod
    (C) Broken piston skirt
    (D) Damaged piston ring lands

50. Which of the following would be the proper repair for an engine block with 0.015 inch of cylinder taper?

    (A) Bore the cylinders to oversize
    (B) Knurl the piston skirts
    (C) Install cylinder liners
    (D) Deglaze the cylinders

51. Technician A says that you should replace torque-to-yield cylinder head bolts with new ones whenever you remove them.

    Technician B says that torque-to-yield cylinder head bolts can be reinstalled if you torque them to specification, then tighten them an additional 90 degrees.

    Who is right?

    (A) A only
    (B) B only
    (C) Both A and B
    (D) Neither A nor B

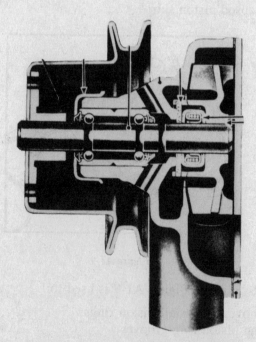

Figure A1-10.

52. The device shown in Figure A1-10 is located in the:

    (A) Transmission
    (B) Fuel system
    (C) Cooling system
    (D) Lubricating system

53. Which of the following engine conditions will cause blow-by?

    (A) Exhaust valves not seating
    (B) Clogged crankcase ventilation system
    (C) Compression leaking past the piston rings
    (D) Worn camshaft lobes

54. Installing a stronger spring in the lubrication system relief valve of an engine in good condition will result in:

    (A) Reduced oil consumption
    (B) Increased oil pressure
    (C) Decreased oil flow to the main bearings
    (D) Increased oil temperature

55. In a running engine, the coolest location will be:

    (A) The top of the radiator
    (B) The bottom of the radiator
    (C) The top of the cylinder head
    (D) The engine block

56. What is the main purpose of a water pump bypass hose?

    (A) To reduce suction and prevent radiator hoses from collapsing
    (B) To prevent air pockets from forming in the water pump housing
    (C) To relieve pressure at the water pump during high speed operation
    (D) To allow circulation of coolant in the engine when the thermostat is closed

57. While assembling a cylinder head, you notice the valve springs are the variable pitch type, the coils are wound tighter together at one end than at the other.

    Technician A says the close wound end of the spring is installed up, toward the tip end of the valve

    Technician B says the close wound end is installed down, toward the cylinder head.

    Who is right?

    (A) A only
    (B) B only
    (C) Both A and B
    (D) Neither A nor B

58. In a four-stroke gasoline engine, the distributor rotor rotates at:

    (A) The same speed as the camshaft
    (B) Twice the speed of the camshaft
    (C) The same speed as the crankshaft
    (D) Half the speed of the camshaft

Figure A1-11.

59. The tool shown in Figure A1-11 is being used to:

    (A) Balance the connecting rod
    (B) Remove metal from the connecting rod parting face
    (C) Straighten a bent connecting rod
    (D) Recondition the big-end bore of the connecting rod

60. In a high mileage engine, cylinder wear is normally greatest at the:

    (A) Top of the cylinder measured parallel to the crankshaft
    (B) Top of the cylinder measured at right angles to the crankshaft
    (C) Bottom of the cylinder measured parallel to the crankshaft
    (D) Bottom of the cylinder measured at right angles to the crank-
        shaft

61. In an OHV engine, excessive valve guide clearance will cause:

    (A) High oil consumption
    (B) High vacuum readings
    (C) A rich fuel mixture
    (D) Low compression readings

62. A pinging sound in an engine occurs on open throttle at low to
    moderate engine speed. This pinging may be caused by which of
    the following conditions?

    (A) Use of high octane fuel
    (B) Heavy carbon deposits in the cylinder
    (C) Low atmospheric temperature
    (D) Intake manifold heater valve stuck closed

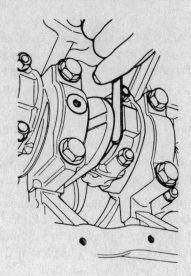

Figure A1-12.

63. The technician in Figure A1-12 is checking the:

    (A) Fillet radius profile
    (B) Crankshaft thrust clearance
    (C) Connecting rod side clearance
    (D) Connecting rod thrust clearance

64. Pressure in a mechanical fuel pump is maintained by:

    (A) An accumulator
    (B) A needle valve
    (C) A vacuum fuel pressure regulator
    (D) A spring under the diaphragm

65. Technician A says that the fuel level in the float bowl of some carburetors is adjusted by bending the arm on the float.

    Technician B says that the fuel level in the float bowl of some carburetors is adjusted by bending the little tab attached to the arm that pushes on the needle valve.

    Who is right?

    (A) A only
    (B) B only
    (C) Both A and B
    (D) Neither A nor B

66. Which of the following is a common cause of excessive back pressure in the engine?

    (A) A muffler with rust holes
    (B) A collapsed exhaust pipe
    (C) A blown exhaust manifold gasket
    (D) A clogged catalytic converter

67. A single diaphragm distributor vacuum advance unit is generally designed to:

    (A) Retard the spark when the engine overheats
    (B) Advance the spark in proportion to engine speed
    (C) Advance the spark completely under part throttle operation
    (D) Retard the spark during acceleration or full throttle operation

68. The block mating surfaces of the cylinder heads from a V-8 engine were machined to remove warpage, 0.030 inch of metal was removed from each head. Which of the following must also be machined before the heads are reinstalled?

    (A) The intake manifold surface of the heads
    (B) The deck surfaces of the cylinder block
    (C) The tops of the lifter valley on the cylinder block
    (D) The head and block mating surfaces of the intake manifold

69. A Hall-Effect switch, or Hall sender, on a computer controlled engine is designed to:

    (A) Monitor and correct fuel mixture
    (B) Signal the computer when to fire the sparkplugs
    (C) Monitor and adjust ignition timing
    (D) Signal the computer when to go to closed-loop mode

70. Technician A says that the knock sensor on a computer controlled engine can be checked using a digital volt-ohm meter or a scan tool.

    Technician B says knock sensor function can often be checked using a timing light and watch for a change as you tap the intake manifold with a hammer to simulate an engine ping.

    Who is right?

    (A) A only
    (B) B only
    (C) Both A and B
    (D) Neither A nor B

71. Stoichiometric ratio on a computer controlled engine is monitored by which of the following?

    (A) Oxygen sensor
    (B) Atmospheric pressure sensor
    (C) Crankshaft position sensor
    (D) Air flow sensor

Figure A1-13.

72. The measurement being taken in Figure A1-13 is used to calculate:

    (A) Connecting rod side clearance
    (B) Fillet radius
    (C) Thrust bearing clearance
    (D) Bearing saddle width

73. A car is in for a maintenance service, it has an engine with variable-valve timing and one of the procedures is to check ignition timing, although timing is not adjustable.

    Technician A says that you have to install a jump wire in the diagnostic connector to disable the variable-valve timing feature before you check the timing.

    Technician B says that by using an adjustable timing light you can compensate for the change so you do not have to disable the system.

    Who is right?

    (A) A only
    (B) B only
    (C) Both A and B
    (D) Neither A nor B

74. Insufficient residual pressure in a port fuel injection system can be caused by all of the following EXCEPT?

    (A) Defective fuel pressure regulator
    (B) Sticking fuel pump check valve
    (C) Leaking injector seals
    (D) Faulty fuel accumulator

75. The primary winding of an ignition coil is connected to the battery through the:

    (A) Condenser
    (B) Sparkplug wiring
    (C) Distributor cap and rotor
    (D) Ignition switch

76. With all types of fuel systems, an overly lean fuel mixture will result in an increase in which type of exhaust emission?

    (A) Oxides of nitrogen
    (B) Carbon monoxide
    (C) Unburned hydrocarbons and carbon monoxide
    (D) Particulate

77. The air flow control meter on a fuel injected engine may contain all of the following components EXCEPT the:

    (A) Canister purge valve
    (B) Throttle potentiometer
    (C) Air charge temperature sensor
    (D) Bypass air bleed

78. Under which of the following conditions is vapor lock most likely to occur?

    (A) With use of a highly volatile fuel
    (B) Driving the engine at low speed
    (C) Operating the engine at low altitudes
    (D) Failure to use antifreeze in the cooling system

79. When repairing a carburetor, the technician accidentally left the accelerator-pump inlet check ball out. What was the likely result?

    (A) Stalling or hesitation when the car is brought to idle
    (B) Excessive burning of oil due to too rich a mixture
    (C) Hard starting and hesitation when the throttle is opened
    (D) Engine backfire and flooding when the throttle is disengaged

80. Technician A says that after grinding valves and seats he laps the valves in with lapping compound to provide a good positive seal and to check the seat contact position.

    Technician B says that lapping the valves is a waste of time because the seating position will change as the engine warms up and the lapped seal will no longer be effective.

    Who is right?

    (A) A only
    (B) B only
    (C) Both A and B
    (D) Neither A nor B

END OF EXAMINATION A1.

SAMPLE EXAM, AUTOMATIC TRANSMISSION/TRANSAXLE TECHNICIAN

TEST A2, 40 Questions

DIRECTIONS: Each question has four suggested answers, lettered A, B, C, and D. Decide which one is the best answer, locate the question number on the sample answer sheet, and with a soft pencil darken the area that corresponds to the answer you have selected.

1. The power train includes all of the following EXCEPT the:

   (A) Clutch
   (B) Differential
   (C) Transmission
   (D) Steering gear

2. In the propeller shaft, a device is used to permit changes in shaft length. This device is called the:

   (A) Shaft joint
   (B) Slip joint
   (C) Length joint
   (D) Idler joint

3. A universal joint in the propeller shaft allows change in the:

   (A) Angle of drive
   (B) Speed of rotation
   (C) Length of the shaft
   (D) Direction of rotation

4. Slippage in the slip joint occurs between externally and internally mated:

   (A) Clutches
   (B) Splines
   (C) Couplings
   (D) Ball joints

5. How does a technician adjust gear-train end play when rebuilding an automatic transmission?

   (A) By removing the clutch plates and installing selective retainer rings
   (B) By changing the selective thrust washer
   (C) By installing different pinion carriers
   (D) By changing the snap ring

6. How many sun gears are used in a compound planetary gear set that has two sets of planetary pinions and two ring gears?

(A) 1
(B) 2
(C) 3
(D) 4

7. Technician A says that in order to produce gear reduction with a single planetary gear set, the carrier is always the output member.

Technician B says that in order to produce reverse gear with a single planetary gear set, the carrier is always the input member.

Who is right?

(A) A only
(B) B only
(C) Both A and B
(D) Neither A nor B

	CLUTCHES					BAND
GEAR RANGES	Low 1-Way Roller	Inter. 1-Way Sprag	Forward	High/ Rev Direct	Inter	Low/ Rev (rear)
Drive Low	**ON**	Off	**ON**	Off	Off	Off
Drive Second	Off	**ON**	**ON**	Off	**ON**	Off
Drive High	Off	Off	**ON**	**ON**	**ON**	Off
Manual Low	—	—	—	—	—	—
Reverse	Off	Off	Off	**ON**	Off	**ON**

Band and Clutch Application

Figure A2-1.

8. The band and clutch application chart shows which components are engaged to provide low, second, high, and reverse speeds. How would the band and clutches be actuated when manual low is selected?

(A)	Off	**ON**	**ON**	Off	Off	**ON**
(B)	Off	**ON**	**ON**	Off	**ON**	Off
(C)	**ON**	Off	**ON**	Off	Off	**ON**
(D)	**ON**	Off	**ON**	Off	**ON**	Off

9. Automatic transmissions use either gear-type or vane-type oil pumps. All of the following apply to both pump designs EXCEPT:

(A) They may provide a variable level of output volume.
(B) They may be driven by the torque converter hub.
(C) They may mount at the front of the transmission case.
(D) They may be driven by a pump driveshaft.

10. The servos of an automatic transmission can best be described as:

(A) Vacuum motors
(B) Planetary gears
(C) Electric switches
(D) Hydraulic pistons and cylinders

11. A car with automatic transmission moves forward in neutral at high engine speeds.

   Technician A says that a faulty clutch check valve ball could be the problem.

   Technician B says the cause of the problem might be a malfunction in the valve body.

   Who is right?

   (A) A only
   (B) B only
   (C) Both A and B
   (D) Neither A nor B

12. The best way to locate an oil pressure leak once the transmission pan has been removed would be to:

   (A) Perform a stall test
   (B) Perform a hydraulic pressure test
   (C) Perform a valve body pressure test
   (D) Perform an air pressure test

13. The sun gear of a single planetary gear set is held while the carrier is driven.

   Technician A says the result is that the sun gear will be driven to provide a reduction ratio.

   Technician B says the pinion gears and ring gear will both turn in the same direction.

   Who is right?

   (A) A only
   (B) B only
   (C) Both A and B
   (D) Neither A nor B

14. Technician A says that if 100 psi of hydraulic pressure is applied to a piston the result is a band application force of 100 pounds.

   Technician B says you divide the hydraulic pressure by the piston surface area of the servo to determine the application force.

   Who is right?

   (A) A only
   (B) B only
   (C) Both A and B
   (D) Neither A nor B

15. A servo is generally used to operate the:
   (A) Bands
   (B) Clutches
   (C) Shift valve
   (D) Governor

16. Which of the following statements about a transmission with electronic shift control is true?

    (A) The gear selector switch controls manual valve position
    (B) The vehicle speed sensor is used in place of the governor
    (C) The valve body is more complex due to the additional solenoids
    (D) The throttle position sensor indicates engine load

17. Technician A says that an air-pressure test can be used to check the operation of the servos and the clutches.

    Technician B says that in an air-pressure test can be used to check the operation of the valves and the accumulator.

    Who is right?

    (A) A only
    (B) B only
    (C) Both A and B
    (D) Neither A nor B

18. The servos in an electronically controlled automatic transmission are actuated by which of the following?

    (A) Vacuum pressure from the modulator
    (B) Centrifugal force from the governor
    (C) An electrical signal from the ECU
    (D) Hydraulic pressure from the pump

19. After installing an automatic transmission, a technician hears a squealing noise when the unit is in operation. What is the most likely source of this trouble?

    (A) Front pump drive sleeve or pump pinion
    (B) Defective torque converter
    (C) Speedometer drive pinion
    (D) Rear output shaft bearing

Figure A2-2.

20. The technician shown in Figure A2-2 is following the typical procedure for checking the transmission oil pump assembly by measuring:

   (A) Gear end to pump body clearance
   (B) Driven gear to crescent clearance
   (C) Driven gear to pump body clearance
   (D) bushing to converter-pump hub clearance

21. Fluid transmission coupling has maximum efficiency when the driven and driving members are turning at a ratio of:

   (A) 1:1
   (B) 1:2
   (C) 1:3
   (D) 1:4

22. The transmission shift lever in a car with automatic transmission has no detent feel. Where should a technician look for the source of trouble?

   (A) Shuttle valve
   (B) Clutch valve ball
   (C) Regulator valve spring
   (D) Manual valve lever

23. A servo is actuated to apply the band by:

   (A) Vacuum pressure
   (B) Pneumatic pressure
   (C) Hydraulic pressure
   (D) Electrical current

24. A three-element torque converter contains all of the following components EXCEPT:

   (A) Impeller
   (B) Stator
   (C) Overrunning sprag
   (D) Turbine

25. An automatic transmission with a vacuum modulator has abrupt and harsh upshifts. A hand vacuum pump connected to the modulator is unable to maintain a constant vacuum level.

   Technician A says the modulator is operating properly and the problem is in the vacuum signal; the cause could be a leaking intake manifold gasket.

   Technician B says the abrupt and harsh upshifts are the result of high throttle pressure caused by a defective modulator not relieving mainline pressure.

   Who is right?

   (A) A only
   (B) B only
   (C) Both A and B
   (D) Neither A nor B

26. In some automatic transmissions, the performance of the torque convertor, stator, clutch, and the transmission clutches may be checked by giving the transmission which of the following tests?

   (A) The stall test
   (B) The braking test
   (C) An acceleration test
   (D) An air-pressure test

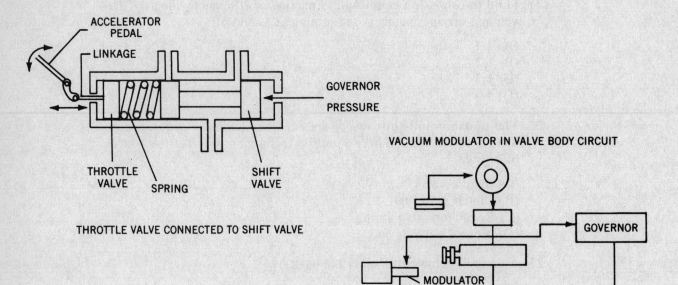

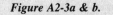

Figure A2-3a & b.

27. The control system pictured in Figure A2-3a & b shows that the shift valve is positioned by pressure from:

   (A) Governor
   (B) Modulator
   (C) Regulator
   (D) Both A and B

28. When the torque converter speed ratio is low, torque multiplication is:

   (A) Zero
   (B) Low
   (C) Variable in cycles
   (D) High

29. Which of the following components senses how fast the vehicle is traveling?

   (A) Governor valve
   (B) Manual valve
   (C) Throttle valve
   (D) Modulator valve

30. Overheating in an automatic transmission can be caused by all of the following EXCEPT:

   (A) Leaking governor seals
   (B) Incorrect engine idle speed
   (C) Improper fluid level
   (D) Faulty band application

31. Clutch apply pressure on an electronically controlled automatic transmission can be checked using:

   (A) A scan tool
   (B) A digital volt-ohm meter
   (C) Air pressure
   (D) A pressure gauge

32. Routine automatic transmission service generally includes all of the following operations EXCEPT:

   (A) Pan gasket replacement
   (B) Screen or filter replacement
   (C) Secondary screen replacement
   (D) Band adjustment

33. A pressure gauge can be use on a transmission installed in a running vehicle to verify all of the following EXCEPT:

   (A) Governor pressure
   (B) Mainline pressure
   (C) Modulator pressure
   (D) Servo apply pressure

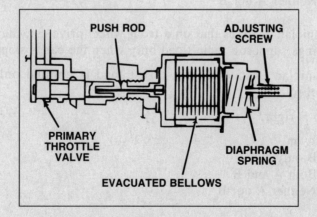

Figure A2-4.

34. The diagram shown in Figure A2-4 illustrates a typical:

    (A) Accumulator
    (B) Vacuum modulator
    (C) Throttle pressure regulator
    (D) Hydraulic servo

35. Technician A says the turbine is locked to the converter cover when a torque converter clutch is applied.

    Technician B says a centrifugally locked torque converter clutch slips to provide torque multiplication during hard acceleration at higher speeds.

    Who is right?

    (A) A only
    (B) B only
    (C) Both A and B
    (D) Neither A nor B

36. The owner of a car states that he hears a "buzzing" noise in the automatic transmission. Of the following, what is the most likely cause?

    (A) Bent pilot shaft
    (B) Clutch plates worn
    (C) Front pump malfunction
    (D) Vacuum leaks

37. Technician A says all modern automatic transmission fluids are basically the same, so any type can be used in any transmission.

    Technician B says transmission fluid operating temperature is the most important factor in determining when to change the fluid.

    Who is right?

    (A) A only
    (B) B only
    (C) Both A and B
    (D) Neither A nor B

38. Technician A states that on a front wheel drive car, the front wheel bearings support a radial load only when the car is stopped.

    Technician B states that a thrust load is applied only when the wheel rotates.

    Who is right?

    (A) A only
    (B) B only
    (C) Both A and B
    (D) Neither A nor B

39. The most common type of universal assembly used in today's front wheel drive cars are:

    (A) Cross and roller
    (B) Double Cardan joint
    (C) Constant velocity assembly
    (D) Ball and Trunion

40. The output shafts of an automatic transaxle are driven by:

    (A) Pinion gears
    (B) Chain drive
    (C) Ring gear assembly
    (D) Side gears

END OF EXAMINATION A2.

SAMPLE EXAM, MANUAL DRIVE TRAIN AND AXLE TECHNICIAN

TEST A3, 40 Questions

DIRECTIONS: Each question has four suggested answers, lettered A, B, C, and D. Decide which one is the best answer, locate the question number on the sample answer sheet, and with a soft pencil darken the area that corresponds to the answer you have selected.

1. The friction facing of a dry-type clutch disc is found to be oil soaked. The technician should:

   (A) Replace the clutch disc
   (B) Replace the main seal
   (C) Clean the disc with solvent
   (D) Increase the clutch spring pressure

2. A heaving growl is heard whenever the clutch pedal is depressed.

   Technician A says a defective pilot bearing could be causing the noise.

   Technician B says the growl could be caused by a defective clutch release bearing.

   Who is right?

   (A) A only
   (B) B only
   (C) Both A and B
   (D) Neither A nor B

3. To properly service a clutch of the type found on most cars, it is important that the face or frictional surface of the flywheel should run true within a tolerance of about:

   (A) 0.006 inch
   (B) 0.012 inch
   (C) 0.018 inch
   (D) 0.025 inch

4. When the clutch is engaged in a car with manual transmission, spring pressure clamps the friction disc between the pressure plate and the?

   (A) Differential
   (B) Sun gear
   (C) Flywheel
   (D) Reaction plate

5. Technician A says that a clutch that spins when disengaged is likely to have incorrect pedal linkage adjustment.

   Technician B says that a clutch that spins when disengaged is likely to have weak or broken pressure springs.

   Who is right?

   (A) A only
   (B) B only
   (C) Both A and B
   (D) Neither A nor B

6. The clutch is replaced on a car that uses a cable to operate the clutch, a typical specification for adjusting the clutch pedal "free play" would be:

   (A) 0.25 to 0.50 inch
   (B) 1.00 to 1.50 inch
   (C) 0.50 to 0.75 inch
   (D) 1.50 to 2.00 inch

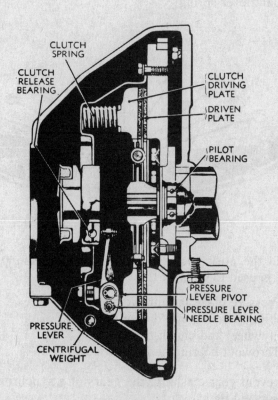

Figure A3-1.

7. Which type pressure plate is used on clutch assembly shown in Figure A3-1?

   (A) Semi-centrifugal
   (B) Diaphragm spring
   (C) Torsion spring
   (D) Coil spring

8. Which of the following clutch parts is located between the engine flywheel and the pressure plate?

   (A) Clutch fork
   (B) Friction disc
   (C) Clutch release lever
   (D) Adjusting screw

9. Clutch linkage binding, misaligned linkage parts, or weak pressure springs may result in all of the following EXCEPT:

   (A) High pedal effort
   (B) Improper clutch release
   (C) Rapid friction disc wear
   (D) Excessive runout

10. In a spring-loaded clutch disc, the torsion springs cushion rotational shock and engagement shock is absorbed by the:

    (A) Anti-rattle springs
    (B) Helical springs
    (C) Diaphragm spring
    (D) Cantilever spring

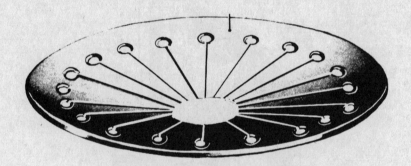

Figure A3-2.

11. When the clutch is engaged, the component pictured in Figure A3-2 is used to connect the:

    (A) Pressure plate and throwout bearing
    (B) Friction facing and driven plate
    (C) Flywheel and clutch plate
    (D) Throwout bearing and clutch cover

12. To prevent gear clashing, the gears of a synchromesh transmission are engaged by a:

    (A) Sliding collar and fork
    (B) Planetary unit
    (C) Slip joint or spline
    (D) Friction and dog clutch

13. Technician A says that you should replace all transmission gears in sets, even if only one gear is bad.

Technician B says that if only one gear on the output shaft is bad you can replace the individual gear, but you must also replace the input shaft gear.

Who is right?

(A) A only
(B) B only
(C) Both A and B
(D) Neither A nor B

14. A customer complains that the manual transmission jumps out of gear.

Technician A says that improperly adjusted shift linkage could be the cause, and a simple adjustment might cure the problem without removing the transmission.

Technician B says that worn main shaft bearings might be at fault, and if so the transmission will have to disassembled to replace them.

Who is right?

(A) A only
(B) B only
(C) Both A and B
(D) Neither A nor B

15. The forward speeds of most fully synchronized manual transmissions are provided by:

(A) Spur gears
(B) Hypoid gears
(C) Helical gears
(D) Double helical gears

16. A sliding gear transmission generally uses an idler gear to:

(A) Connect the input shaft to the output shaft
(B) Obtain an overdrive gear ratio
(C) Reverse the direction of rotation
(D) Obtain a gear reduction ratio

17. The counter shaft drive gear in a manual transmission is meshed with a gear on which of the following?

(A) Main shaft
(B) Idler shaft
(C) Drive shaft
(D) Output shaft

18. Technician A says that in the fully synchronized three-speed transmission first gear is always in mesh.

Technician B says that in the fully synchronized three-speed transmission second gear is always in mesh.

Who is right?

(A) A only
(B) B only
(C) Both A and B
(D) Neither A nor B

19. The gears on a standard transmission clash when the clutch pedal is depressed and the transmission is shifted from neutral into low gear. The most likely cause would be:

    (A) Worn synchronizers and sliding collars
    (B) A warped clutch disc
    (C) Excessive clutch pedal free travel
    (D) Broken springs in the clutch hub

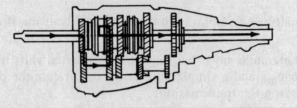

Figure A3-3.

20. What gear is engaged in the transmission shown as figure A3-3?

    (A) First gear
    (B) Second gear
    (C) Third gear
    (D) Fourth gear

21. If the transmission shown in Figure A3-3 is fully synchronized, how many synchronizer assemblies would be required?

    (A) 5
    (B) 4
    (C) 3
    (D) 2

22. In a car equipped with overdrive, Technician A says failure of the system to go into overdrive can be due to a misaligned clutch plate.

    Technician B says the overdrive electric control momentarily interrupts sun gear mesh as the transmission comes out of overdrive.

    Who is right?

    (A) A only
    (B) B only
    (C) Both A and B
    (D) Neither A nor B

23. A customer with a FWD car complains that it makes a clicking noise that sounds like the transmission as it is driven around corners.

    Technician A says too much backlash in the differential side gears could be the source of the noise.

    Technician B says that a worn CV joint is the likely cause.

    Who is right?

    (A) A only
    (B) B only
    (C) Both A and B
    (D) Neither A nor B

24. In most syncromesh transmissions, the drive gears are helical cut gears and the synchronizer gears are:

    (A) Spur cut gears
    (B) Hypoid cut gears
    (C) Bevel cut gears
    (D) Dog cut gears

25. In a four-speed fully synchronized transmission that uses two shifting forks for all forward speeds, the synchronizer closest to the input shaft must be engaged when the transmission is in:

    (A) First and fourth gears
    (B) First and reverse gears
    (C) Second and third gears
    (D) Third and fourth gears

26. A continuous noise was heard coming from the rear axle when the transmission was shifted into neutral while the car was moving.

    Technician A said this can be caused by a worn pinion bearing.

    Technician B said this could be caused by a worn axle bearing.

    Who is right?

    (A) A only
    (B) B only
    (C) Both A and B
    (D) Neither A nor B

27. A differential pinion gear has eleven teeth. The ring gear has thirty-nine teeth.

    Technician A says the gear ratio is 3.54 to 1.

    Technician B says the gear ratio is 4.11 to 1.

    Who is right?

    (A) A only
    (B) B only
    (C) Both A and B
    (D) Neither A nor B

28. A overdrive gear ratio can be obtained with a planetary gear set by locking either the ring gear or the?

    (A) Overrunning clutch
    (B) Pinion gear
    (C) Sun gear
    (D) Planet carrier

29. In a final drive assembly, the ring gear is bolted to the:

    (A) Carrier
    (B) Pinion shaft
    (C) Drive axle
    (D) Differential case

30. In a limited slip differential, a chatter is felt as the vehicle starts to move.

    Technician A says that the problem could be caused by the wrong lubricant.

    Technician B says that the backlash being out of adjustment could be the cause.

    Who is right?

    (A) A only
    (B) B only
    (C) Both A and B
    (D) Neither A nor B

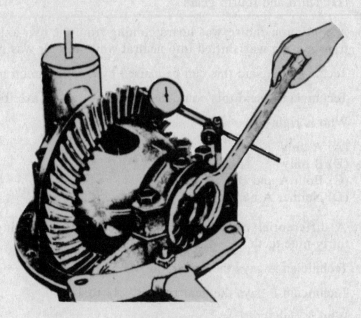

Figure A3-4.

31. Figure A3-4 shows a typical setup for checking:

    (A) Pinion bearing preload
    (B) Pinion to ring gear backlash
    (C) Ring gear end play
    (D) Ring gear runout

32. A dye check on the gear teeth of a reconditioned differential shows heavy flank contact on the drive gear teeth.

    Technician A says you can correct the gear mesh by adjusting the pinion height.

    Technician B says you have to move the ring gear out from the pinion to get the right gear contact.

    Who is right?

    (A) A only
    (B) B only
    (C) Both A and B
    (D) Neither A nor B

33. Heavy heel contact on the differential gear teeth can produce a noise that is most noticeable when the vehicle?

    (A) Decelerates
    (B) Accelerates
    (C) Drives around corners
    (D) Undergoes a gear change

34. Which of the following does the Hotchkiss drive use to absorb torque from the rear-end?

    (A) A Panhard rod
    (B) Springs
    (C) Torsion bars
    (D) A torque tube

35. A car with manual transaxle will not shift into third gear, while all of the other gears can be selected and there is no unusual noise.

    Technician A says that a worn torque strut can allow the engine to twist and prevent engagement.

    Technician B says that worn shift linkage bushings or damaged linkage could cause the problem.

    Who is right?

    (A) A only
    (B) B only
    (C) Both A and B
    (D) Neither A nor B

36. A continuous noise comes from a rear axle when a RWD car pulls straight ahead. What is the most likely cause?

    (A) Excessive axle play
    (B) Worn differential pinions
    (C) Loose pinion shaft bearings
    (D) Excessive side gear backlash

37. In a differential, when the pinion gear engages the ring gear below the center line of the axle, the gear tooth cut must have a:

    (A) Hypoid face
    (B) Spur bevel
    (C) Spiral bevel
    (D) Double helix

38. Which of the following statements best applies to the differential carrier of a conventional differential?

    (A) It carries the drive pinion bushing
    (B) It is supported by roller bearings
    (C) It is stamped with the bearing cap marking
    (D) It is completely machined from a forging

39. Improper tooth contact between the drive pinion and drive gear can be identified by which of the following sounds?

(A) Pinging
(B) Tapping
(C) Clanking
(D) Whining

40. Worn or damaged axle carrier bearings will generally produce a constant whirring or humming noise when:

(A) A gear change is made
(B) The car is moving
(C) The car is accelerating
(D) The car is decelerating or coasting

END OF EXAMINATION A3.

SAMPLE EXAM, SUSPENSION AND STEERING TECHNICIAN

TEST A4, 40 Questions

DIRECTIONS: Each question has four suggested answers, lettered A, B, C, and D. Decide which one is the best answer, locate the question number on the sample answer sheet, and with a soft pencil darken the area that corresponds to the answer you have selected.

1. Which of the following is the most common cause of spring breakage on an automobile?

   (A) Overloading
   (B) Faulty lubrication
   (C) Spring misalignment
   (D) Deterioration of rubber mountings

2. In a typical steering mechanism linkage, the idler arm is normally attached to the:

   (A) Spindle
   (B) Tie rod
   (C) Center link
   (D) Pitman arm

3. To obtain initial preload, which tool should be used to adjust front bearings on most RWD cars with conventional front suspensions?

   (A) A spring scale
   (B) A torque wrench
   (C) A dial indicator
   (D) A tension gauge

4. A car with torsion bar front suspension is in the shop for a wheel alignment.

   Technician A says the torsion bars should be adjusted before the caster and camber are adjusted.

   Technician B says that you should set the toe angle to specifications after you adjust the torsion bars.

   Who is right?

   (A) A only
   (B) B only
   (C) Both A and B
   (D) Neither A nor B

5. Which of the following is likely to cause steering gear damage?

(A) Hitting curbs
(B) Sudden stops
(C) Fast acceleration
(D) Excessive lubrication

6. Which would be the most probable cause of a car wandering from side to side as it is being driven on a level road?

(A) Bent stub axle
(B) Bent steering arm
(C) Loose or worn steering connections
(D) Front wheels out of alignment

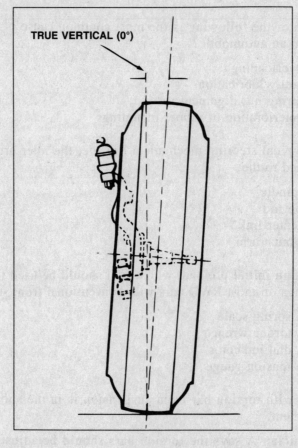

TRUE VERTICAL (0°)

Figure A4-1.

7. Which of the following alignment angles is illustrated by the wheel shown in Figure A4-1?

(A) Positive caster
(B) Negative caster
(C) Positive camber
(D) Negative camber

8. The steering geometry of modern cars is designed so that during a turn the chassis will lift slightly. Which of the following causes the vehicle to lift?

(A) Toe angle
(B) Roll steer
(C) Steering axis inclination
(D) Positive camber settings

9. A customer has a car equipped with manual steering and complains that it has recently become difficult to steer and requires considerable effort to turn the steering wheel.

Technician A says that insufficient preload on the steering gear could be the cause and an adjustment might cure the problem.

Technician B says to check the tire pressures first, the cause could simply be low inflation pressure.

Who is right?

(A) A only
(B) B only
(C) Both A and B
(D) Neither A nor B

10. Which of the following would be a typical steering gear reduction for passenger vehicles?

(A) 4-to-1
(B) 8-to-1
(C) 12-to-1
(D) 16-to-1

11. The reason for adjusting toe-in by turning the adjusting sleeves on the tie rods equal amounts in opposite directions would be to:

(A) Prevent excessive play in the steering wheel
(B) Center the steering wheel
(C) Keep the vehicle tracking straight
(D) Avoid an excessive adjustment

12. A buzzing noise occurs in a car with power steering when the engine is running at fast idle. The noise is heard when the wheels are straight, but disappears when the wheels are turned. Which of the following is the most likely cause of the noise?

(A) A broken relief spring
(B) Low fluid level
(C) A clogged high-pressure line
(D) A sticking pressure control valve

13. A technician tests a ball joint that is unloaded and finds slightly more than ¼ inch of play. This indicates that the ball joint:

(A) Should be replaced
(B) Should be tightened
(C) Should be lubricated
(D) Is within tolerable limits

14. The steering knuckle is rigidly attached to which of the following components?

(A) Kingpin
(B) Pitman arm
(C) Center link
(D) Wheel spindle

15. To remove a rack and pinion steering gear from most cars you will have to perform all of the following EXCEPT:

(A) Disconnect the outer tie rod ends from the steering knuckles
(B) Disconnect and remove the rack mounting bolts from the frame
(C) Disconnect the inner tie rods from the steering rack
(D) Disconnect the steering shaft coupler from the pinion

16. Which of the following is the most likely cause of a FWD vehicle pulling to one side whenever the it is brought to a stop?

(A) A defective CV joint
(B) A binding front wheel bearing
(C) A sticking brake caliper
(D) A worn strut or collapsed spring

17. Which of the following statements about a front antiroll bar is true?

(A) It applies force opposite to that of the springs when the springs are deflected equally
(B) The bar normally connects to both lower control arms
(C) The bar is adjustable to level the vehicle
(D) One end attaches to the lower control arm and the other end connects to the frame of the vehicle

18. Technician A says that in order to properly adjust a recirculating ball worm and nut steering gear, you should have the gear in the center position when making the pitman shaft gear over-center adjustment.

Technician B says that in order to properly adjust a recirculating ball worm and nut steering gear, you center the steering gear, then check gear mesh preload by turning the worm shaft with a torque wrench.

Who is right?

(A) A only
(B) B only
(C) Both A and B
(D) Neither A nor B

19. In order to check ball joint wear on a vehicle that has the coil spring between the front crossmember and the lower control arm, it is usually necessary to:

(A) Place a support wedge between the upper arm and the frame and jack up the lower arm
(B) Place a support wedge between the upper arm and the frame and jack up the frame
(C) Lower the control arm
(D) Disconnect the steering knuckle

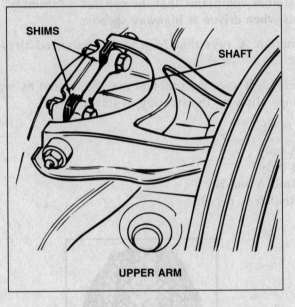

SHIMS

SHAFT

UPPER ARM

Figure A4-2.

20. When adjusting the alignment on the left front wheel of a vehicle as shown in Figure A4-2, the technician removes shims from the bolt at the front of the shaft only. This adjustment would move the:

(A) Caster in the negative direction and the camber in the negative direction
(B) Caster in the negative direction and the camber in the positive direction
(C) Caster in the positive direction and the camber in the negative direction
(D) Caster in the positive direction and the camber in the positive direction

21. Which of the following adjustments helps the steering of a car by returning it to a straight position after cornering?

(A) Camber
(B) Caster
(C) Toe-in
(D) Toe-out

22. A technician measures the distance from the right lower ball joint to a point on the left side of the rear axle. This is one of the measurements used to check which of the following?

(A) Vehicle tracking
(B) Vehicle wheelbase
(C) Toe-out on turns
(D) Suspension concentricity

23. When an automobile makes a sharp turn, the inside rear wheel will:

    (A) Rotate at a faster speed than the outside rear wheel
    (B) Rotate at a slower speed than the outside rear wheel
    (C) Rotate at the same speed as the outside rear wheel
    (D) Slip slightly to prevent axle wind-up

24. A customer complains that the car has a "shimmy" from the front wheels when driven at highway speeds.

    Technician A says that improperly balanced tires are the likely cause.

    Technician B says the problem may be caused by worn control arm bushings allowing the steering to flex at speed.

    Who is right?

    (A) A only
    (B) B only
    (C) Both A and B
    (D) Neither A nor B

Figure A4-3.

25. The tire shown in Figure A4-3 shows wear in the center of the track. This generally indicates which of the following?

    (A) Over-inflated tires
    (B) Worn shock absorbers
    (C) Improper wheel balance
    (D) Incorrect toe setting

26. A technician cannot correct the alignment on a FWD vehicle equipped with MacPherson struts. The problem is most likely caused by which of the following?

    (A) Worn tie rod ends
    (B) Bent strut
    (C) Weak springs
    (D) Worn strut cartridge valves

27. Technician A says that after installing new lower control arm pivot bushings you should tighten the bolts until the bushings just begin to bulge.

Technician B says that after installing new lower control arm pivot bushings you preload the bushings by tighten the bolts with the control arm resting against the frame.

Who is right?

(A) A only
(B) B only
(C) Both A and B
(D) Neither A nor B

28. Both front tires show shoulder wear on both sides of the treads. This condition is probably caused by:

(A) Over-inflation
(B) High cornering loads
(C) Under-inflation
(D) Incorrect toe-in

29. If a loud, dull thump can be heard when a car hits a small rise in the road, the noise is likely to be caused by which of the following?

(A) Over-inflated tires
(B) Worn antiroll bar bushings
(C) Poorly lubricated suspension
(D) Sagging front springs

30. Technician A says that when performing a four-wheel alignment on a car you should always make adjustments to the rear wheels first, then set the front wheel angles.

Technician B says that setting the camber angle should be the first adjustment you make when aligning either the front or rear wheels.

Who is right?

(A) A only
(B) B only
(C) Both A and B
(D) Neither A nor B

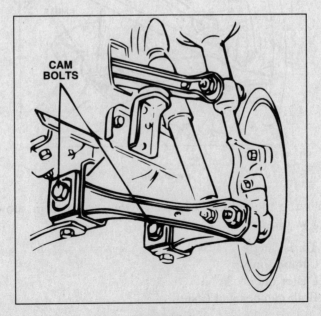

Figure A4-4.

31. The cam bolts on the front control arm shown in Figure A4-4 can be used to adjust:

   (A) Thrust angle
   (B) Camber only
   (C) Caster only
   (D) Both camber and caster

32. The steering gear may be connected to the steering column by all of the following EXCEPT:

   (A) A universal joint
   (B) A Rzeppa joint
   (C) A pot joint
   (D) A flexible coupling

33. A customer complains that the steering wheel on a car with power rack and pinion steering does not return to center after driving around corners.

   Technician A says the problem could be caused by a sticking pressure relief valve.

   Technician B says that low fluid level could be the cause.

   Who is right?
   (A) A only
   (B) B only
   (C) Both A and B
   (D) Neither A nor B

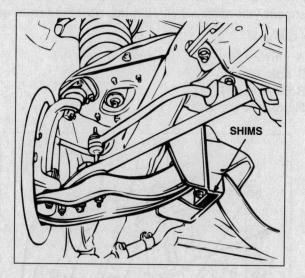

Figure A4-5.

34. Removing the shims from the lower control arm shown in figure A4-5 would change:

   (A) Thrust angle
   (B) Camber only
   (C) Caster only
   (D) Both camber and caster

35. Improperly adjusted caster angles can cause all of the following problems EXCEPT:

    (A) Hard steering
    (B) Rapid tire wear
    (C) Pulling to one side
    (D) High speed instability

36. A technician adjusting alignment of the front wheels to obtain maximum tire mileage will adjust the wheels so the rolling tire will:

    (A) Have toe-in
    (B) Have positive camber
    (C) Have camber to compensate for toe-in
    (D) Be perpendicular and have zero toe-in

37. Technician A says that most cars are aligned with a certain amount of toe-in to counteract the effect of positive camber.

    Technician B says that most cars are aligned with a certain amount of positive caster for better stability and to help the steering return to center.

    Who is right?
    (A) A only
    (B) B only
    (C) Both A and B
    (D) Neither A nor B

38. When caster, camber, and toe-in have been adjusted, steering axis inclination and toe-out figures should be correct. If the steering axis inclination and toe-out figures are not correct, a likely cause could be all of the following EXCEPT:

    (A) Bent suspension components
    (B) Worn ball joints
    (C) Worn steering parts
    (D) Severely worn tires

39. A car with heavy loads in the rear will show:

    (A) An increase in camber
    (B) An increase in caster
    (C) A decrease in camber
    (D) A decrease in caster

40. A radial tire has a "P 285/60 ZR 16" designation. What does the "60" indicate?

    (A) Tread width
    (B) Aspect ratio
    (C) Section height
    (D) Rim width

END OF EXAMINATION A4.

SAMPLE EXAM, BRAKE TECHNICIAN

TEST A5, 50 Questions

DIRECTIONS: Each question has four suggested answers, lettered A, B, C, and D. Decide which one is the best answer, locate the question number on the sample answer sheet, and with a soft pencil darken the area that corresponds to the answer you have selected.

1. When the brakes are applied on a car with a vacuum power booster the pedal drops slightly when the engine is started.

   Technician A says a leaking power booster diaphragm could be the cause of the problem.

   Technician B says the problem could be from a sticking manifold vacuum check valve or a collapsed vacuum hose.

   Who is right?

   (A) A only
   (B) B only
   (C) Both A and B
   (D) Neither A nor B

2. Which of the following is likely to result from excessive wear of the brake linings?

   (A) Brake drag
   (B) Warped drums
   (C) High pedal effort
   (D) Scoring of drums

3. While a running test of a braking system is being made, it is found that the brake drum on one of the wheels runs abnormally cool. This condition is most likely caused by:

   (A) A worn brake lining
   (B) An inoperative brake
   (C) A broken return spring
   (D) A scored or worn brake drum

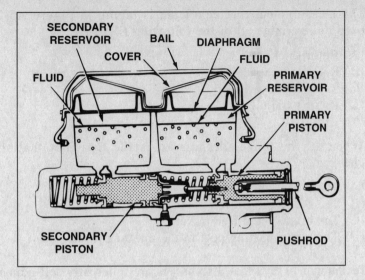

Figure A5-1.

4. Figure A5-1 shows a cut-a-way drawing of a typical:

   (A) Quick-take-up master cylinder
   (B) Dual-piston master cylinder
   (C) Stepped-bore master cylinder
   (D) Central hydraulic master cylinder

5. If the rear wheels lock when heavy brake pressure is applied in a dual braking system, a likely source of trouble might be:

   (A) Worn brake bands
   (B) Brake fluid leak
   (C) A defective proportioning valve
   (D) Frozen star adjuster

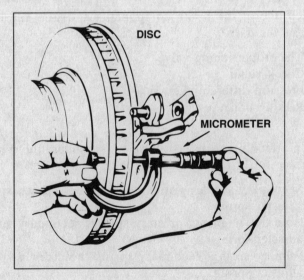

Figure A5-2.

6. The measurement the technician is taking in Figure A5-2 can be used to determine all of the following EXCEPT:

   (A) Rotor thickness
   (B) Rotor lateral runout
   (C) Rotor taper variation
   (D) Rotor parallelism

7. When all the brakes drag, what is the first part that should be checked?

   (A) The wheel cylinders
   (B) The brake fluid level
   (C) The brake pedal free travel
   (D) The compensating port in the master cylinder

8. Technician A says that disc brakes are inherently self-adjusting.

   Technician B says that disc brakes have superior cooling to drum brakes.

   Who is right?

   (A) A only
   (B) B only
   (C) Both A and B
   (D) Neither A nor B

9. If a technician hears noise when the brakes are applied, the cause could be any of the following EXCEPT:

   (A) Linings not fully broken in
   (B) Use of improper lining or pad
   (C) Disc with excessive lateral runout
   (D) Linings or pads soiled with grease or oil

10. Which one of the brake components activates the brake warning light on the dash?

    (A) The proportioning valve
    (B) Check valve
    (C) Pressure differential switch
    (D) Parking brake lever

11. When a technician is installing brake shoes, the most convenient sequence for installing the springs is:

    (A) Secondary spring, primary spring, hold down spring, and star adjuster spring
    (B) Hold down spring, primary spring, secondary spring, and star adjuster spring
    (C) Primary spring, secondary spring, hold down spring, and star adjuster spring
    (D) Star adjuster spring, primary spring, secondary spring, and hold down spring

12. Of the following, which will most likely cause the front brakes on a disc-drum brake system to be overly sensitive to light pedal pressure?

   (A) Air in the system
   (B) A defective metering valve
   (C) A malfunctioning cylinder in the brakes
   (D) Clogged compensating port in the master cylinder

13. A sliding or floating caliper is more advantageous than a fixed caliper for all of the following EXCEPT:

   (A) Improved heat transfer
   (B) Lighter weight
   (C) Smaller size
   (D) Ease of service

14. Technician A says that hydraulic brake boosters that are pressurized by the power steering pump often use a gas charged accumulator to store pressure.

   Technician B says that brake systems that use a dedicated electric pump to supply pressure generally have an accumulator that stores pressure that is only used for reserve braking.

   Who is right?

   (A) A only
   (B) B only
   (C) Both A and B
   (D) Neither A nor B

15. Technician A says that brake torque is absorbed on the front wheels by the knuckle and suspension control arms.

   Technician B says that brake torque is absorbed on the rear wheels by the differential and drive shaft.

   Who is right?

   (A) A only
   (B) B only
   (C) Both A and B
   (D) Neither A nor B

16. When replacing the brake shoes in a single anchor duo-servo system the primary shoe should be installed to:

   (A) Face the front on all brakes
   (B) Face the rear on all brakes
   (C) Face the front on the right-side brakes and face the rear on the left-side brakes
   (D) Face the rear on the right-side brakes and face the front on the left-side brakes

17. Semi-metallic brake linings offer all of the following EXCEPT:

    (A) Increased fade resistance
    (B) Improved heat dissipation
    (C) Improved cold performance
    (D) Increased service life

18. When disc brake pads are retracted so that they are not touching the brake rotor surface, the amount of retraction:

    (A) Is affected by the piston seals
    (B) Is limited by the metering valve
    (C) Is hydraulically controlled
    (D) Is affected by the piston return springs

19. Which of the following is the primary advantage of an anti-lock brake system?

    (A) Brake pad wear is greatly reduced
    (B) Directional control is allowed during maximum braking
    (C) To stop the car in a short distance on wet pavement
    (D) To maintain stability on irregular surfaces

20. The brake pedal on a car with four-wheel disc brakes pulsates rapidly when the brakes are applied. This condition could be caused by any of the following EXCEPT:

    (A) A loose wheel bearing
    (B) An uneven rotor thickness
    (C) Excessive rotor runout
    (D) Sticking caliper slides

21. Which of the following is the correct procedure to test the brake system warning lights?

    (A) Use an ammeter to check circuit continuity
    (B) Use jump wires at the brake distributor switch assembly
    (C) Remove the warning light bulb and test it with an ohmmeter
    (D) Hold the brake pedal in a depressed position and open a bleed screw at one of the wheels

22. As a general rule, how much free action should there be at the brake pedal?

    (A) ¼ inch
    (B) ¾ inch
    (C) 1 inch
    (D) 1½ inch

23. In order to perform properly, brake fluid must have which of the following properties?

    (A) Low viscosity and volatility
    (B) High "wetting" characteristics
    (C) High boiling point
    (D) Detergent properties to keep parts clean

24. Technician A says that a dial indicator can be used to check a disc brake rotor for taper variation and parallelism.

Technician B says that disc brake rotor lateral runout can be checked either on the vehicle or on a brake lathe using a dial indicator.

Who is right?

(A) A only
(B) B only
(C) Both A and B
(D) Neither A nor B

25. When a technician loosens the locknut on the equalizer yoke, located under the ear, and turns the adjusting nut. He is making an adjustment to which of the following?

(A) Disc brake
(B) Pedal free play
(C) Parking brake
(D) Rear brake shoes

26. Technician A says that riveted brake shoe linings are advantageous because they have a squeak-resisting tendency and are easy to reline.

Technician B says that bonded brake shoe linings are advantageous because they give long life.

Who is right?

(A) A only
(B) B only
(C) Both A and B
(D) Neither A nor B

27. Technician A says to use an 80-grit abrasive to finish rotors that will be installed with semi-metallic pads, a fairly rough surface finish allows the new pads to grip and seat in rapidly.

Technician B says rotors that will be installed with semi-metallic pads the should by finished on a lathe using a 120-grit abrasive to get the smooth surface needed for proper break-in.

Who is right?

(A) A only
(B) B only
(C) Both A and B
(D) Neither A nor B

28. When pressure bleeding the hydraulics of a disc-drum brake system the pressure tank should be charged to approximately:

(A) 40 psi
(B) 30 psi
(C) 20 psi
(D) 10 psi

29. Upon applying the foot brakes of a car, the brake pedal goes to the floorboard, but it can be pumped up. This condition could be caused by all of the following EXCEPT:

(A) Air in the hydraulic system
(B) An internal master cylinder leak
(C) A clogged quick-take-up valve
(D) Rear drum brakes out of adjustment

30. Technician A says that when bleeding brakes you should always start with the bleeder farthest from the master cylinder and work your way in order to the bleeder closest to the master cylinder.

Technician B says that with diagonal-split brakes you bleed the right side brakes first, then bleed the left side.

Who is right?

(A) A only
(B) B only
(C) Both A and B
(D) Neither A nor B

31. What would be the proper procedure when a technician discovers that the brake fluid is contaminated?

(A) Flush the system with alcohol
(B) Replace all hydraulic rubber cups and seals, and fluid
(C) Add a decontamination oil to the system
(D) Bleed and flush the hydraulic system

32. The steering wheel of a car with disc-drum brakes shimmies as the brakes are applied.

Technician A says that the problem could be caused by excessive rotor runout or loose wheel bearings.

Technician B says worn suspension parts or out-of-balance wheels could cause the shimmy.

Who is right?

(A) A only
(B) B only
(C) Both A and B
(D) Neither A nor B

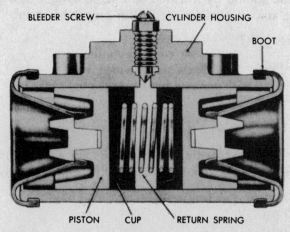

Figure A5-3.

33. The device shown in Figure A5-3 is used to change:

   (A) Electrical energy to mechanical force
   (B) Rotational torque to direct line pressure
   (C) Hydraulic pressure to mechanical force
   (D) Heat energy to electrical energy

34. On vehicles equipped only with hydraulic braking, the most serious danger that may occur is:

   (A) Unequal braking
   (B) Loss of the brake fluid
   (C) A defect in the metering valve
   (D) A dirty or clogged wheel cylinder

35. Technicians check the hydraulic system for leaks by:

   (A) Using a pressure gauge
   (B) Using a metering device
   (C) Checking the master cylinder
   (D) Applying steady pressure to the pedal

36. Where is the anchor pin in self-energizing drum brakes usually located?

   (A) At the end of the shoe
   (B) At the mid point of the shoe
   (C) As close to the cam as possible
   (D) As near the drum center as possible

37. When the brake pedal operating a hydraulic brake system is released quickly, the initial makeup fluid is supplied to the pressure chamber of the master cylinder through the:

   (A) Check valve
   (B) Port hole
   (C) Compensating port
   (D) Bleeder holes in the piston

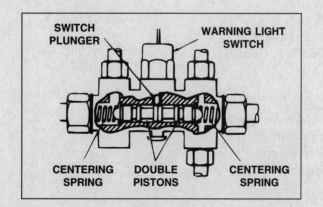

Figure A5-4.

38. Figure A5-4 illustrates a typical:

    (A) Proportioning valve
    (B) Combination valve
    (C) Metering valve
    (D) Pressure differential valve

39. Which of the following statements about the use of proportioning and metering valves in hydraulic brake systems is correct?

    (A) The proportioning valve is installed in the line to the front brakes of a four-drum brake system to balance the pressures on the front and rear brake shoes
    (B) The metering valve is installed directly after the master cylinder to prevent brake lock-up during panic stops
    (C) The proportioning valve is placed in the line to the rear drum brakes when disc brakes are used in the front
    (D) The metering valve is placed in the line to the rear drum brakes when disc brakes are used in the front

40. A force of 50 pounds is applied to the push rod of the one-inch bore master cylinder in a properly operating hydraulic brake system. The master cylinder is connected to a 1-½-inch bore wheel cylinder. The fluid pressure in the wheel cylinder is approximately:

    (A) 50 psi
    (B) 75 psi
    (C) 100 psi
    (D) 25 psi

41. On a vacuum assisted disc-drum type brake system the brake pedal slowly goes to the floor as the vehicle is brought to a stop.

    Technician A says that a leaking primary cup in the master cylinder could be causing the problem.

    Technician B says that the problem could be a faulty residual check valve in the master cylinder.

    Who is right?

    (A) A only
    (B) B only
    (C) Both A and B
    (D) Neither A nor B

42. Most modern brake systems use which type of brake fluid?

    (A) Hydraulic System Mineral Oil (HMSO)
    (B) Ethylene glycol
    (C) Polyglycol
    (D) Silicone

43. Brake fluid should be periodically flushed from the system and replaced because it:

    (A) Causes rubber deterioration when it gets old
    (B) Is hygroscopic and loses its performance capability
    (C) Chemically breaks down due to extreme temperatures
    (D) Turns to sludge and becomes slow to react

44. The pad on the piston side of a single piston floating caliper disc brake is worn to minimum thickness, the pad on the opposite side of the same caliper is only slightly worn.

    Technician A says that the uneven wear could be caused by too much rotor runout.

    Technician B says that a leaking caliper piston seal may be causing the problem.

    Who is right?

    (A) A only
    (B) B only
    (C) Both A and B
    (D) Neither A nor B

45. When pressure bleeding a disc-drum system there is no fluid flow when the front caliper bleed screw is opened, the pressure bleeding equipment is properly connected and charged. Which of the following is the most likely cause?

    (A) The pressure differential valve is faulty
    (B) The metering valve release button is not activated
    (C) The proportioning valve release button is not activated
    (D) The compensating port of the master cylinder is restricted.

46. Technician A says that any type of brake fluid can be used to top off a system as long as it meets or exceeds the DOT grade specified by the manufacturer.

    Technician B says that not all brake fluids are compatible and that mixing them can cause serious damage to the seals and rubber parts of the system.

    Who is right?

    (A) A only
    (B) B only
    (C) Both A and B
    (D) Neither A nor B

47. A customer complains of a squeal from the front disc brakes when the car is brought to a stop, the car has only been driven several hundred miles since new brake pads were installed. The noise may be caused by all of the following EXCEPT:

    (A) Sticking calipers slides or frozen piston
    (B) Glazed friction material or poor quality lining
    (C) Improperly installed, missing, or weak anti-rattle clips, springs, or shims
    (D) Outboard brake pad retaining tabs not tightly secured to the caliper.

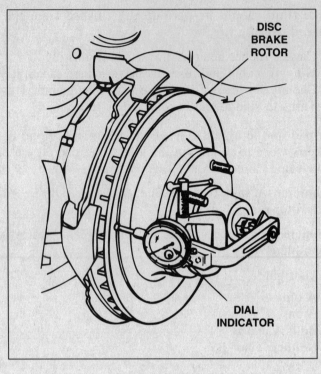

Figure A5-5.

48. The dial indicator shown in Figure A5-5 is set-up to measure:

(A) Rotor parallelism
(B) Rotor axial runout
(C) Rotor lateral runout
(D) Wheel bearing pre-load

49. An anti-lock brake system performs all of the following EXCEPT:

(A) Monitors vehicle speed
(B) Computes the rate of wheel rotation
(C) Electronically applies the brakes as needed
(D) Modulates brake hydraulic pressure

50. How many wheel speed sensors are generally used with a three-channel anti-lock brake system that operates on the select low principal?

(A) 2
(B) 3
(C) 4
(D) Either 2 or 4

END OF EXAMINATION A5.

SAMPLE EXAM, ELECTRICAL SYSTEMS TECHNICIAN

TEST A6, 50 Questions

DIRECTIONS: *Each question has four suggested answers, lettered A, B, C, and D. Decide which one is the best answer, locate the question number on the sample answer sheet, and with a soft pencil darken the area that corresponds to the answer you have selected.*

1. Sparks and open flames should be kept away from batteries that are being charged because of the danger of explosion or fire resulting from the generation of:

   (A) Argon gas
   (B) Fluorine gas
   (C) Nitrogen gas
   (D) Hydrogen gas

2. In zero degree (F) weather, a 100 ampere-hour battery that is in good condition will supply 300 amperes for about:

   (A) 5 minutes
   (B) 10 minutes
   (C) 15 minutes
   (D) 20 minutes

3. Before charging the battery, the ground cable should be disconnected at the battery in order to protect the:

   (A) Ignition coil
   (B) Ignition module
   (C) Alternator diodes
   (D) Voltage regulator

4. If the cut-out relay points in the generator relay remain closed after the engine is switched off, all of the following could occur EXCEPT:

   (A) A dead battery
   (B) Damage to the generator field
   (C) Motorization of the generator
   (D) Shorted stator windings

5. What is the first item a technician should check or test to analyze a no charge condition?

   (A) Regulator operation
   (B) Field continuity
   (C) Belt tension
   (D) Supply voltage

6. Technician A says that a charged battery with a low charging rate is a normal condition.

   Technician B says that a charged battery with a high charging rate can be the result of a poor regulator ground.

   Who is right?

   (A) A only
   (B) B only
   (C) Both A and B
   (D) Neither A nor B

7. Worn starter motor brushes should be replaced when they are:

   (A) ¼ of original length
   (B) ½ of original length
   (C) ¾ of original length
   (D) None of the above

8. When the starting motor of an engine is engaged with the head lamps on, the technician notices that the lamps go out as the starter solenoid is energized. What is the most likely cause?

   (A) The battery has one dead cell
   (B) The solenoid switch is not closing the circuit
   (C) The solenoid windings are shorted
   (D) There is a poor connection at one of the battery terminals

9. A technician tested the starting circuit on car with a 5.0-liter V8 engine and observed the following results: the engine cranked slowly, the starter current draw was 90 amps, and the battery voltage was 11 volts while cranking. What should the technician do next?

   (A) Check the voltage drop of the starter motor circuit.
   (B) Test the battery capacity
   (C) Replace the starter motor because a short is indicated
   (D) Determine the condition of the engine

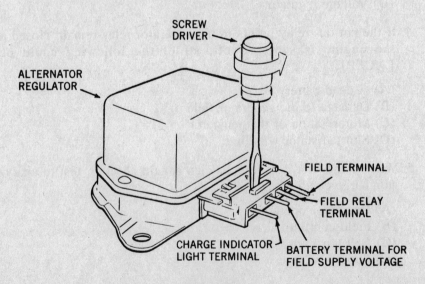

Figure A6-1.

10. Figure A6-1 shows the procedure for:

    (A) adjusting voltage output
    (B) adjusting amperage output
    (C) Removing the regulator from the car
    (D) Disconnecting the wiring connector

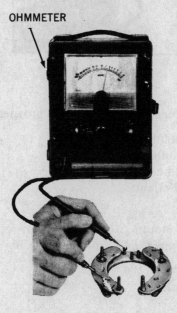

OHMMETER

Figure A6-2.

11. The technician in Figure A6-2 is checking:

    (A) The alternator stator for short circuit
    (B) The alternator rotor for open circuit
    (C) The alternator diode
    (D) The alternator slip ring

12. There is no output from the charging system of a vehicle. When a jump wire is connected between the B (battery) terminal and F (field) terminal of the alternator the system begins charging.

Technician A says a bad stator winding in the alternator could be the problem.

Technician B says the problem could be caused by an open circuit between the ignition switch and the B terminal of the alternator.

Who is right?

    (A) A only
    (B) B only
    (C) Both A and B
    (D) Neither A nor B

Figure A6-3.

13. The technician in Figure A6-3 is using a growler to check a starter for:

(A) A shorted armature circuit
(B) An open armature circuit
(C) A shorted field circuit
(D) An open field circuit

14. With most starter motors, a technician can separate the commutator end frame, field frame, and drive housing by removing the:

(A) Cover band
(B) Overrunning clutch
(C) Through bolts
(D) Bendix drive

15. A gasoline engine runs when the ignition key in the "START" position, but stops running when the key is returned to the "ON" position. The most likely cause would be:

(A) An open ignition resistor
(B) A shorted ignition condenser
(C) A defective ignition coil
(D) An shorted neutral safety switch

16. When a vehicle equipped with an alternator is started, battery current generally flows to the alternator:

(A) Commutator
(B) Rectifier
(C) Rotor windings
(D) Stator windings

17. Technician A says that in an alternator system, a discharged battery with a low charging rate could be caused by a low current setting.

Technician B says that a discharged battery with a low charging rate could be caused by a low voltage setting.

Who is right?

(A) A only
(B) B only
(C) Both A and B
(D) Neither A nor B

18. Which alternator component converts alternating current to direct current?

   (A) Diodes
   (B) Field relay
   (C) Rotor slip rings
   (D) Stator windings

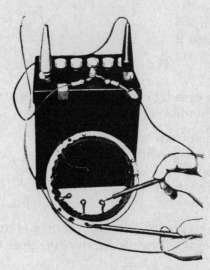

Figure A6-4.

19. What type of test is the technician in Figure A6-4 performing?

   (A) A stator connection test
   (B) A stator ground test
   (C) A stator voltage test
   (D) A stator continuity test

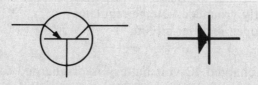

Figure A6-5.

20. The two electrical symbols shown in Figure A6-5 are used in a wiring diagram to represent:

   (A) A switch and a ground
   (B) A fuse and a capacitor
   (C) A transistor and a diode
   (D) A resistor and ground connection

21. Which of the following methods does a voltage regulator use to control alternator output?

   (A) Momentarily grounding the stator windings
   (B) Limiting voltage output at the "B" terminal
   (C) Controlling current feed to the rotor
   (D) Momentarily grounding the negative diodes

22. A vehicle with a fully charged battery shows a high charging rate.

   Technician A says that a poor ground connection on the engine may be at fault.

   Technician B says the a grounded stator in the alternator may be causing the problem.

   Who is right?
   (A) A only
   (B) B only
   (C) Both A and B
   (D) Neither A nor B

23. An armature growler can be used to test a starting motor armature for all of the following EXCEPT:

   (A) Condition of insulation
   (B) Commutator condition
   (C) Short circuits
   (D) Circuit resistance

24. After the engine starts, the overrunning clutch drive is moved out of mesh from the flywheel starter ring gear teeth by which of the following:

   (A) The bendix pinion
   (B) The plunger return spring
   (C) Centrifugal force
   (D) A deenergized electromagnet

25. A battery requires frequent recharging. The cause could be all of the following EXCEPT:

   (A) The battery is sulphated
   (B) Wrong size alternator drive pulley
   (C) Poorly grounded voltage regulator
   (D) An open rectifier circuit

26. A fully charged 12-volt battery is discharged for 15 seconds at a rate three times its ampere hour rating. What is indicated if the voltage drops to 10.0?

   (A) The battery has one bad cell
   (B) The battery has adequate capacity
   (C) The battery connections are bad
   (D) The battery should be recharged and tested again

27. A heat sink is usually used in connection with which of the following?

   (A) Regulators
   (B) Alternators
   (C) Starter motors
   (D) Ignition coils

28. Which of the following types of electric starting motors is frequently used because of its high starting torque?

    (A) Capacitor-type
    (B) Series wound-type
    (C) Shunt wound-type
    (D) Compound wound-type

29. Which of the following is a part of the regulator used to control the output of an alternator?

    (A) Load relay
    (B) Current limiter
    (C) Voltage limiter
    (D) Cut-out relay

30. Which of the following statements about the pinion gear of an overrunning clutch-type of starting motor is most nearly correct?

    (A) A screw action operates the pinion
    (B) The pinion is disengaged by a single spring
    (C) The pinion must always be meshed with the flywheel
    (D) The pinion gear is always connected to the clutch housing

31. A technician can use a battery hydrometer to test the battery for:

    (A) Voltage capacity
    (B) General state of charge
    (C) Total capacity
    (D) Potential output amperage

32. During a three-minute battery test of a 12-volt battery, if the cell voltages are uneven by more than 0.1-volt to 0.15-volt, the technician should:

    (A) Replace the battery
    (B) Test the electrolyte specific gravity and charge the battery
    (C) Top-off the electrolyte, slow charge the battery, and re-test the battery
    (D) Test the total battery voltage with a battery charger operating at a fast charge

33. For a vehicle equipped with an alternator and a two-unit voltage regulator, the regulator will contain which of the following components?

    (A) A field relay and a current limiter
    (B) A field relay and a voltage limiter
    (C) A voltage limiter and a current limiter
    (D) A reverse current relay and a current limiter

34. The slip rings on an automotive alternator transmit:

    (A) Direct current to the field coils
    (B) Alternating current to the field coils
    (C) Alternating current from the stator windings
    (D) Direct current to the alternator output terminals

35. A customer complains that the head lights on his car flare up when engine speed is increased. Which of the following may be a cause?

    (A) Voltage regulator adjusted too low
    (B) Electrolyte in battery is weak
    (C) Shorted alternator stator winding
    (D) Idle speed is too low

36. To polarize a DC generator that has an externally grounded field winding, a technician should momentarily jump the:

    (A) Armature and field terminals on the generator
    (B) Battery and the field terminals on the regulator
    (C) Generator and battery terminals on the regulator
    (D) Generator and the field terminals on the regulator

37. When the DC generator is running slow or not operating at all, the cutout relay is designed to:

    (A) Close the circuit between the generator and battery
    (B) Prevent the battery from discharging back through the generator
    (C) Send residual current through the circuit to supply the electrical devices
    (D) Prevent any damaging current from flowing from the battery to the electrical devices

38. A technician who is undercutting a cranking motor commutator will do which of the following?

    (A) Leave a thin edge of mica next to the segments
    (B) Take heavy cuts to remove all of the hard mica
    (C) Cut the mica away cleanly from the top of the segments
    (D) Use a tungsten-carbide cutting tool to remove the mica and sandpaper to smooth the segments

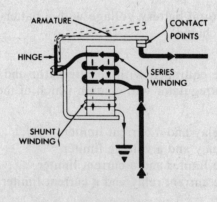

Figure A6-6.

39. The schematic wiring circuit shown in Figure A6-6 illustrates which of the following?

    (A) A relay
    (B) An ignition switch
    (C) An ignition coil
    (D) An amplifier

40. Heating a thermistor will cause its resistance to:

    (A) Fluctuate in cycles
    (B) Stabilize
    (C) Increase
    (D) Decrease

41. A battery has a specific gravity of 1.200 at 80°F (25°C), what is its state of charge?

    (A) Completely discharged
    (B) About ½ charged
    (C) About ¾ charged
    (D) Fully charged

42. The oil pressure warning light remains on whenever the engine is running, an oil pressure test has been performed and actual pressure is within specification.

    Technician A says that the problem may be caused by a ground in the circuit between the indicator light and the oil pressure switch.

    Technician B says that an internal open in the pressure switch could cause the light to stay on.

    Who is right?

    (A) A only
    (B) B only
    (C) Both A and B
    (D) Neither A nor B

43. The alternator is noisy whenever the engine is running.

    Technician A says the noise could be caused by a bad diode.

    Technician B says that a worn bearing is a likely source of the noise.

    Who is right?

    (A) A only
    (B) B only
    (C) Both A and B
    (D) Neither A nor B

44. Which of the following statements is true about a charging system with an alternator?

    (A) The output current increases when the field current increases
    (B) The output current decreases when the field current increases
    (C) The alternator output current is high when the battery is fully charged
    (D) The alternator output voltage is high when the battery is discharged

45. An integrated circuit that uses a combination of individual transistors, diodes, capacitors, and other electronic parts is known as a:

    (A) Compound circuit
    (B) Discrete circuit
    (C) Digital circuit
    (D) Hybrid circuit

46. To test a circuit using an ammeter, the ammeter must be connected to the circuit in:

    (A) Relay
    (B) Series
    (C) Parallel
    (D) Series-parallel

47. When checked with an ohmmeter, the resistance of an open circuit will be:

    (A) Zero
    (B) Unstable
    (C) Infinite
    (D) Extremely low

48. To check the primary resistance of an ignition coil, an ohmmeter is connected to the:

    (A) Coil negative terminal and high tension terminal
    (B) Coil positive terminal and high tension terminal
    (C) Coil negative terminal and coil positive terminal
    (D) Coil positive terminal and battery ground

49. A low current-draw reading during a coil current-draw test could indicate all of the following EXCEPT:

    (A) A loose primary lead at the positive coil terminal
    (B) A poor secondary lead at the positive coil terminal
    (C) Loose or corroded primary circuit connections
    (D) High resistance in the coil primary winding

50. A voltmeter is connected to the battery positive and negative terminals. While cranking the engine, the reading on the voltmeter is below specification.

    Technician A says the low reading can be caused by a bad battery.

    Technician B says a bad starter could be drawing too much current.

    Who is right?

    (A) A only
    (B) B only
    (C) Both A and B
    (D) Neither A nor B

END OF EXAMINATION A6.

SAMPLE EXAM, HEATING AND AIR CONDITIONING TECHNICIAN

TEST A7, 50 Questions

DIRECTIONS: Each question has four suggested answers, lettered A, B, C, and D. Decide which one is the best answer, locate the question number on the sample answer sheet, and with a soft pencil darken the area that corresponds to the answer you have selected.

1. Which of the following is a part of the cooling system thermostat that functions to open and close the valve?

   (A) The compensating spring
   (B) The bellows
   (C) The vacuum valve
   (D) The pressure valve

2. All of the following can be used to detect leaks in an air conditioning system that uses R-12 refrigerant EXCEPT:

   (A) An argon leak detector
   (B) Leak detection dye
   (C) A halide leak detector
   (D) A halogen leak detector

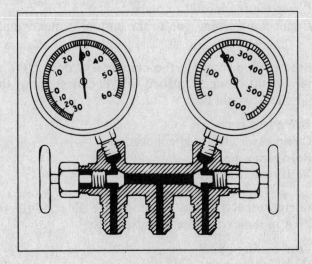

Figure A7-1.

129

3. The manifold gauge set shown in Figure A7-1 is connected to an operating air conditioning system. The gauge readings would indicate:

   (A) A low state of charge
   (B) Normal operation
   (C) High low side pressure
   (D) Low high side pressure

4. As the refrigerant in the air conditioning system passes through the condenser it changes state from:

   (A) Low pressure liquid to high-pressure vapor
   (B) High-pressure vapor to low-pressure liquid
   (C) High-pressure liquid to high-pressure vapor
   (D) High-pressure vapor to high-pressure liquid

5. A heater which has been repaired still does not deliver sufficient heat. The blower operates and the coolant is at the proper level.

   Technician A says the trouble could be an improperly adjusted heater control valve.

   Technician B says a defective thermostat could be the problem.

   Who is right?

   (A) A only
   (B) B only
   (C) Both A and B
   (D) Neither A nor B

6. To properly reverse flush a clogged engine block, radiator, and cooling system, a technician would:

   (A) Use air and water
   (B) Use low pressure steam
   (C) Leave the thermostat in place
   (D) Connect a flushing gun to the bottom of the engine block

7. With the engine running, the compressor does NOT engage when the air conditioning is turned on. The first thing the technician should check would be:

   (A) Drive belt tension
   (B) Compressor electrical connections
   (C) Refrigerant level
   (D) Verify controls are set at full cold

8. The refrigerant R-12 used in automobile air conditioning systems is effective in removing heat because of its:

   (A) Low boiling point
   (B) High boiling point
   (C) Stability under pressure
   (D) Catalytic properties

9. An air conditioning blower operates properly, but the system output is still inadequate. The most likely cause is in the:

   (A) Condenser
   (B) Evaporator core
   (C) Receiver-drier
   (D) Temperature control

10. The use of a pressure cap on the radiator tank of an automotive cooling system permits all of the following EXCEPT:

    (A) Relief of excess pressure
    (B) Increased cavitation in the pump
    (C) Admission of air to the system when the system is cooling
    (D) The rise of water temperature to a temperature above 212°F

11. To check the line that carries the refrigerant from the condenser to the expansion valve, a technician would:

    (A) Use his fingers to check for cold spots
    (B) Use compressed air to blow out the lines
    (C) Use a vacuum gauge to see if there is pressure
    (D) Look for discoloration or frost on the line

12. The clutch drive in the air conditioning compressor will wear according to:

    (A) The speed at which the air conditioner operates
    (B) The number of clutch applications that are made
    (C) The amount of pressure maintained within the system
    (D) The temperature at which the air conditioning operates

13. Technician A says that when the discharge and suction lines of an air conditioning unit are at about the same temperature, the entire refrigerant charge may have leaked out.

    Technician B say that when the sight glass foams at start-up the entire refrigerant charge may have leaked out.

    Who is right?

    (A) A only
    (B) B only
    (C) Both A and B
    (D) Neither A nor B

14. The operation of an air conditioning compressor is controlled by which of the following?

    (A) A free wheeling clutch
    (B) A centrifugal clutch
    (C) A mechanical clutch
    (D) A magnetic clutch

15. Which of the following statements would apply when there is maximum heat transfer in the air conditioning system of the vehicle?

    (A) Refrigerant leaving the receiver will be vapor
    (B) Refrigerant leaving the condenser will be vapor
    (C) Refrigerant leaving the evaporator will be vapor
    (D) Refrigerant leaving the expansion valve will be vapor

16. An air conditioner on a car performs satisfactorily for about 20 to 40 minutes, then begins to loose efficiency. What is the most likely cause?

(A) A blocked air passage
(B) A defective clutch coil
(C) A slipping compressor belt
(D) A malfunctioning suction throttle valve

17. The expansion valve in the air conditioning system of a car is controlled by the temperature and:

(A) Humidity of the interior
(B) Pressure within the compressor
(C) Pressure within the condenser
(D) Pressure at the evaporator outlet

18. Technician A says that in a closed refrigeration system the pressure after the system has been recently operated will be higher on the condenser side than it is on the evaporator side.

Technician B says that in a closed refrigeration system the pressure after the system has been idle for some time will tend to equalize.

Who is right?

(A) A only
(B) B only
(C) Both A and B
(D) Neither A nor B

19. In an automotive air conditioning system, the conditioned air is cooled as it passes through the:

(A) Receiver
(B) Condenser
(C) Evaporator
(D) Compressor

20. Technician A says the receiver-drier in an air conditioning system separates liquid refrigerant from any gas that might have left the condenser.

Technician B says any moisture the refrigerant may contain is absorbed as it passes through the receiver-drier in an air conditioning system.

Who is right?

(A) A only
(B) B only
(C) Both A and B
(D) Neither A nor B

21. Technician A says that as air passes over the evaporator coil, heat is removed from the air.

    Technician B says that as air passes over the evaporator coil, humidity condenses on the coil to remove moisture from the air.

    Who is right?

    (A) A only
    (B) B only
    (C) Both A and B
    (D) Neither A nor B

22. An expansion valve is used in the air conditioning system to control which of the following?

    (A) Quantity of refrigerant in the evaporator
    (B) Temperature of refrigerant in the condenser
    (C) Pressure of refrigerant in the compressor
    (D) Temperature of the air in the interior of the car

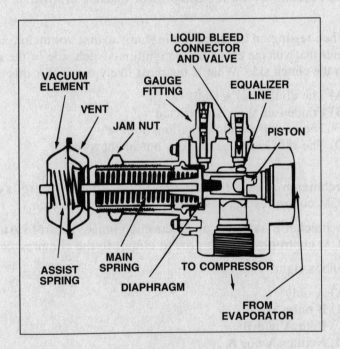

Figure A7-2.

23. The component shown in figure A7-2 is designed to restrict outlet suction and maintain a constant pressure level in the evaporator. This part is known as the:

    (A) Expansion valve
    (B) Restricted orifice
    (C) Suction throttling valve
    (D) Pressure cycling switch

24. Technician A says that to check the blower operation of an air conditioning system the blower should be operating at high speed.

Technician B says that the temperature control should be set at the lowest setting to check the blower operation of the air conditioning system.

Who is right?

(A) A only
(B) B only
(C) Both A and B
(D) Neither A nor B

25. The compressor clutch is engaged on an automotive air conditioning unit when:

(A) A plunger is forced against a cylinder
(B) Magnetism is formed by an electric circuit
(C) Heat load in the system reaches 15,000 BTU
(D) Pressure within the compressor reaches 115 psi.

26. When testing an air conditioning unit with a voltmeter, a technician finds that voltage exists on the ignition-switch side of the unit but not on the clutch side. What is the most likely reason for this condition?

(A) The clutch has seized
(B) Condenser flow is restricted
(C) The cutoff switch is malfunctioning
(D) The refrigerant has leaked out of the system

27. Technician A says that an electronic climate control system with BCM control cycles power to the compressor clutch.

Technician B says that an electronic climate control system without BCM control cycles the ground circuit to the compressor clutch.

Who is right?

(A) A only
(B) B only
(C) Both A and B
(D) Neither A nor B

28. When an automotive air conditioning system is operating, refrigeration will be at its highest pressure between the:

(A) Compressor and condenser
(B) Throttling valve and compressor
(C) Evaporator and throttling valve
(D) Expansion valve and evaporator

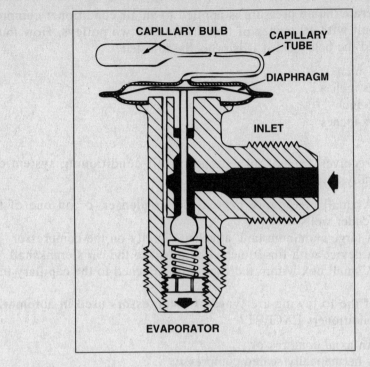

Figure A7-3.

29. The component shown in figure A7-3 is:

    (A) A combination valve
    (B) An expansion valve
    (C) An evaporator pressure regulator
    (D) An evaporator temperature regulator

30. In some air conditioning systems, a suction throttling valve is used. The purpose of this valve is to

    (A) Control compressor cycling
    (B) Control the expansion valve
    (C) Prevent evaporator freeze-up
    (D) Maintain low condenser pressures

31. Not enough heat is being supplied to the passenger compartment by the heater. The engine coolant level is correct and the blower motor is functioning properly.

    Technician A says a misadjusted heater control could be the cause.

    Technician B says a bad thermostat could be the cause.

    Who is right?

    (A) A only
    (B) B only
    (C) Both A and B
    (D) Neither A nor B

32. Moderate thumb pressure is applied to an air conditioner compressor belt with 10 inches of travel between two pulleys. How much should the belt yield if it is properly adjusted?

 (A) 1 inch
 (B) 5/8 inch
 (C) 1/4 inch
 (D) 1/8 inches

33. The receiver-drier of an automotive air conditioning system can generally be found by looking for:

 (A) A small black tank next to the condenser, or on one of the fender wells
 (B) A large aluminum tank attached directly on the compressor
 (C) A device with fins attached by a belt to the car's crankshaft
 (D) A small box within the condenser attached to the capillary tube

34. All of the following are types of compressors used in automotive air conditioners EXCEPT?

 (A) An axial compressor
 (B) A hermetically sealed compressor
 (C) A variable-displacement non-cycling type
 (D) A two-cylinder in-line unit

35. In the air conditioning cycle, high pressure liquid is most likely to be found between the:

 (A) Compressor and the condenser
 (B) Condenser and the thermal expansion valve
 (C) Thermal expansion valve and the evaporator
 (D) Evaporator and the compressor

36. The refrigerant in most automotive applications is R-12, which has a boiling point at atmospheric pressure of:

 (A) −22°F
 (B) −12°F
 (C) 37°F
 (D) 212°F

37. A valve, other than the expansion control valve, that helps prevent freeze-up of an automotive air conditioner is located between the:

 (A) Evaporator and blower
 (B) Receiver and evaporator
 (C) Compressor and condenser
 (D) Evaporator and compressor

38. After a few minutes of air conditioner operation bubbles appear in the sight gauge. Which of the following is indicated?

    (A) Normal operation
    (B) Low refrigerant
    (C) Low compressor pressure
    (D) Leaking valves

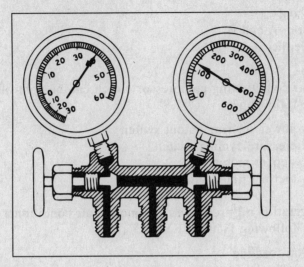

Figure A7-4.

39. The manifold gauge set shown in figure A7-4 is connected to an operating air conditioning system.

    Technician A says the gauge readings could indicate either a malfunctioning POA valve or an internal compressor problem.

    Technician B says the problem may be the expansion valve stuck in the closed position or a low refrigerant charge.

    Who is right?

    (A) A only
    (B) B only
    (C) Both A and B
    (D) Neither A nor B

40. After starting an engine in cold weather, to warm it up as fast as possible with least harm, the best technique would be which of the following?

    (A) Pump the accelerator pedal up and down for about a minute before driving off at normal speed
    (B) Hold down the accelerator steadily for about 10 seconds before driving off at normal speed
    (C) Let the engine idle normally for about a minute before driving off at normal speed
    (D) Let the engine idle normally for about a minute before driving off at slow speed

41. Technician A says that stem-type valves are more common than Schrader valves on air conditioning systems.

   Technician B says Schrader valves may contain calibrated springs that release at specific levels.

   Who is right?

   (A) A only
   (B) B only
   (C) Both A and B
   (D) Neither A nor B

42. The air conditioning compressor clutch can be controlled by which of the following?

   (A) A power steering cutout switch
   (B) A pressure cycling switch
   (C) A stepper motor
   (D) A thermal time switch

43. Refrigeration oil used in an automotive air conditioner will have all of the following features EXCEPT:

   (A) Non-foaming
   (B) Sulphur-free
   (C) Variable viscosity
   (D) Wax-free

44. The BILEVEL mode in a typical automotive air conditioning system divides the discharge air to flow:

   (A) 60% from the dash and 40% to the floor
   (B) 40% from the dash and 60% to the floor
   (C) 50% from the dash and 50% to the floor
   (D) 80% from the dash and 20% to the floor

45. Technician A says that the fixed-orifice tube relieves pressure on the refrigerant and allows it to evaporate quickly.

   Technician B says the fixed-orifice tube is used to absorb latent heat as the refrigerant changes state

   Who is right?

   (A) A only
   (B) B only
   (C) Both A and B
   (D) Neither A nor B

46. An Automatic Temperature Control (ATC) system controls all of the following EXCEPT?

   (A) Recirculation air door
   (B) Engine coolant fan
   (C) Blend door actuator
   (D) Panel/defroster door actuator

47. The major cause of air conditioner compressor malfunctions would be which of the following?

    (A) Leaks in the compressor cylinder
    (B) Loss of lubricant
    (C) Inadequate operating pressure
    (D) Excessive operating pressure

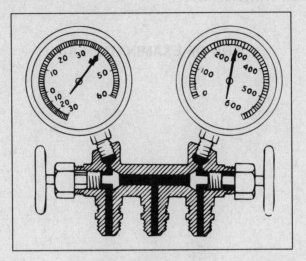

Figure A7-5.

48. The manifold gauge set shown in figure A7-5 is connected to an operating air conditioning system.

    Technician A says the gauge readings could be caused by restricted air flow through the condenser or an overcharged system.

    Technician B says either a leaking temperature-sensing bulb or an open bypass valve could be the cause of the problem.

    Who is right?

    (A) A only
    (B) B only
    (C) Both A and B
    (D) Neither A nor B

49. The air conditioning system high side pressure is too high.

    Technician A says the problem could be caused by restricted air flow through the condenser.

    Technician B says a leaking thermal bulb or an open bypass valve could cause high high side pressure.

    Who is right?

    (A) A only
    (B) B only
    (C) Both A and B
    (D) Neither A nor B

50. No heat is flowing from the passenger compartment vent on a car with a blend air heating system. This condition could result from all of the following EXCEPT:

(A) Faulty vacuum circuit to the control valve
(B) Incorrect cable adjustment
(C) Incorrect thermostat installed
(D) Low refrigerant level

END OF EXAMINATION A7.

SAMPLE EXAM, ENGINE PERFORMANCE TECHNICIAN

TEST A8, 80 Questions

DIRECTIONS: Each question has four suggested answers, lettered A, B, C, and D. Decide which one is the best answer, locate the question number on the sample answer sheet, and with a soft pencil darken the area that corresponds to the answer you have selected.

1. A technician sets the proper electrode gap on a sparkplug most accurately if he uses a:

   (A) Dial gauge
   (B) Round wire feeler gauge
   (C) Square wire feeler gauge
   (D) Flat feeler gauge

2. An internal combustion engine emits three major air pollutants from the tail pipe. These three pollutants would be:

   (A) Sulfates, particulate, carbon monoxide
   (B) Sulfates, carbon monoxide, nitrous oxide
   (C) Carbon monoxide, oxides of nitrogen, hydrocarbons
   (D) Hydrocarbons, carbon dioxide, nitrous oxide

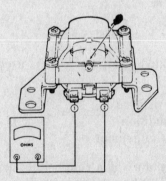

Figure A8-1.

3. The set-up illustrated in Figure A8-1 is used to test the ignition coil:

   (A) Ground circuit
   (B) Secondary circuit
   (C) Polarity
   (D) Primary circuit

4. The air injection systems used with electronic engine controls may have all of the following components EXCEPT:

(A) An integrator valve
(B) An air switching valve
(C) A gulp valve
(D) A diverter valve

5. An artificial enrichment test is performed and the rpm gain measured is below specification.

Technician A says that the low rpm gain could result from the air-fuel ratio being too lean

Technician B says a malfunctioning air injection system could be causing the problem.

Who is right?

(A) A only
(B) B only
(C) Both A and B
(D) Neither A nor B

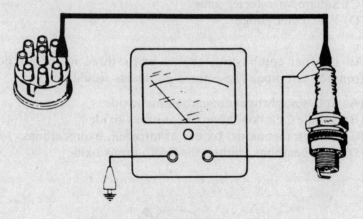

Figure A8-2.

6. The set-up illustrated in Figure A8-2 is used to test the:

(A) Coil polarity
(B) Condenser resistance
(C) Sparkplug condition
(D) Contact point alignment

7. A customer complains of a rough idle and the engine stalling on light acceleration. When the vacuum line is disconnected from the EGR valve, the problem disappears.

Technician A says the problem may by the EGR valve is incorrectly opening when the engine is at idle.

Technician B says the problem could be caused by a broken diaphragm spring in the EGR valve and the valve is stuck closed.

Who is right?

(A) A only
(B) B only
(C) Both A and B
(D) Neither A nor B

8. To which number sparkplug is a timing light connected during all timing operations on a six cylinder engine?

   (A) One
   (B) Two
   (C) Four
   (D) Six

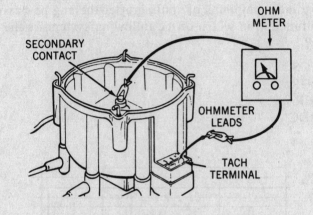

Figure A8-3.

9. The technician in Figure A8-3 is using an ohmmeter to test:

   (A) Coil polarity
   (B) Coil primary circuit
   (C) Coil secondary circuit
   (D) Coil ground

10. The condition of a resistance-type sparkplug can quickly be checked using which of the following?

    (A) An ammeter
    (B) A voltmeter
    (C) An ohmmeter
    (D) A potentiometer

11. Electronic fuel injection systems reduce vehicle emissions by:

    (A) Using the intake manifold to vaporize the fuel charge
    (B) Reducing fuel consumption at high engine speeds
    (C) Matching engine speed to load conditions
    (D) Matching the air-fuel ratio to engine requirements

12. A technician is performing a power balance test. When a sparkplug is shorted out there is no change in engine speed. This would indicate which of the following:

    (A) The sparkplug is defective
    (B) The cylinder is missing
    (C) The high-tension lead is bad
    (D) Coil output is low

13. A light load test is performed on a battery, and the battery is found to have *less* than 1.95 volts on all cells. What conclusion can be made?

    (A) The battery is in good condition
    (B) The battery is too discharged to test
    (C) The battery is defective and should be replaced
    (D) The battery is in good condition but needs charging

14. A customer complains of stalling after the engine has warmed up. A malfunction in which of the following systems is the most likely cause?

    (A) TCS
    (B) EGR
    (C) AIR
    (D) BDC

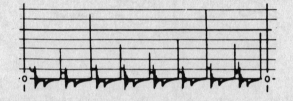

Figure A8-4.

15. What corrective action should the technician take to eliminate the problem indicated by the scope pattern shown in Figure A8-4?

    (A) Replace the coil
    (B) Adjust the dwell angle
    (C) Replace the sparkplugs
    (D) Replace the contact points

16. A spark test reveals no spark. The ammeter shows a small fluctuating reading. These findings indicate trouble in which of the following?

    (A) Battery
    (B) Ignition switch
    (C) Primary circuit
    (D) Secondary circuit

17. Technician A says that in a test of combustion efficiency a tachometer is connected to the engine.

    Technician B says that in a test of combustion efficiency a vacuum gauge is connected to the intake manifold.

    Who is right?

    (A) A only
    (B) B only
    (C) Both A and B
    (D) Neither A nor B

18. An occasional drop of about four inches in a vacuum gauge test indicates:

    (A) Sticky valves
    (B) Retarded timing
    (C) Incorrect fuel mixture
    (D) Weak valve springs

19. Technician A says that a hot-wire, or heated-film, air mass sensor measures the velocity of the airflow entering the engine.

    Technician B says that a hot-wire, or heated-film, air mass sensor regulates fuel delivery based on barometric absolute pressure and air charge temperature

    Who is right?

    (A) A only
    (B) B only
    (C) Both A and B
    (D) Neither A nor B

20. Fuel vapors from the fuel tank that are stored in the charcoal canister are:

    (A) Filtered by the charcoal canister and released to the atmosphere
    (B) Slowly released to the atmosphere through a check valve
    (C) Become part of the air fuel mixture when the engine is started
    (D) Condensed to liquid by the charcoal canister and returned to the fuel tank

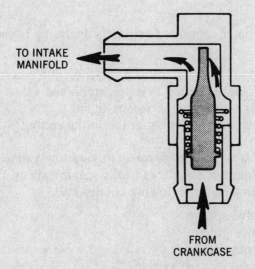

TO INTAKE MANIFOLD

FROM CRANKCASE

Figure A8-5.

21. The PCV valve shown in Figure A8-5 is in what mode of operation?

    (A) Idle
    (B) Cruise
    (C) Acceleration
    (D) Engine off

22. Technician A says that a defective sparkplug wire will cause high hydrocarbon readings.

    Technician B says that a defective sparkplug wire will cause high carbon monoxide readings.

    Who is right?

    (A) A only
    (B) B only
    (C) Both A and B
    (D) Neither A nor B

23. While performing a vacuum test on an engine, the technician notices a sudden periodic drop of the needle by 1 or 2 points. This could be caused by:

    (A) A vacuum leak
    (B) An incorrect fuel mixture
    (C) Worn valve guides
    (D) A sparkplug misfire

24. Technician A says that a throttle position sensor is a digital device.

    Technician B says that a throttle position sensors is a potentiometer.

    Who is right?

    (A) A only
    (B) B only
    (C) Both A and B
    (D) Neither A nor B

25. When a computer controlled engine is operating in the "open loop" mode, it:

    (A) Ignores the input signal from the coolant temperature sensor
    (B) Controls fuel metering to a predetermined value
    (C) Responds to the oxygen sensor signal
    (D) Maintains ignition timing at the initial setting

26. A vacuum test is performed on an engine, the gauge needle rapidly vibrates at idle but stabilizes out as engine speed increases. This indicates which of the following conditions?

    (A) Weak valve springs
    (B) Worn valve guides
    (C) A valve not seating
    (D) A restricted exhaust system

27. The ignition points of a conventional ignition system are adjusted to increase the point gap. This adjustment will:

    (A) Increase the dwell angle
    (B) Retard the ignition timing
    (C) Advance the ignition timing
    (D) Not change dwell angle

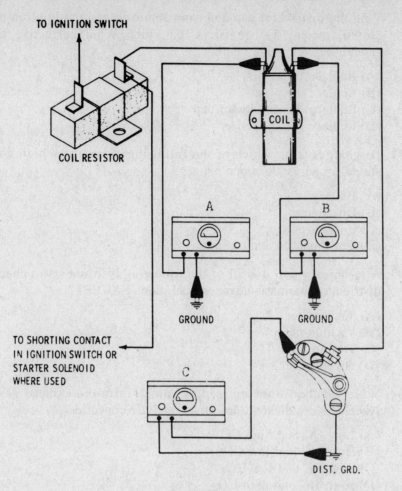

TO IGNITION SWITCH

COIL RESISTOR

COIL

A

B

GROUND

GROUND

TO SHORTING CONTACT
IN IGNITION SWITCH OR
STARTER SOLENOID
WHERE USED

C

DIST. GRD.

Figure A8-6.

Questions 28 through 31 refer to Figure A8-6.

28. Meter "A" is arranged to test the condition of which of the following?

(A) Distributor
(B) Condensers
(C) Resistors
(D) Wiring

29. The leads to meter "B" are connected, the ignition switch is in the "ON" position, the engine is not running, and the ignition points are closed. A reading of 0.0 to 0.2 volts on meter "C" would indicate:

(A) A defective coil
(B) A short in the distributor
(C) A short in the coil circuit
(D) Normal distributor electrical condition

30. With the distributor cap and rotor removed and the ignition points open, meter "C" registers 0.0 volts. This reading would indicate:

(A) A shorted condenser circuit
(B) Shorted ignition wiring
(C) An open condenser circuit
(D) A shorted coil resistor

31. With the distributor cap and rotor removed and the ignition points closed, meter "C" registers 0.4 volts. What corrective action should the technician take?

    (A) Replace the coil
    (B) Replace the points
    (C) Replace the distributor cap
    (D) Replace the condenser

32. Discharges from which of the following show up as high voltage surges on an oscilloscope pattern?

    (A) Battery
    (B) Distributor
    (C) Contact points
    (D) Coil high-tension terminal

33. A technician will use all of the following instruments to check the distributor automatic advance operations EXCEPT?

    (A) Tachometer
    (B) Vacuum pump
    (C) Timing light
    (D) Dwell meter

34. Which of the following readings on an infra-red exhaust gas analyzer would indicate a defective catalytic converter?

    (A) Low HC and high CO
    (B) High HC and low CO
    (C) Low HC and low CO
    (D) High HC and high CO

35. On the scope it is observed that there are uneven firing voltages. Of the following, this condition is most likely caused by

    (A) Worn distributor rotor
    (B) Weak ignition coil
    (C) Worn distributor bushings
    (D) Worn sparkplugs

36. As compared to a conventional-type of sparkplug, a resistor-type of sparkplug will:

    (A) Have an auxiliary air gap
    (B) Reduce the inductive portion of the spark
    (C) Lengthen the capacitive portion of the spark
    (D) Require a higher voltage to function properly

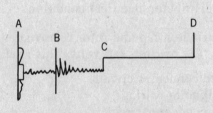

Figure A8-7.

37. Referring to the scope pattern in Figure A8-7, dwell would be indicated by the portion of the pattern between which two letters?

(A) A and B
(B) C and D
(C) A and C
(D) B and C

38. The vapors of an activated charcoal canister may be drawn off by all of the following methods EXCEPT:

(A) Constant purging
(B) Variable purging
(C) Computer-controlled purging
(D) Percolation purging

39. An ignition system test is made by taking the end of the high tension wire from the coil and holding it near the engine block. At the same time, the movable ignition point arm is shorted to the breaker plate with the points open and the ignition on. No spark is obtained at the end of the high tension wire. Of the following, which is the most likely cause?

(A) Defective coil
(B) Defective rotor
(C) Defective ignition points
(D) Defective distributor cap

40. An ignition system test is made by taking the end of the high tension wire from the center tower of the distributor cap and holding it near the engine block. At the same time, the movable ignition point arm is shorted to the breaker plate with the points open and the ignition on. A good spark is obtained at the end of the high tension wire. No spark is obtained at any of the sparkplugs when cranking the engine with the ignition on. Of the following, the most likely cause would be a?

(A) Defective coil
(B) Defective condenser
(C) Defective ignition switch
(D) Defective plug wires

41. Technician A says that the dwell angle of a solid-state ignition system can be checked using an ammeter.

Technician B says you can use an ohmmeter to measure dwell angle on a solid-state ignition system

Who is right?

(A) A only
(B) B only
(C) Both A and B
(D) Neither A nor B

42. Which of the following statements would apply to a solid-state ignition system that uses a Hall-effect switch?

   (A) A magnetic field expands and collapses as the trigger wheel teeth move past the pole piece
   (B) A variable digital voltage is provided in proportion to rotational speed
   (C) A uniform digital voltage is provided regardless of rotational speed
   (D) An on/off signal is transmitted as a slotted disc passes over a light-emitting diode

43. If an engine is operating at 1500 rpm, the distributor would be operating at:

   (A) 3000 rpm
   (B) 1500 rpm
   (C) 1000 rpm
   (D) 750 rpm

44. Setting the sparkplug gap opening tighter than specification will result in:

   (A) A smooth idle and lack of power
   (B) A rough idle and hard starting
   (C) A smooth idle and occasional backfire
   (D) A rough idle only

45. Technician A says that some electronic ignition distributors have an adjustable air gap between pick-up and reluctor.

   Technician B says that most air gaps can be adjusted with a standard 0.008 inch feeler gauge.

   Who is right?

   (A) A only
   (B) B only
   (C) Both A and B
   (D) Neither A nor B

46. Which of the following is the most common firing order for an inline 6-cylinder engine?

   (A) 1-3-2-6-4-5
   (B) 1-2-5-6-3-4
   (C) 1-5-3-6-2-4
   (D) 1-6-3-5-4-2

47. Technician A says that a 4-gas analyzer will measure not only CO and HC, but the amount of O_2 and CO_2 in the exhaust as well.

   Technician B says an advantage of the 4-gas analyzer is that it can accurately measure emissions at the tailpipe, rather than upstream of the catalytic converter.

   Who is right?

   (A) A only
   (B) B only
   (C) Both A and B
   (D) Neither A nor B

48. An engine with electronic port fuel injection has high fuel pressure at idle. Which of the following could be the cause?

    (A) A plugged fuel injector
    (B) A leaking fuel pump check valve
    (C) Low manifold vacuum
    (D) High manifold vacuum

49. The firing order of a V-8 engine is 1-5-4-2-6-3-7-8. Which of the following would be companion cylinders on this engine?

    (A) 3 and 4
    (B) 2 and 8
    (C) 7 and 1
    (D) 5 and 6

50. The proper procedure for performing a compression test on an automotive engine includes:

    (A) Having the throttle blocked open
    (B) Performing the test when the engine is cold
    (C) Cranking the engine for a maximum of two compression strokes
    (D) Removing one sparkplug at a time and reinstalling it after completing the test on that cylinder

51. A vacuum test is performed on an idling engine and the gauge reads a steady 9 inches of vacuum. Which of the following could cause this low reading?

    (A) A broken piston ring or valve spring
    (B) A burnt or sticking intake valve
    (C) Worn valve guides or late ignition timing
    (D) Late valve timing or worn piston rings

52. An emissions test was performed on a car with a fuel injected engine using a 2-gas analyzer. The following results were noted: at idle both CO and HC readings were high, at 2500 rpm the HC reading returned to normal but the CO level remained high.

    Technician A says that a leaking fuel injector may be causing the problem.

    Technician B says the condition may be caused by a clogged air filter element.

    Who is right?

    (A) A only
    (B) B only
    (C) Both A and B
    (D) Neither A nor B

53. A rapidly fluctuating reading on a vacuum gauge that shows up only at high engine speeds may indicate which of the following?

    (A) An incorrect fuel mixture
    (B) Weak valve springs
    (C) Advanced ignition timing
    (D) A leaking cylinder head gasket

54. Detonation can be caused by all of the following EXCEPT:

    (A) Retarded ignition timing
    (B) EGR valve stuck closed
    (C) Lean air-fuel mixture
    (D) Excess combustion chamber carbon deposits

55. A vacuum test is performed on a car's engine. The engine is operating at 2000 rpm. If the engine is in good operating condition the vacuum should read:

    (A) Slightly lower than the idle reading
    (B) Slightly higher than the idle reading
    (C) Considerably lower than the idle reading
    (D) The same as the idle reading

56. A technician removes the air cleaner and starts the engine. He sets the speed at approximately 750 rpm. He slides a flat plate partially over the air horn and notes the reading on a tachometer. The technician is performing a test of which of the following?

    (A) Timing advance
    (B) Vacuum advance
    (C) Air-fuel ratio
    (D) Cylinder balance

57. Technician A says that when a compression test is made on the engine the throttle should be wide open.

    Technician B says that when a compression test is made on the engine the starter should pump the piston five times and no more.

    Who is tight?

    (A) A only
    (B) B only
    (C) Both A and B
    (D) Neither A nor B

58. In a typical automotive engine, the intake valve begins to open when the piston:

    (A) Passes top dead center on the intake stroke
    (B) Approaches top dead center on the exhaust stroke
    (C) Approaches bottom dead center of the intake stroke
    (D) Passes bottom dead center of the exhaust stroke

59. The set-up shown in Figure A8-8 is used to check the:

    (A) Distributor mechanical advance
    (B) Ignition secondary continuity
    (C) Ignition module
    (D) Pick-up coil

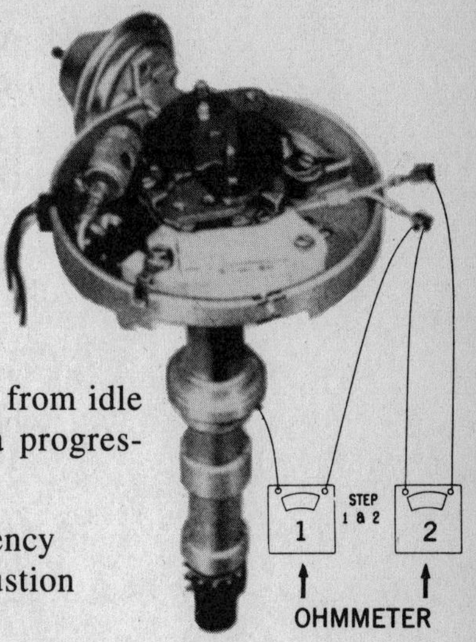

Figure A8-8.

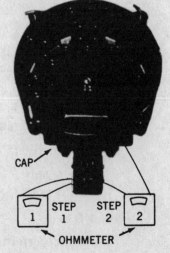

60. As the engine speed of a gasoline engine slowly increases from idle to cruising, the combustion test meter should indicate a progressively:

    (A) Leaner fuel mixture   (C) Lower thermal efficiency
    (B) Higher fuel-air ratio   (D) Higher rate of combustion

61. Intake manifold leaks can be detected using a vacuum gauge by which of the following methods?

    (A) Putting the engine on full choke, and checking for a change in the gauge reading
    (B) Accelerating the engine to a fast speed, and checking for a change in the gauge reading
    (C) Pumping the accelerator, and checking for instant response in the gauge reading
    (D) Spraying a non-combustible solvent around the flange and manifold gaskets, and watching for a change in the gauge reading

62. The set-up shown in Figure A8-9 is used to check the:

    (A) Distributor cap high tension terminals
    (B) Distributor cap continuity
    (C) Ignition coil
    (D) Electronic ignition module within the cap

Figure A8-9.

63. Backfiring is an explosion in the intake manifold. One possible cause could be:

    (A) A restricted air flow
    (B) A lean fuel mixture and a cold engine
    (C) A burnt exhaust valve or damaged piston
    (D) Late valve timing

64. A no-load carburetor mixture test indicates that the mixture is too lean. The fault might lie in any of the following EXCEPT

(A) High float level
(B) Plugged metering jets
(C) Air leak in the manifold
(D) Incorrect metering rod adjustment

65. Technician A says that after performing a test series with a combustion tester the unit should be disconnected and operated about 10 minutes in order to remove moisture.

Technician B says that after performing a test series with a combustion tester the unit can be serviced using compressed air to remove moisture.

Who is right?

(A) A only   (C) Both A and B
(B) B only   (D) Neither A nor B

66. With the engine operating at 2000 rpm it is observed that the combustion meter reading is 10 percent greater with the air cleaner in place than when it is removed. This result indicates which of the following?

(A) Normal operation   (C) A dirty air filter
(B) Excessive blow-by   (D) A by-pass air restriction

67. Technician A says the combustion tester should NOT be used on an engine that is burning oil because oily smoke will eventually decrease the sensitivity of the tester.

Technician B says the combustion tester should NOT be used on an engine that is burning oil because the meter will not give an accurate reading under that condition.

Who is right?

(A) A only   (C) Both A and B
(B) B only   (D) Neither A nor B

68. While performing a vacuum test, the throttle is quickly opened to attain an engine speed of 2000 rpm. The gauge drops to one inch of vacuum while the engine is accelerating, then jumps to 25 inches when the throttle is suddenly closed. These test results indicate:

(A) Incorrect ignition timing   (C) A restricted exhaust system
(B) Normal operation   (D) A lean fuel mixture

69. Which of the following advantages of the fuel injection system is most related to emission control?

(A) Starting is faster and easier
(B) Fuel flow is cut off completely on deceleration
(C) Engine response to load changes is quicker and better
(D) Horsepower output per cubic inch piston displacement is higher

70. A technician performing a compression test on an engine finds that the addition of a tablespoon of SAE 40 motor oil causes no significant increase in the low compression pressure. Based on these results, low compression pressure could be caused by all of the following EXCEPT:

(A) Sticking valves   (C) Worn piston rings
(B) A broken piston   (D) A leaking head gasket

71. An auto technician has performed an automotive fuel system test and reports a fuel flow of ½ pint/min. at 500 rpm, a static fuel pump discharge pressure of 6 psi, and a 15 in-Hg vacuum at the pump inlet line. These results indicate that the next step the technician would take would be to:

(A) Replace the defective fuel pump
(B) Check for a plugged inlet fuel line
(C) Check for a leaking pump diaphragm
(D) Consider the system to be operating properly

72. A positive type crankcase ventilating system will contain all of the following EXCEPT:

(A) A metering valve
(B) An intake breather
(C) A road draft tube
(D) A manifold suction tube

73. The PCV valve is installed between the:

(A) Crankcase and intake manifold
(B) EGR valve and intake manifold
(C) Exhaust manifold heat riser and air cleaner
(D) Exhaust pipe and intake manifold

Figure A8-10.

74. Which of the following components is illustrated in Figure A8-10?

(A) A positive crankcase ventilating valve
(B) A temperature sensing valve
(C) A air cleaner temperature sensing valve
(D) A thermal time switch

75. The component illustrated in Figure A8-11 is part of which system?

(A) Positive crankcase ventilation
(B) Early fuel evaporation
(C) Exhaust gas recirculation
(D) Controlled fuel/air mixture

Figure A8-11.

76. An air injection system used to control emissions may use all of the following components EXCEPT:

(A) A diverter valve
(B) A gulp valve

(C) An anti-backfire valve
(D) A blow-off valve

77. A malfunctioning PCV valve may cause which of the following conditions?

(A) Improper idling
(B) Poor acceleration

(C) Increased oil consumption
(D) Increased fuel consumption

78. Automotive exhaust gas analyzers used in emission control maintenance will normally indicate the percentage of:

(A) NO
(B) SO_2

(C) CO_2
(D) CO

79. Which of the following conditions may result when the evaporation control system is not working?

(A) Excessive pressure in fuel tank
(B) Collapsed fuel tank
(C) Vapor flow from air cleaner
(D) Improper engine idle

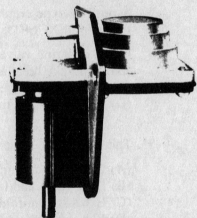

Figure A8-12.

80. The component illustrated in figure A8-12 is used to control:

(A) PCV vacuum
(B) EGR actuation
(C) EFE switching
(D) Distributor advance vacuum

END OF EXAMINATION A8.

ANSWERS TO SAMPLE EXAMINATIONS

EXAMINATION A1, ENGINE REPAIR

1. A	11. C	21. C	31. C	41. C	51. A	61. A	71. A
2. C	12. D	22. D	32. B	42. D	52. C	62. B	72. C
3. A	13. C	23. D	33. D	43. A	53. C	63. C	73. D
4. B	14. D	24. B	34. B	44. B	54. B	64. D	74. C
5. B	15. D	25. A	35. B	45. D	55. B	65. C	75. D
6. A	16. A	26. D	36. C	46. A	56. D	66. D	76. A
7. C	17. A	27. A	37. D	47. B	57. B	67. D	77. A
8. A	18. C	28. D	38. A	48. C	58. A	68. A	78. A
9. C	19. C	29. B	39. D	49. D	59. B	69. B	79. C
10. D	20. C	30. A	40. D	50. A	60. B	70. C	80. B

EXAMINATION A2, AUTOMATIC TRANSMISSION/TRANSAXLE

1. D	6. A	11. C	16. D	21. A	26. A	31. D	36. C
2. B	7. A	12. D	17. A	22. D	27. D	32. C	37. B
3. A	8. C	13. B	18. D	23. C	28. D	33. C	38. B
4. B	9. A	14. D	19. A	24. C	29. A	34. B	39. C
5. B	10. D	15. A	20. B	25. D	30. A	35. C	40. D

EXAMINATION A3, MANUAL DRIVE TRAIN AND AXLE

1. A	6. B	11. A	16. C	21. D	26. B	31. B	36. D
2. B	7. D	12. D	17. B	22. C	27. D	32. B	37. C
3. A	8. B	13. A	18. C	23. B	28. C	33. D	38. D
4. C	9. D	14. C	19. C	24. A	29. D	34. B	39. B
5. A	10. D	15. C	20. C	25. A	30. C	35. B	40. B

EXAMINATION A4, SUSPENSION AND STEERING

1. A	6. C	11. B	16. C	21. D	26. B	31. D	36. D
2. C	7. C	12. D	17. B	22. A	27. D	32. B	37. C
3. B	8. C	13. A	18. C	23. B	28. C	33. D	38. D
4. C	9. B	14. D	19. C	24. A	29. D	34. B	39. B
5. A	10. A	15. C	20. A	25. A	30. C	35. B	40. B

EXAMINATION A5, BRAKES

1. D	6. B	11. B	16. A	21. D	26. C	31. B	36. A	41. A	46. B
2. D	7. C	12. B	17. C	22. A	27. B	32. C	37. B	42. C	47. A
3. B	8. C	13. A	18. A	23. C	28. B	33. C	38. D	43. B	48. C
4. B	9. D	14. A	19. B	24. B	29. C	34. C	39. C	44. D	49. C
5. C	10. D	15. A	20. D	25. C	30. D	35. D	40. B	45. B	50. C

EXAMINATION A6, ELECTRICAL SYSTEMS

1. D	6. C	11. C	16. C	21. C	26. B	31. B	36. C	41. B	46. B
2. A	7. B	12. D	17. B	22. D	27. B	32. A	37. B	42. A	47. C
3. C	8. D	13. A	18. A	23. D	28. B	33. B	38. C	43. C	48. C
4. D	9. A	14. C	19. B	24. B	29. C	34. A	39. A	44. A	49. B
5. C	10. D	15. A	20. C	25. D	30. D	35. B	40. D	45. D	50. C

EXAMINATION A7, HEATING AND AIR CONDITIONING

1. B	6. A	11. A	16. D	21. C	26. D	31. C	36. A	41. D	46. B
2. A	7. D	12. B	17. D	22. A	27. D	32. B	37. D	42. A	47. B
3. B	8. A	13. A	18. C	23. C	28. A	33. A	38. B	43. C	48. A
4. D	9. D	14. D	19. C	24. C	29. B	34. B	39. A	44. A	49. A
5. C	10. B	15. C	20. C	25. B	30. C	35. B	40. D	45. C	50. D

EXAMINATION A8, ENGINE PERFORMANCE

1. B	11. D	21. A	31. B	41. A	51. D	61. D	71. B
2. C	12. B	22. A	32. D	42. C	52. A	62. C	72. C
3. D	13. B	23. D	33. D	43. D	53. B	63. B	73. A
4. A	14. B	24. B	34. D	44. D	54. A	64. D	74. B
5. D	15. C	25. C	35. D	45. A	55. A	65. A	75. B
6. A	16. D	26. B	36. B	46. C	56. C	66. C	76. D
7. A	17. C	27. C	37. B	47. C	57. C	67. A	77. A
8. A	18. A	28. C	38. D	48. C	58. B	68. B	78. D
9. C	19. D	29. D	39. A	49. B	59. D	69. B	79. C
10. C	20. C	30. A	40. D	50. A	60. A	70. C	80. D

GLOSSARY OF TERMS

This is some of the language you are likely to see on your examination. Of course, not all of these terms will appear on the tests, but reading through them will help refresh your memory. Perhaps the greatest benefit from this list will be to put you in the right frame of mind for taking the exams. Without reading a lot of technical text you will steep yourself in just the right atmosphere for high test scores.

[A]

ABS: *See*: Anti-lock brakes.

AC: Alternating current, or current that reverses its direction at regular intervals.

Accelerator Pump: A device in the carburetor that supplies an additional amount of fuel, temporarily enriching the fuel-air mixture when the throttle is suddenly opened.

Acceleration: The process of increasing velocity. Average rate of change of increasing velocity, usually measured in feet per second.

Accumulator: A device that absorbs the shock of sudden pressure surges within a hydraulic system. Accumulators are used in transmission hydraulic systems, some brake hydraulic systems, and air conditioning systems.

Ackerman Steering: The steering-system design that permits the front wheels to round a turn without sideslip, by turning the inner wheel in more than the outer wheel.

Actuator: A device that receives an electrically coded command from a computer and responds by performing a mechanical action.

Adaptive Memory: A feature of computer memory that allows the microprocessor to adjust its memory for computing open-loop operation, based on changes in engine operation.

Air Bleed: A passage in the carburetor through which air can seep or bleed into fuel moving through a fuel passage.

Air Brakes: Vehicle brakes actuated by air pressure.

Air Charge Temperature (ACT) Sensor: A thermistor used to measure intake air temperature or air-fuel mixture temperature.

Air Cleaner: A device, mounted in the intake air stream, through which air must pass before entering the engine. A filtering device in the air cleaner removes dust and dirt particles from the air.

Air Filter: A filter that removes dust and dirt particles from air that passes through it.

Air Horn: That part of the air passage in the carburetor, or throttle body that is on the atmospheric side of the assembly.

Air Injection: A way of reducing exhaust emissions by injecting air into each of the exhaust ports of an engine. The air mixes with the hot exhaust and oxidizes the HC and CO to form H_2O and CO_2.

Air-Fuel Ratio: The ratio of air to gasoline by weight in the air-fuel mixture drawn into an engine.

Air-Hydraulic System: An air brake system that uses a single air chamber to power a hydraulic master cylinder that applies the wheel friction assemblies through conventional brake calipers and wheel cylinders.

Alternating Current: A flow of electricity through a conductor, first in one direction, then in the opposite direction.

Alternator: In the electrical system, the device that changes mechanical energy to alternating current electrical energy.

Ammeter: An electric meter that measures current, in amperes, in an electric circuit.

Amperage: The amount of current flow through a conductor.

Ampere: Unit of electric current flow measurement. One ampere equals the current that will flow through a one-ohm resistance when one volt is impressed across the resistance.

Analog: A voltage signal or processing action that varies continuously with the variable being measured or controlled.

Analog Computer: A computer that works with information in the form of signals that vary in strength.

Angle of Approach: The maximum angle of an incline onto which a vehicle can move from a horizontal plane without interference; as, for instance, from front bumpers.

Angle of Departure: The maximum angle of an incline from which a vehicle can move onto a horizontal plane without interference; as, for instance, from rear bumpers.

Annulus Gear: Another name for the internal ring gear in a planetary gear set.

Antifreeze: A substance, usually ethylene glycol, added to the cooling system to prevent freezing.

Anti-friction Bearing: A bearing of the type that supports the imposed load on rolling surfaces (balls, rollers, needles), to minimizing friction.

Antiknock: Refers to substances that are added to automotive fuel to decrease the tendency to knock when fuel-air mixture is compressed and ignited in the engine cylinder.

Anti-Lock Brakes: A braking system that automatically regulates hydraulic pressure under heavy pedal applications to prevent wheel lock-up and maintain steering control.

Antiroll Bar: A transverse suspension link that transfers some of the load on one wheel to the opposite wheel. Its main purpose is to prevent body roll during cornering. Also called an "anti-sway bar" or "stabilizer bar".

Armature: A current-carrying conductor inside a motor, which reacts to the magnetic field of the motor by moving to a weaker area of the field. Armature movement provides mechanical energy to perform work.

Asbestos: The generic name for a group of minerals used in brake friction materials and made up of millions of individual fibers. The fibers pose a serious health hazard if inhaled or ingested.

Aspect Ratio: The ratio of tire section height to section width expressed as a percentage.

Aspirator: A regulator and venturi installed in the air cleaner to provide EGR flow under low engine vacuum conditions to control detonation.

Asymmetrical: Different on both sides of center.

ATDC: After Top Dead Center, the position of a piston after it has passed its highest point of travel, usually expressed in degrees.

Atmosphere: The mass of air that surrounds the earth.

Atmospheric Pressure: The pressure on the Earth's surface caused by the weight of air in the atmosphere. At sea level, this pressure is 14.7 psi at 32°F (0°C).

Atom: The smallest part of an element that still has all the characteristics of that element.

Atomization: The spraying of a liquid through a nozzle so that the liquid is broken into tiny globules or particles.

Automatic Adjusters: Brake adjusters that use shoe movement, or parking brake application, to continually reset the lining-to-drum clearance.

Automatic Choke: A choke that operates automatically in accordance with certain engine conditions (usually temperature and intake manifold vacuum). It is also electrically controlled.

Automatic Transmission: A transmission that reduces or eliminates the necessity of shifting gears by hand to secure different gear ratios in the transmission.

Available Voltage: The peak voltage that a coil can produce.

Axial Motion: Movement along, or parallel to, the centerline (axis) of a shaft.

Axis: A center line. The line about which something rotates or about which something is evenly divided.

Axle: The rod on which a wheel or wheels spin. In an automobile, the axle may or may not link the two wheels directly, depending on the suspension design.

Axle Windup: In a rear, drive axle, the reaction of the axle housing against axle shaft rotation, in which the axle housing tries to rotate in the opposite direction. Axle windup creates a lifting force on the driveshaft.

[B]

Backfire: The accidental combustion of gases in an engine's intake or exhaust system.

Backlash: The backward rotation of a driven gear that is permitted by clearance between meshing teeth of two gears.

Backing Plate: The fixed part of a drum brake that is attached to the vehicle suspension. The wheel cylinder and brake shoes are mounted on the backing plate.

Backpresssure: A pressure that tends to slow the exit of exhaust gases from the combustion chamber; usually caused by restrictions in the exhaust system.

Baffle: A plate or shield to divert the flow of liquid or gas.

Balance Valve: A spool valve and spring combination used to regulate hydraulic system pressure. Some balance valves also use auxiliary lever force or fluid force in doing their jobs.

Ball Bearing: A type of bearing which contains steel balls that roll between inner and outer races.

Battery: A device consisting of two or more cells for converting chemical energy into electrical energy.

Ball Joint: A type of coupling whose two main parts are a ball and socket.

Ball Nut: A part of a recirculating ball steering gear that has a groove cut inside it corresponding to the groove on the worm gear, creating a tunnel through which steel balls roll to move the ball nut and sector gear.

Ballast (Primary) Resistor: A resistor in the primary circuit that stabilizes ignition system voltage and current flow.

Banjo Fitting: A banjo-shaped connector with a hollow bolt through its center that enables fluid lines to exit components at a right angle.

Barometric Pressure: Atmospheric pressure, as measured with a barometer.

Battery Charging: The process of supplying a battery with a flow of electric current to produce chemical actions in the battery; these actions reactivate the chemicals in the battery so that they can again produce electrical energy.

BDC: Bottom Dead Center; the position of the piston when it reaches the lower limit of travel in the cylinder.

Beam Axle: A bar or tube running from one wheel to the other on a non-drive axle.

Bearing: A part in which a journal pivot, or pin, turns or revolves. A part on, or in which, another part slides.

Belleville Spring: A diaphragm-type spring sometimes used to help apply and release a multiple-disc clutch.

Bendix Drive: A type of drive used in a starter which provides automatic coupling with the engine flywheel for cranking and automatic uncoupling when the engine starts.

Bevel Gear: A gear with teeth cut at an angle on its outer surface. Bevel gears often transmit motion between two shafts at an angle to one another.

Bimetallic Temperature Sensor: A device that uses two strips of different metals welded together. When heated, one side will expand more than the other, causing the strip to bend, which makes or breaks a pair of contact points.

Bipolar: A transistor which uses both holes and electrons as current carriers.

Block: *See*: Cylinder block.

Blow-By: Leakage of the compressed fuel-air mixture or burned gases from combustion, passing piston and rings and into the crankcase.

Blowoff Valve: A spring-loaded valve that opens when boost pressure overcomes the spring tension.

Bleeder Screw: A hollow screw that is tightened to close a bleed valve, and loosened to open the valve, allowing air and fluid to be purged.

Blower: A mechanical device for compressing and delivering air to the engine at higher than atmospheric pressure.

Body: The assembly of sheet-metal sections, framework, doors, windows, etc., which provides an enclosure for passengers or carriage space for freight.

Bond: To bind together.

Boost: A measure of the amount of air pressurization, above atmospheric, that a supercharger can deliver.

Booster Valve: A valve in an automatic transmission that increases mainline pressure when driveline loads are high to prevent apply devices from slipping.

Boot: A protective cover, pleated to allow compression and expansion, made of rubber or plastic. Also called a "bellows".

Bore: The internal diameter of any machined hole.

Boss: An extension or strengthened section, such as the projections within a piston which support the piston pin.

Brake Adjuster: A device or mechanism used to set and maintain the proper clearance between the brake lining and drum.

Brake Balance: The split of braking power between the front and rear axles. Proper brake balance allows the driver to use the full braking ability at all four wheels when stopping the car.

Brake Band: A flexible band, usually of metal with an inner lining of brake fabric, which is tightened on a drum to slow, or stop rotation.

Brake Caliper: The device in a disc brake that converts hydraulic pressure back into the mechanical force used to apply the brake pads against the rotor.

Brake Drum: The rotating part of a drum brake assembly that is contacted by the brake shoes to create the friction necessary to stop the vehicle.

Brake Fade: The partial or total loss of braking power that occurs when excessive heat reduces friction between the brake linings and the rotor or drum.

Brake Fluid: A compounded fluid used in a hydraulic braking system; it transmits hydraulic force from the brake master cylinder to the wheel cylinder and should be impervious to heat or freezing.

Brake Horsepower: The power actually delivered by the engine which is available for driving the vehicle.

Brake Lathe: A machine that rotates drums and/or rotors, and uses cutting bits to remove metal from the friction surfaces.

Brake Lines: The network of steel tubing and rubber hoses used to transmit brake system hydraulic pressure from the master cylinder to the wheel friction assemblies.

Brake Lining: A material that is good at generating friction and resisting heat. The lining is molded, bonded, or riveted to the rubbing surfaces of brake shoes and pads.

Brake Pads: The parts of a disc brake assembly that are faced with the lining material that rubs against the rotor to create the friction necessary to stop the vehicle.

Brake Shoes: The curved metal parts, faced with brake lining, which are forced against the brake drum to produce braking or retarding action.

Brake: The mechanism that slows or stops a moving object when a pedal or other control is operated.

Breakdown Voltage: The voltage above which a zener diode will allow reverse current flow.

Breaker Points: The metal contact points that act as an electrical switch in a distributor. They open and close the ignition primary circuit.

Bronze: A soft-metal alloy consisting essentially of copper and tin often used for bushings.

Brushes: The carbon or carbon and metal parts in a motor or generator that contact the rotating armature commutator or rings.

BTDC: Before Top Dead Center, the position of a piston before it has reached its highest point of travel, usually expressed in degrees.

Bump Stop: A rubber cushion that keeps the suspension from compressing or extending excessively.

Bump Steer: A steering condition in which a tie rod resists steering arm movement during suspension travel and either jerks the steering arm inward or pushes it outward, effectively steering the wheel in a direction not intended by the driver.

Bushing: A sleeve placed in a bore to serve as a bearing surface.

Buss Bar: A solid metal strip, or bar, used as a conductor in a fuse panel.

Bypass: A separate passage which permits a liquid, gas, or electric current to take a path other than that normally used.

[C]

Cam: A stepped or curved eccentric wheel mounted on a rotating shaft. As a cam is turned, objects in contact with it are raised or lowered.

Camber: To curve or bend; the amount in inches or degrees that the front wheels of a vehicle are tilted from a true vertical at the top.

Camber Roll: The amount that camber changes when wheels are steered to either side. Caster determines camber roll.

Capacitance: The ability of two conducting surfaces, separated by an insulator, to store an electric charge.

Capacitor: A device that can store voltage without affecting the voltage in any way. Formed by bringing two conductive surfaces close together, separated only by an insulator. Also called condenser.

Capillary Tube: A long, narrow tube used to transmit internal gas pressure from a remote sensing bulb to a thermostatic expansion valve diaphragm.

Carbon Monoxide (CO): An odorless, colorless, tasteless poisonous gas. A major pollutant given off by an internal combustion engine.

Carbon-pile Regulator: A type of regulator for regulating or controlling voltage or amperage in a circuit, which makes use of a stack, or pile, of carbon disks.

Carburetor: The device in a fuel system which mixes fuel with air and delivers the combustible mixture to the intake manifold.

Caster: The amount in degrees that the steering knuckle pivots are tilted forward or backward from a true vertical.

Caster Trail: The distance between where the caster line intersects the ground and the center of the tire contact patch.

Catalyst: A substance that causes a chemical reaction, without being changed by the reaction.

Cell: A combination of electrodes and electrolyte which converts chemical energy into electrical energy. Two or more cells connected together form a battery.

Center Link: The part of a parallelogram steering linkage that transmits movement from the pitman arm to the tie rods.

Centrifugal Advance: The mechanism in an ignition distributor by which the spark is advanced or retarded as the engine speed varies.

Centrifugal Force: The force acting on a rotating body, which tends to move its parts outward and away from the center of rotation.

Charging Rate: The rate of flow, in amperes, of electric current flowing through a battery while it is being charged.

Chassis: An assembly of mechanisms, attached to a frame, that make up the major operating part of an automobile, the vehicle less the body.

Check Valve: A valve that permits fluid or vacuum flow in one direction but prevents it in the opposite direction.

Check Ball: A type of hydraulic valve consisting of a ball that seals an orifice when it is seated and can be unseated to open the orifice.

Choke: A device in the carburetor that chokes off, or reduces, the flow of air into the intake manifold; this produces a partial vacuum in the intake manifold and, consequently, a richer fuel-air mixture.

Circuit: A closed path or combination of paths through which passage of the medium (electric current, air, liquid, etc.) is possible.

Circuit Breaker: In electric circuits, a mechanism designed to break or open the circuit when certain conditions exist.

Clearance: The space between mechanical parts.

Clearance Volume: The volume of a combustion chamber when the piston is at top dead center.

Closed-Loop: An operational mode in which the engine control microprocessor reads and responds to feedback signals from the oxygen sensor, adjusting system operation accordingly.

Clutch: A mechanism used to connect, disconnect, and regulate slippage between a driving and driven member.

Clutch Pack: The assembly of clutch plates and pressure plates that provides the friction surfaces in a multiple-disc clutch.

Coil: In electrical circuits, turns of wire, usually on a core and enclosed in a case, through which electric current passes.

Coil Spring: A type of spring made of an elastic metal such as steel, formed into a wire or bar and wound into a coil.

Combustion: A chemical action, or burning, of a fuel.

Combustion Chamber: The space at the top of the cylinder and in the head in which combustion of the fuel-air mixture takes place.

Commutation: The process of converting alternating current which flows in the armature windings of direct current generators into direct current.

Commutator: A device that changes the direction of electrical current flow. In many motors, the commutator is a ring split into two or more pieces, and as it rotates past the brushes that bring current to and from the commutator, the current flow reverses.

Compensating Port: The opening between the fluid reservoir and high-pressure chamber that allows fluid to enter or exit the hydraulic system to adjust for changes in volume.

Compression: Act of pressing into a smaller space or reducing in size or volume by pressure.

Compression Ratio: The ratio between the volume in the cylinder with the piston at bottom dead center and with the piston at top dead center.

Compression Rings: The upper rings on a piston; the rings designed to hold the compression in the cylinder and prevent blow-by.

Compression Stroke: The piston stroke from bottom dead center to top dead center during which both valves are closed and the gases in the cylinder are compressed.

Concentric: Having a common center, as circles or spheres, one within the other.

Condenser (air conditioning): A radiator-like tube-and-fin heat exchanger exposed to outside airflow. As gaseous refrigerant flows through the tubes, it condenses to liquid and releases heat that the airstream carries away.

Condenser (electrical): *See*: Capacitor.

Conductor: A material through which electricity will readily flow.

Connecting Rod: Linkage between the crankshaft and piston, usually attached to the piston by a pin and toy the crankshaft journal by a split bearing and bearing cap.

Constant Velocity (CV) Joint: A shaft coupling, consisting either of a ball and cage assembly or a tripod and tulip, that allows changes in the angle between two rotating shafts without affecting the rate of rotation.

Continuity: Continuous, unbroken. Used to describe a working electrical circuit or component that is not open.

Continuous Injection System: A fuel injection system in which fuel is injected constantly whenever the engine is running.

Control Unit: In an automotive electronic system, a small on-board computer that processes information received from sensors and sends signals to various actuators so they operate in response to the driving conditions. Also called a "control module".

Control Arm: A suspension link attached to the knuckle or wheel flange at one end and pivoting on a frame member at the opposite end.

Control Valve: The valve in a power steering system that controls the application of pressurized fluid against the power piston.

Controller: A device that uses a variable resistor to regulate current flow to an electric brake friction assembly based on hand, foot, hydraulic, or air pressure.

Cooling Fan: The fan in the engine cooling system that provides a forced circulation of air through the radiator or around the engine cylinders so that cooling is effected.

Cooling Fins: Thin metal projections on an engine casting that greatly increase the heat-radiating surfaces to improve cooling by increasing heat dissipation.

Core: An iron mass, generally the central portion of a coil or electromagnet or armature around which wire is coiled.

Core Plug: Also called a freeze plug. A shallow metal cup inserted into the engine block to seal holes left by manufacturing.

Corrosion: The chemical dissolving or etching away of metals. Also, the name given the residue left by the process.

Cowl: The front portion of the vehicle body or cab which partially encloses the dash panel and forms the windshield frame.

Crank: A device for converting reciprocating motion into rotary motion, and vice versa.

Crankcase: The lower part of the engine in which the crankshaft rotates.

Crankcase Breather: The opening or tube that allows air to enter the crankcase to permit ventilation and relieve pressure.

Crankcase Dilution: Dilution of the lubricating oil in the oil pan by liquid gasoline seeping down the cylinder walls past the piston rings.

Crankcase Ventilation: The circulation of air through the crankcase which removes water and other vapors, thereby preventing the formation of water sludge and other unwanted substances.

Cranking Motor: *See*: Starter.

Crankshaft: The main rotating member or shaft of the engine, with journals to which connecting rods are attached.

Cross-Firing: Ignition voltage jumping from the distributor rotor to the wrong spark plug electrode inside the distributor cap. Also, ignition voltage jumping from one spark plug cable to another due to worn insulation.

Cross-Groove Joint: A plunging, ball-and-cage CV joint that uses angled grooves in the inner and outer races to allow plunge.

Crossmember: A lateral, or transverse, steel rail in the automobile frame, running from one side member to the other.

Cup Seals: Circular rubber seals with a depressed center surrounded by a raised sealing lip. Cup seals can contain high pressure in one direction, but do not seal in the other.

Current Regulator: A magnetic-controlled relay by which the field circuit of the generator is made and broken very rapidly to secure even current output and prevent generator overload from excessive output.

Cutout Relay: An automatic magnetic switch attached to the generator to cut out generator circuit and prevent overcharging of battery. *See*: Circuit breaker.

Cycle: A series of events with a start and finish, during which a definite train of events takes place. In the engine, the four piston strokes (or two piston strokes on 2-stroke cycle engine) that complete the working process and produce power.

Cycling Clutch: A pressure-control system that maintains air conditioning refrigerant pressure by engaging and disengaging the compressor with its electromagnetic clutch.

Cylinder: A tubular-shaped structure. In the engine, the tubular opening in which the piston moves up and down.

Cylinder Block: That part of an engine to which, and in which, other engine parts and accessories are attached or assembled.

Cylinder Head: The part of the engine that encloses the cylinder bores. Contains water jackets (on liquid-cooled engine) and valves.

[D]

DC: Direct current, or current that flows in one direction only.

D'Arsonval Movement: A small, current-carrying coil mounted within the field of a permanent horseshoe magnet. Interaction of the magnetic fields causes the coil to rotate. Used as a measuring device within electrical gauges and test meters.

Damper: A device for reducing the motion or oscillations of moving parts, air, or liquid.

Damping Force: The total resistance of a shock absorber. Also called "control force".

Dead Axle: An axle that simply supports and does not turn or deliver power to the wheel or rotating member.

Deceleration: The process of slowing down. Opposite to acceleration.

Delta-Type: An alternator stator design in which the three windings of a 3-phase alternator are connected end-to-end. The beginning of one winding is attached to the end of another winding. A delta-type stator is used in an alternator that must give high-current output.

Detented: Positions in a switch that allow the switch to stay in that position. In an ignition switch, the On, Off, Lock, and Accessory positions are detented.

Detonation: In the engine, excessively rapid burning of the compressed fuel-air mixture so that knocking results.

Dew-Point: The temperature at which air becomes 100 percent saturated with moisture at a given absolute humidity.

Diaphragm: A flexible membrane, usually made of fabric and rubber in automotive components, clamped at the edges and usually spring loaded.

Dielectric: The insulating material between the two plates of a condenser, or capacitor.

Diesel Engine: An engine using the diesel cycle of operation; air alone is compressed and diesel fuel is injected at the end of the compression stroke. Heat of compression produces ignition.

Dieseling: A condition in which extreme heat in an engine's combustion chamber continues to ignite fuel after the ignition has been turned off.

Differential: A mechanism between axles that permits one axle to turn at a different speed from the other and, at the same time, transmits power from the driving shaft to the axles.

Differential Winding: In electrical machinery, a winding in a reverse or different direction than the main operating windings. The differential winding acts to modify or change the action of the machine under certain conditions.

Digital: A voltage signal or processing function that has only two levels: on/off or high/low.

Diode: An electronic semiconductor device that acts as a switch. A diode allows current flow in one direction but not the other.

Direct Current: A flow of electricity in one direction through a conductor.

Disc Brake: A type of brake in which friction is generated by brake pads rubbing against the sides of a brake rotor.

Discard Dimension: The thinnest width at which a rotor can safely operate.

Discard Diameter: The largest inside diameter at which a brake drum can safely operate.

Distributor: *See*: Ignition distributor.

Diverter Valve: A valve used in an air injection system to prevent backfire. During deceleration it "dumps" the air from the air pump into the atmosphere. Also called a dump valve.

Double-Cardan Universal Joint (U-Joint): A shaft coupling, consisting of two sets of yokes with two crosspieces joining them together, that allows changes in the angle between two rotating shafts with minimal effect on the rate of rotation.

Double-Offset Joint: A plunging, ball-and-cage CV joint that uses long grooves in the outer race to allow plunge.

Downshift Valve: An auxiliary shift valve that increases throttle pressure to force a downshift under high driveline loads. Also called a kick-down valve or detent valve.

Drag Link: An intermediate link in the steering system between the Pitman arm and an intermediate arm, or drag-link arm.

Drive Axle: An axle that transmits torque from a differential or transaxle to the wheels.

Drum Brake: A type of brake in which friction is generated by brake shoes rubbing against the inside of a brake drum.

Dual Master Cylinder: A master cylinder that contains two pistons that supply the hydraulic pressure for a dual-circuit braking system.

Dual-Circuit Brake System: A brake system that actuates the wheel friction assemblies using two separate hydraulic circuits.

Dual-Servo Brake: A drum brake that has servo action in both the forward and reverse directions.

Duty Cycle: The percentage of the total time that a solenoid is energized during pulse width modulation as determined by a timed voltage pulse from the computer.

Dwell Angle: Also called cam angle, or dwell. The measurement in degrees of how far the distributor cam rotates while the breaker points are closed.

Dynamic Friction: The coefficient of friction between two surfaces that have relative motion between them. Also called kinetic friction.

Dynamic Seal: A seal that prevents fluid passage between two parts that are in motion relative to one another.

Dynamometer: A device for measuring power output of an engine.

[E]

Early Fuel Evaporation (EFE): A system that preheats the incoming air-fuel mixture to improve driveability when the engine is cold.

Eccentric: Off center or out of round. A part whose center section is offset from its primary axis.

Eddy Currents: Currents which are induced in an iron core and circulate in the core.

Efficiency: Ratio between the effect produced and the power expended to produce the effect.

Elastic Limit: The point beyond which a deformed piece of metal will no longer return to its original shape.

Electricity: A form of energy that involves the movement of electrons from one place to another, or the gathering of electrons in one area. Either terminal of an electric source; either conductor by which the current enters and leaves an electrolyte.

Electro-Hydraulic Booster: A power booster that uses an electric motor and pump to create hydraulic pressure which is then used to increase brake application force.

Electrochemistry: In a battery, voltage caused by the chemical action of two dissimilar materials in the presence of a conductive chemical solution.

Electrolyte: The chemical solution in a battery that conducts electricity and reacts with the plate materials.

Electromagnet: Temporary magnet constructed by winding a number of turns of insulated wire into a coil or around an iron core; it is energized by a flow of electric current through the coil.

Electron: Negative charged particle that is a basic constituent of matter and electricity. Movement of electrons is an electric current.

Electron Theory: The current flow theory which says that electricity flows from negative to positive.

Electronic Fuel Injection (EFI): A computer-controlled fuel injection system which gives precise mixture control and almost instant response to all operating conditions at all speed ranges.

Emergency Brakes: Another name sometimes given to the parking brakes because of their limited ability to stop the car in the event of total failure of the service brakes.

Emitter: The outside layer of semiconductor material in a transistor that conducts current to the base.

Endplay: Axial play, when measured at the end of a shaft.

Energy: The capacity for performing work.

Engine: An assembly that burns fuel to produce power, sometimes referred to as the power plant.

Engine Displacement: A measurement of the volume of air displaced by a piston as it moves from bottom to top of its stroke. Engine displacement is the piston displacement multiplied by the number of pistons in an engine.

Engine Mapping: A process of vehicle and engine simulation used to establish variable values for the computer to work with in determining system control.

Equal-Arm Suspension: A suspension system that uses two control arms of equal length, upper and lower, at each wheel. Also called "parallelogram suspension". Equal-arm suspensions have been obsolete for many years.

Ethanol: Ethyl alcohol distilled from grain or sugar cane.

Ethylene Glycol: A chemical compound that forms a good engine coolant when mixed with water, increasing the coolant's resistance to both freezing and boil over.

Evaporation: The action that takes place when a liquid changes to a vapor or gas.

Evaporative Emission Control (EEC): A way of controlling HC emissions by collecting fuel vapors from the fuel tank and carburetor fuel bowl vents and directing them through an engine's intake system.

Evaporator: A radiator-like tube-and-fin heat exchanger, exposed to airflow into the passenger compartment. As liquid refrigerant flows through the tubes, it vaporizes and absorbs heat from the air flowing between the fins.

Exhaust Gas Recirculation (EGR): A pollution control system that injects a small quantity of exhaust gasses into the air-fuel mixture to lower combustion temperatures and limit the formation of oxides of nitrogen (NO_x).

Exhaust Manifold: That part of the engine that provides a series of passages through which burned gases from the engine cylinders may flow to the muffler.

Exhaust Stroke: The piston stroke from bottom dead center to top dead center during which the exhaust valve is opened so that burned gases are forced from the engine cylinder.

Exhaust Valve: The valve which opens to allow the burned gases to escape from the cylinder during the exhaust stroke.

[F]

Fail-Safe System: Any component or group of components that enables a vehicle to operate safely in the event that one of its systems, such as a hydraulic or an electronic system, malfunctions.

Fan: *See*: Cooling fan.

Farad: The unit of measurement of a condenser's ability to store electrical energy.

Fast-Burn Combustion Chamber: A compact combustion chamber with a centrally located spark plug. The chamber is designed to shorten the combustion period by reducing the distance of flame front travel.

Feedback: The return of a portion of the output (actuator) to the input (computer), used to maintain an output device within predetermined limits.

Field: In an alternator, generator, or electric motor, the area in which a magnetic flow occurs.

Field Coil: A coil of wire, wound around an iron core, which produces the magnetic field in an alternator, generator, or electric motor when current passes through it.

Field Circuit: The charging system circuit that delivers current to the alternator field.

Field Frame: The frame in an alternator, generator, or electric motor into which the field coils are assembled.

Field Relay: A magnetic switch used to open and close the alternator field circuit or, in a charging circuit with a warning lamp, to control the lamp circuit.

Field Winding: *See:* Field coil.

Filter: A device through which gas or liquid is passed; dirt, dust, and other impurities are removed by the separating action.

Final Drive: The last set of reduction gears the power flow passes through on its way to the drive axles.

Firewall: The bulkhead that separates the engine bay from the passenger compartment.

Firing Order: The order in which combustion occurs in the cylinders of an engine.

Firing Voltage (Required Voltage): The voltage level that must be reached to ionize and create a spark in the air gap between the spark plug electrodes.

First Law of Thermodynamics: The natural law that states energy cannot be created or destroyed; it can only be converted into another form.

Fixed Tripod Joint: A tripod CV joint in which the tripod is fixed to the tulip in such a way as to prevent plunging action of the joint.

Fixed Brake Caliper: A brake caliper whose body is solidly attached to the vehicle suspension and does not move when the brakes are applied.

Fixed Dwell: The ignition dwell period begins when the switching transistor turns on and remains relatively constant at all speeds.

Flat Spot: The brief hesitation or stumble of an engine caused by a momentary overly lean air-fuel mixture due to the sudden opening of the throttle.

Flexible Coupling: A shaft coupling, made of rubber or reinforced rubber and a solid safety connection, that allows changes in the angle between two rotating shafts.

Flexplate: The thin metal plate, used in place of a flywheel, that joins the engine crankshaft to the fluid coupling or torque converter.

Float: In a carburetor, the hollow shell that is suspended by the fuel in the float bowl and controls a needle valve that regulates the fuel level in the bowl.

Float Valve: A valve that is controlled by a hollow ball floating in a liquid, such as in the fuel bowl of a carburetor.

Floating Caliper: A caliper whose body moves on the anchor plate but does not make metal-to-metal contact with it. Floating calipers are supported by bushings and O-rings that slide on guide pins and sleeves.

Flooding: A condition caused by heat expanding the fuel in a fuel line. The fuel pushes the carburetor inlet needle valve open and fills up the fuel bowl even when more fuel is not needed. Also, the presence of too much fuel in the intake manifold.

Flow Control Valve: Another name for a modulator valve.

Fluid: A liquid; in an automotive hydraulic system, a liquid that can convey pressure from one surface to another. Automotive fluids also frequently have the secondary purpose of lubricating and cooling moving parts.

Fluid Shear: The internal friction that occurs within a fluid when its rate or direction of flow is suddenly changed. Fluid shear in the torque converter is the major source of transmission fluid heat buildup.

Fluid Coupling: A coupling in the power train that connects between the engine and other power train members through a fluid.

Flywheel: The rotating metal wheel, attached to the crankshaft, that helps level out the power surges from the power strokes and also serves as part of the clutch and engine-cranking system.

Foot-Pound: A unit of work done in raising one pound of weight against the force of gravity to the height of one foot.

Force: The action that one body may exert upon another to change its motion or shape. Force is usually measured in pounds or Newtons.

Four-Wheel Drive (4WD): An automotive drive layout in which all four wheels provide the power to move the vehicle.

Four-Wheel Alignment: A wheel alignment procedure performed on all four wheels of a vehicle, rear wheels first, then front wheels.

Four-Wheel Steering (4WS): A type of steering system that can operate all four wheels when the driver turns the steering wheel.

Frame: An assembly of metal structural parts and channel sections that support the engine and body and that is supported by the vehicle wheels.

Free Electrons: Three or fewer loosely held electrons in an atom's valence ring.

Frequency: The number of vibrations, cycles, or changes in direction in a unit of time.

Free play: The portion of travel of an actuating component that is not converted into movement in the reacting component.

Friction: The resistance to motion between two bodies in contact with each other.

Friction Material: A blend of substances with a relatively consistent friction coefficient over a wide range of conditions.

Friction Modifiers: Additives that enable lubricants to maintain their viscosity over a wide range of temperatures.

Front-Wheel Drive (FWD): An automotive drive layout in which the front wheels provide the power to move the vehicle.

Fuel: The substance that is burned to produce heat and create motion of the piston on the power stroke in an engine.

Fuel Filter: A device placed in the fuel line of the fuel system to remove dirt and other harmful solids.

Fuel Gauge: An indicating device in the fuel system that indicates the amount of fuel in the fuel tank.

Fuel Line: The tube or tubes connecting the fuel tank and the carburetor and through which the fuel passes.

Fuel Passage: Drilled holes in the carburetor body and tubes through which fuel passes from the float bowl to the fuel nozzles.

Fuel Pump: The mechanism in the fuel system that transfers fuel from the fuel tank to the carburetor or injectors.

Fuel Tank: The storage tank for fuel on the vehicle.

Fulcrum: The support, as a wedge-shaped piece or a hinge, about which a lever turns.

Full-Floating Axle: A solid, drive axle in which the wheel bearings and brake drum ride on the axle housing, the axle shaft attaches to the brake drum through a flange at that end, and the wheel mounts onto the brake drum hub.

Full-Wave Rectification: A process by which all of an alternating current sine wave voltage is rectified and allowed to flow as direct current.

Fuse: A circuit-protecting device that uses a substance with a low melting point. The substance melts if an overload occurs, thus protecting other devices in the system.

[G]

G: A unit of measurement for gravitational forces. One G equals the force of gravity on an object.

G-Force: The force of gravity on an object, which resists changes in speed or direction.

G-Lader: A type of supercharger pump which compresses air by squeezing it through an internal spiral, then forcing it through ports into the engine.

Galvanic Battery: A direct current voltage source, generated by the chemical action of an electrolyte.

Gas: A state of matter of no definite shape or volume, easily compressed, with a high tendency to disperse.

Gas Shock Absorber: A hydraulic shock absorber in which the air in the reserve tube is replaced by pressurized gas.

Gas Fade: Brake fade caused by hot gases and dust particles that reduce friction between the brake linings and drum or rotor under hard, prolonged braking.

Gasohol: A blend of ethanol and unleaded gasoline, usually at a one to nine ratio.

Gasket: A flat strip, usually of cork, metal, composite material, or a combination of materials, placed between two surfaces to provide a tight seal between them.

Gasoline: A liquid hydrocarbon, obtained from petroleum, which is suitable as an internal combustion engine fuel.

Gear: Mechanical device to transmit power or turning effort from one shaft to another; more specifically, gear which contains teeth that engage or mesh upon turning.

Gear Mesh Preload: The resistance that the drive gear of a gear set exerts against the driven gear, or the force required to move the driven gear against that resistance.

Gear Oil: A petroleum-based oil of the proper viscosity and chemical make-up for use in gear boxes. Gear oils cling to gear surfaces to reduce gear train friction and heat.

Gear Lash: A lack of mesh between two gears, resulting in a lag between when one gear moves and when it engages the other.

Gear Pump: A pump that uses two meshed gears inside the pump body to produce fluid flow. The meshing and unmeshing of the gears as they rotate creates fluid chambers of varying volumes.

Gear Ratio: The relative speeds at which two gears turn; the proportional rate of rotation.

Gear Reduction: A condition in which the drive gear rotates faster than the driven gear. Output speed of the driven gear is reduced, while output torque is increased.

Gearshift: A mechanism by which the gears in a transmission system are engaged.

Gear Train: A series of two or more gears meshed together so that power is transmitted between them.

Generator: In the electrical system, the device that changes mechanical energy to direct current electrical energy.

Generator Regulator: In the electrical system, the unit which is composed of the current regulator, voltage regulator, and circuit breaker relay.

Geometric Centerline: An imaginary line that bisects the front and rear axles of a vehicle.

Governor: A mechanism that controls, or limits speed or another variable.

Governor Pressure: The automatic transmission hydraulic pressure that is directly related to vehicle speed. Governor pressure increases with vehicle speed and is one of the principle pressures used to control shift points.

Governor Valve: The valve that regulates governor pressure in relation to vehicle road speed. Commonly called a governor.

Grease: A thick, non-pourable lubricant, usually made of oil thickened with a soap. Automotive greases are usually petroleum-based and contain additives related to their intended use.

Greenhouse Effect: In our usage, the warming of an enclosed space by trapped heat, resulting from sunlight entering through windows.

Grinding: The process of using a power-driven abrasive stone to remove metal from parts.

Grommets: Ring-shaped parts made of a third material that prevent problems where two other dissimilar materials come into contact.

Gross Vehicle Weight Rating (GVWR): The manufacturer's specified maximum allowable weight for a vehicle including passengers and cargo.

Ground: Connection of an electrical unit to the engine or frame to return the current to its source.

Ground Cable: The battery cable that provides a ground connection from the vehicle chassis to the battery.

Group Number: A battery identification number that indicates battery dimensions, terminal design, holddown location, and other physical features.

Gulp Valve: A valve used in an air injection system to prevent backfire. During deceleration it redirects air from the air pump to the intake manifold where the air leans out the rich air-fuel mixture.

Gusset Plate: A plate at the joint of a frame structure of steel used to strengthen the joint.

[H]

Half-Wave Rectification: A process by which only one-half of an alternating current sine wave voltage is rectified and allowed to flow as direct current.

Hall-Effect Switch: A signal-generating switch that develops a transverse voltage across a current-carrying semiconductor when subjected to a magnetic field.

Handbrake: A brake operated by hand. Also referred to as the parking brake.

Hard Spots: Circular, bluish/gold, glassy areas on friction surfaces where extreme heat has altered the structure of the metal. Hard spots are also called chill spots.

Heat: The disorganized energy in any substance caused by the rapid vibration of the atoms and molecules making it up.

Heat Exchanger: A component in which heat is transferred from one medium (such as hot coolant) to another (such as the surrounding air) through conduction.

Heat Range: The measure of a spark plug's ability to dissipate heat from its firing end.

Heat Checking: Small cracks on a friction surface. Heat checks do not penetrate through the friction surface, and can usually be machined out of it.

Heater Core: A heat exchanger in the HVAC system through which hot coolant passes and releases its heat by conduction.

Helical: In the shape of a helix, which is the shape of a screw thread or coil spring.

Helical Gear: A gear on which the teeth are at an angle to the gear's axis of rotation.

High Side: The portion of the air conditioning system in which the refrigerant is under high pressure and at high temperature. It includes the compressor outlet, condenser, receiver-drier (if used), and expansion device inlet.

High-speed circuit: In the carburetor, the passages through which fuel flows when the throttle valve is fully opened.

High-Speed Surge: A sudden increase in engine speed caused by high manifold vacuum pulling in an excess air-fuel mixture.

High-Swirl Combustion Chamber: A combustion chamber in which the intake valve is shrouded or masked to direct the incoming air-fuel charge and create turbulence that will circulate the mixture more evenly and rapidly.

Hill Holder: A device in the transmission that automatically prevents the vehicle from rolling backwards down a hill when the vehicle is brought to a stop.

Hold-In Winding: The coil of small-diameter wire in a solenoid that is used to create a magnetic field to hold the solenoid plunger in position inside the coil.

Homogeneous: Being of a similar nature. Homogeneous liquids blend together completely; no part of either liquid remains separate.

Horsepower: A measure of a definite amount of power; 550 foot-pound per second.

Hotchkiss Drive: Type of rear live axle suspension in which the springs serve as torque members.

Humidity: Water vapor in the air.

HVAC: An acronym for heating-ventilation-air conditioning systems.

Hydraulic Circuit: An arrangement of an input source, fluid passages, control valves, and an output device that is used to transmit motion and force to do work.

Hydraulic Brakes: A braking system that uses a fluid to transmit hydraulic pressure from a master cylinder to wheel cylinders, which then cause brake movement and braking action.

Hydraulically Operated Switching Valve: A spool valve whose position is determined by hydraulic pressures acting on its faces. The shift valves that control most gear changes in an automatic transmission are hydraulically operated switching valves.

Hydraulic Shock Absorber: A shock absorber that provides hydraulic friction to damp the oscillation of the suspension spring. Typically, this term refers to the most basic hydraulic shock design.

Hydraulic Steering: A steering system that uses a fluid to produce an assisting hydraulic pressure on the steering linkage, thus reducing the steering effort on the part of the driver.

Hydraulic Valve Lifter: Valve lifter that uses hydraulic pressure to maintain zero valve clearance to reduce noise and periodic adjustment.

Hydraulics: The study of liquids and their use to transmit force and motion.

Hydrocarbon (HC): A chemical compound made up of hydrogen and carbon. A major pollutant given off by an internal combustion engine. Gasoline itself is a hydrocarbon compound.

Hydrodynamics: The study, or science, of the mechanical movement and action of liquids or fluids in motion.

Hydrometer: A device to determine the specific gravity of a liquid. This indicates the freezing point of the coolant in a cooling system or, as another example, the state of charge of a battery.

Hygroscopic: An affinity or attraction for water. Polyglycol brake fluids are hygroscopic.

Hydrovac Brakes: A type of braking system using vacuum to assist in brake operation. The vacuum action reduces the effort required from the driver to operate the vehicle brakes.

Hypoid Gear Set: A combination of a ring gear and pinion gear in which the pinion meshes with the ring gear below the centerline of the ring gear. Commonly used in automotive final drives.

[I]

I-Beam: A solid, metal axle whose cross-section looks like the capital letter I.

Idle: Engine speed when accelerator pedal is fully released; generally assumed to mean when engine is doing no work.

Idle Circuit: The circuit in the carburetor through which fuel is fed when the engine is idling.

Idler Arm: The part of a parallelogram steering linkage that helps the pitman arm support the center link. The idler arm allows center link movement but does not transmit any movement.

Idler Gear: A gear placed between a driving and a driven gear to make them rotate in the same direction. It does not affect the gear ratio.

Ignition: The action of setting fire to, In an engine, the initiating of the combustion process in the engine cylinders.

Ignition Advance: Refers to the spark advance produced by the distributor in accordance with engine speed and intake manifold vacuum.

Ignition Coil: That component of the ignition system that acts as a transformer and steps up battery voltage, the high voltage then produces a spark across the spark plug gap.

Ignition Distributor: That component of the ignition system that closes and opens the circuit between the battery and ignition coil, and distributes the resultant high-voltage surges from the coil to the proper spark plugs.

Ignition Interval (Firing Interval): The number of degrees of crankshaft rotation between ignition sparks.

Ignition Switch: The switch in the ignition system that can be operated to open or close the ignition primary circuit.

Ignition Timing: Refers to the timing of the spark at the spark plug as related to the piston position in the engine cylinder.

Impeller: A rotor or rotor blade used to force a gas or liquid in a certain direction under pressure.

Inboard Brakes: Brakes mounted near the differential rather than out at the wheels.

Inch-Pound: A unit of work done in raising one pound of weight against the force of gravity to the height of one inch.

Included Angle: The steering axis inclination angle plus or minus the camber angle.

Independent Suspension: A suspension design that allows each wheel on an axle to travel vertically without affecting the opposite wheel.

Indicated Horsepower: A measurement of engine power based on power actually developed in the engine cylinders.

Induced Voltage: The voltage which appears in a conductor when relative motion exists between it and magnetic flux lines.

Induction: The action or process of producing voltage by the relative motion of a magnetic field and a conductor.

Inductive-Discharge Ignition: A method of igniting the air-fuel mixture in an engine cylinder. It is based on the induction of a high voltage in the secondary winding of a coil.

Inert: A substance that exhibits no chemical activity, or does so only under extreme conditions.

Inertia: The property of a body at rest to remain at rest, and a body in motion to remain in motion in a straight line unless acted upon by an outside force.

Injection Pump: A pump used on diesel engines to deliver fuel under high pressure at precisely timed intervals to the fuel injectors.

Injector: The mechanism, including nozzle, which injects fuel into the engine combustion chamber on fuel injected engines.

In-line Engine: An engine in which all engine cylinders are in a single row, or line.

Input: Information that a control unit receives and uses to carry out its program. In an automotive electronic system, input comes from sensors and switches throughout the vehicle.

Input Member: The drive member of a planetary gear set.

Input Gear: The gear that provides input motion to, or drives, the rest of the gears in a gear system.

Input Source: The piston or pump that supplies the input force in a hydraulic system.

Insert: A form of screw thread insert to be placed in a tapped hole into which a screw or bolt will be screwed. The insert protects the part into which the hole was tapped, preventing enlargement due to repeated removal and replacement of the bolt.

Insulation: Substance that stops movement of electricity (electrical insulation) or heat (heat insulation).

Insulator: A substance (usually of glass or porcelain) that will not conduct electricity.

Intake Manifold: That component of the engine which provides a series of passages from the carburetor to the engine cylinders through which fuel-air mixture can flow.

Intake Manifold Vacuum: The low pressure area (vacuum) located below the throttle butterfly valve in the engine intake manifold.

Intake Stroke: The piston stroke from top dead center to bottom dead center during which the intake valve is open and the cylinder receives a charge of fuel-air mixture.

Intake Valve: The valve in the engine which is opened during the intake stroke to permit the entrance of fuel-air mixture into the cylinder.

Integral: Whole; entire; lacking nothing of completeness.

Integrator: The ability of the computer to make short-term—minute-by-minute—corrections in fuel metering.

Intercooler: An air-to-air or air-to-liquid heat exchanger used to lower the temperature of the air-fuel mixture by removing heat from the intake air charge.

Interference: In radio, any signal received that overrides or prevents normal reception of the desired signal. In mechanical practice, anything that causes mismating of parts so they cannot be normally assembled.

Internal Combustion Engine: An engine in which the fuel is burned inside the engine, as opposed to an external combustion engine where the fuel is burned outside the engine, such as a steam engine.

Internal Gear: A gear in which the teeth point inward rather than outward as with a standard spur gear.

Internal Ring Gear: A gear with a hole through its center and teeth cut on the inner circumference. Also called an "annulus gear".

Ion: An atom which has become unbalanced by losing or gaining an electron. It can be positively or negatively charged.

Ionize: To break up molecules into two or more oppositely charged ions. The air gap between the spark plug electrodes is ionized when the air-fuel mixture is changed from a non-conductor to a conductor.

Isolated Field Circuit: A variation of the A-circuit. Field current is drawn from the alternator output outside of the alternator and sent to an insulated brush. The other brush is grounded through the voltage regulator.

[J]

Jackshaft: An intermediate driving shaft.

Jam Nuts: Two nuts that are tightened against each other to lock them in position.

Jet: A metered opening in an air or fuel passage to control the flow of fuel or air.

Jounce: Suspension compression, occurring when the wheel and tire go over a bump, or pressure is applied to the top of the suspension.

Junction: The area where two types of semiconductor materials are joined.

Journal: That part of a shaft that rotates in a bearing.

[K]

Keep-Alive Memory (KAM): A form of long-term RAM used mostly with adaptive strategies. Requires a separate power supply circuit to maintain voltage when the ignition is off.

Kickback: Vibrations and road shocks transmitted through the steering system so that the driver feels them at the steering wheel.

Kinetic Energy: The energy of mass in motion. All moving objects posses kinetic energy.

Kinetic Friction: The amount of friction that exists between two surfaces in motion.

Kingpin: A metal cylinder used in the steering knuckle of some beam axles so the knuckle can pivot when the steering linkage moves the steering arm.

Kingpin Inclination: The number of degrees that the kingpin, which supports the front wheel, is tilted from the vertical.

Knock: In the engine, a rapping or hammering noise resulting from excessively rapid burning or detonation of the compressed fuel-air mixture.

Knockback: Brake caliper piston retraction caused by rotor runout driving a piston back into its bore when the brakes are released.

Knockoff Wheel: A wheel secured to the hub by a single center nut.

Knuckle: A metal casting that supports the wheel, joins the suspension to the wheel, and provides pivot points between them.

[L]

Laminated: Made up of layers of thin sheets, leaves, or plates bonded together.

Land: The large, outer circumference of a valve spool, or piston, that slides against the bore. Most spool valves have several lands that are used to block fluid passages, pistons use lands to support the piston rings.

Lap Winding: A method of wiring a motor armature. The two ends of a conductor are attached to two commutator bars that are next to each other.

Latent Heat: Heat that is absorbed or given off during a change of state of a material without changing its temperature.

Lateral Horizontal Axis: An imaginary line, running from side-to-side of a vehicle and intersecting the center of gravity, around which the car body rotates (pitches) during acceleration or deceleration.

Lateral Runout: The side-to-side movement of a rotating part.

Lead: A driving condition in which the vehicle steers to one side if the driver takes his or her hands off the steering wheel.

Leading-Trailing Brake: A non-servo brake with one energized and one de-energized shoe.

Leaf Spring: A spring made of one or more long, thin strips of steel alloy or plastic composite material.

Lean mixture: A fuel-air mixture that has a high proportion of air and a low proportion of fuel.

Lever: A rigid bar or beam of any shape capable of turning about one point, called the fulcrum; used for transmitting or changing force or motion.

Leverage: The mechanical advantage obtained by use of lever; also an arrangement or combination of levers.

Light-Emitting Diode (LED): A gallium-arsenide diode that emits energy as light. Often used in automotive indicators.

Lining Fade: Brake fade caused by a drop in the brake lining coefficient of friction as a result of excessive heat.

Link: A joining piece; in a suspension, any of the metal rods or arms that are part of the linkage between the frame and the wheels.

Liquid Crystal Display (LCD): An indicator consisting of a sandwich of glass containing electrodes and polarized fluid. Voltage applied to the fluid allows light to pass through it.

Liquid-Vapor Separator Valve: A valve in some fuel systems that separates liquid fuel from fuel vapors.

Live Axle: A solid, drive axle.

Load-Carrying Ball Joint: A ball joint that links a suspension arm to a knuckle and transfers sprung weight from the arm to the wheel.

Lobes: The rounded (eccentric) protrusions on a camshaft that force, and govern, the opening of the intake and exhaust valves.

Longitudinal Axis: A imaginary line, running the length of a vehicle front to rear and intersecting the front and rear roll centers, around which the car body rotates (rolls) during cornering.

Low Side: The portion of the air conditioning system in which the refrigerant is under low pressure and at low temperature. It includes the expansion device outlet, evaporator, accumulator (if used), and compressor inlet.

Lower Control Arm: In an A-arm suspension, the lower and longer of the control arms linking the knuckle to the frame.

Lubrication: The process of supplying a coating of oil between moving surfaces to prevent actual contact between them. The oil film permits relative movement with little frictional resistance.

[M]

MacPherson Strut: A strut that is solidly mounted to the knuckle and that includes the suspension spring as part of its construction.

MacPherson Strut Suspension: A strut suspension in which a coil spring is integral to each strut and the strut base mounts rigidly to the knuckle.

Magnet: Any body that has the ability to attract iron.

Magnetic Field: The space around a magnet which the magnetic lines of force permeate.

Magnetic Flux: The invisible directional lines of force which make up a magnetic field.

Magnetic Pole: Focus of magnetic lines of force entering or emanating from magnet.

Magnetic Pulse Generator: A signal-generating switch that creates a voltage pulse as magnetic flux changes around a pickup coil.

Magnetic Saturation: The condition when a magnetic field reaches full strength and maximum flux density.

Magnetic Shunt (Magnetic Bypass): A piece of metal on a voltage regulator coil that controls voltage output at varying temperatures by affecting the coil's magnetic field.

Magnetism: The property exhibited by certain substances and produced by electron (or electric current) motion which results in the attraction of iron.

Main Bearing: In the engine, the bearings that support the crankshaft in the cylinder block.

Mainline Pressure: The pressure developed from the fluid output of the pump and controlled by the pressure regulator valve. Mainline pressure operates the apply devices in the transmission and is the source of all other pressures in the hydraulic system.

Manifold: *See*: Intake manifold or Exhaust manifold.

Manifold Absolute Pressure (MAP): Pressure in the intake manifold that is a combination of atmospheric pressure and manifold vacuum or boost pressure.

Manifold Vacuum: Low air pressure in the intake manifold of a running engine, caused by the descending pistons creating empty space in the cylinders faster than the entering air can fill it.

Manual Valve: The valve in an automatic transmission that is moved manually, through the shift linkage, to select the drive range. The manual valve directs and blocks fluid flow to various hydraulic circuits.

Mass: The property of a object that leads to the concept of inertia.

Master Cylinder: The device that converts mechanical pressure from the brake pedal into hydraulic pressure that is routed to the wheels to operate the friction assemblies.

Matter: Anything which has weight and occupies space.

Mechanical Efficiency: In an engine, the ratio between brake horsepower and indicated horsepower.

Mechanical Fade: Brake fade caused by heat expansion of the brake drum away from the brake linings. Mechanical fade is not a problem with disc brakes.

Mechanical-Hydraulic Booster: A power booster that uses hydraulic pressure from the power steering pump to increase brake application force.

Mechanism: A system, of parts or appliances which acts as a working agency to achieve a desired result.

Member: Any essential part of a machine or structure.

Meshing: The mating or engaging of the teeth of two gears.

Metering Rod: A small rod, having a varied diameter, operated within a jet to vary the flow of fuel through the jet.

Methanol: Methyl alcohol distilled from wood or made from natural gas sometimes used as an additive in gasoline.

Micro-Inches: A measurement system used to express the roughness of a machined or ground surface.

Micron: A unit of length equal to one millionth of a meter, one one-thousandth of a millimeter.

Millisecond: One one-thousandth of a second.

Misfire: Failure of the air-fuel mixture to ignite during the power stroke.

Modified Strut: A strut that is solidly mounted to the knuckle but does not include the suspension spring as part of its construction.

Modulator Valve: The valve in a power steering pump that controls fluid flow into the pressure hose.

Module: A self-contained, sealed unit that houses the solid-state circuits which control certain electrical or mechanical functions.

Molecule: Two or more atoms chemically bonded together.

Monoleaf Spring: A leaf spring using only one leaf. Monoleaf springs are usually made of plastic composite material.

Monolith: A large block. In a catalytic converter, the monolith is made like a honeycomb to provide several thousand square yards or meters of catalyst surface area.

Monotube Shock Absorber: A hydraulic shock absorber that uses only one tube, along with two pistons.

Motor: A machine that converts electrical, vacuum, or other energy into mechanical energy.

Muffler: In the exhaust system, a device through which the exhaust gases must pass; in the muffler, the exhaust sounds are greatly reduced.

Multi-Link Suspension: A generic term, generally applied to unique suspension designs that do not fit into common categories. Multi-link suspensions are generally used at the rear of sports or performance cars.

Multigrade: An oil that has been tested at more than one temperature, and so has more than one SAE viscosity number.

Multiple-Disc Clutch: A clutch that consists of alternating friction discs and steel discs that are forced together hydraulically to lock one transmission part to another.

Multipoint (Port) Injection: A fuel injection system in which individual injectors are installed in the intake manifold at a point close to the intake valve. Air passing through the manifold mixes with the injector spray just as the intake valve opens.

Mutual Induction: Induction associated with more than one circuit, as two coils, one of which induces current in the other as the current in the first changes.

[N]

Negative: A term designating the point of lower potential when the potential difference between two points is considered.

Negative Offset: A characteristic of a wheel in which the face of the wheel disc is behind, or further inboard than, the rim centerline.

Negative Temperature Coefficient (NTC): A type of resistor often used in automobiles. Its resistance decreases as temperature increases.

Negative Terminal: The terminal from which electrons depart when a circuit is completed from this terminal to the positive terminal of generator or battery.

Needle Valve: Type of valve with rod-shaped, needle-pointed valve body which works into a valve seat so shaped that the needle point fits into it and closes the passage; the needle valve in the carburetor float circuit is an example.

Neutron: A particle in an atom that has no charge and is electrically neutral.

No-Load Oscillation: The rapid, back-and-forth, peak-to-peak oscillation of voltage in the ignition secondary circuit when the circuit is open.

Non-Load-Carrying Ball Joint: A ball joint that links a suspension arm to a knuckle but does not transfer sprung weight from the arm to the wheel. Also called a "follower joint".

Noble Metals: Metals, such as platinum and palladium, that resist oxidation.

Nonvolatile RAM: Random access memory (RAM) that retains its information when current to the chip is removed.

Normally Aspirated: An engine that uses normal vacuum to draw in its air-fuel mixture. Not supercharged or turbocharged.

North Pole: The pole of a magnet from which the lines of force are assumed to emanate.

Nozzle: An orifice or opening in a carburetor through which fuel feeds into the passing air stream on its way to the intake manifold.

Nucleus: The center core of an atom that contains the protons and neutrons.

[O]

Octane Rating: A measure of the antiknock value of engine fuel.

Odometer: The part of the speedometer that measures, accumulatively, the number of vehicle miles traveled.

Ohm: A measure of electrical resistance. A conductor of one ohm resistance will allow a flow of one ampere of current when one volt is imposed on it.

Ohmmeter: A meter used to measure resistance to current flow.

Oil: A liquid lubricant derived from petroleum and used in machinery to provide lubrication between moving parts.

Oil Control Rings: The lower rings on the piston which are designed to prevent excessive amounts of oil from working up into the combustion chamber.

Oil Cooler: A heat exchanger through which hot oil passes, air allowed to circulate around the unit draws off heat to cool the oil.

Oil Galleries: Passages in the block and head that carry pressurized oil to various parts of the engine.

Oil Gauge: Device that indicates the pressure of oil in the lubrication system.

Oil Pan: The lower part of the crankcase in which a reservoir of oil is maintained.

Oil Pump: The pump that transfers oil from the oil pan to the various moving parts in the engine that require lubrication.

Oil Strainer: A strainer placed at the inlet end of the oil pump to strain out dirt and other particles, preventing these from getting into moving engine parts.

One-Way Clutch: A mechanical holding device that prevents rotation in one direction, but overruns to allow it in the other. One-way clutches are either roller clutches or sprag clutches.

One-Way Check Valve: A type of switching valve that allows fluid to pass in one direction only, and then only when the pressure is sufficient to unseat the valve.

Open Loop: An operational mode in which the computer adjusts a system to function according to pre-determined instructions and does not always respond to feedback signals from its sensors.

Orifice: A small opening or restriction in a line or passage that is used to regulate pressure and flow.

Oscillating: Moving back and forth with a steady rhythm.

Out-of-Round: A term used to describe a circular part with radial runout, or a bore that has worn to an oval shape.

Output: Electrically coded commands that a control unit sends to an actuator or actuators. In an automotive electronic system, the output causes a change in some aspect of the car's operation.

Output Circuit: The charging system circuit that sends voltage and current to the battery and other electrical systems and devices.

Output Device: A piston or motor that transmits output force created by the pressure in a hydraulic system.

Output Member: The driven member of a planetary gear set.

Output Gear: The final gear in a gear system, which transmits motion to another component.

Overdrive: A condition in which the drive gear rotates slower than the driven gear. Output speed of the driven gear is increased, while output torque is reduced.

Overflow Tank: Special tank in cooling system (a surge tank) to permit expansion and contraction of engine coolant without loss.

Overhead Valve: Valve mounted in head above combustion chamber.

Overload Breaker: In an electrical circuit, a device that breaks or opens a circuit if it is overloaded by a short, ground, use of too much equipment, etc.

Overrunning Clutch: A type of drive mechanism used in a starter which transmits cranking effort but overruns freely when engine tries to drive starter. Also, a special clutch used in several mechanisms that permits a rotating member to turn freely under some conditions, but not under other conditions.

Oversteer: A driving condition, resulting from greater slip angles at the rear tires than the front, in which the vehicle turns more sharply than steering system input demands.

Overturning Moment: The tendency of a vehicle to overturn during cornering. The greater the tendency becomes, the closer the vehicle is to its overturning moment.

Oxidation: A form of corrosion caused by combining a substance with oxygen. Rust, more precisely called iron oxide, is a common type of oxidation.

Oxides of Nitrogen (NO$_x$): Chemical compounds of nitrogen given off by an internal combustion engine which combine with hydrocarbons to produce smog.

[P]

Panhard Rod: A transverse link, used in rear suspensions, joined to the frame at one end and to a beam axle or axle housing at the other end.

Parallel Circuit: The electrical circuit formed when two or more electrical devices have like terminals connected together (positive to positive and negative to negative) so that each may operate independently of the other.

Parallelism: The state that exists when two surfaces are an equal distance apart at every point.

Parking Brake: *See*: Handbrake.

Particulate: Small pieces (particles) of matter. Liquid or solid particles such as lead and carbon that are given off by an internal combustion engine as pollution.

Pascal's Law: The principle that pressure on a confined fluid is transmitted equally in all directions and acts with equal force on equal areas.

Pawl: A hinged or pivoted part that fits into a toothed wheel to provide rotation in one direction while preventing it in the other.

Peak Inverse Voltage (PIV): The highest reverse bias voltage that can be applied to a junction of a diode before its atomic structure breaks down and allows current to flow.

Percolation: The bubbling and expansion of a liquid. Similar to boiling.

Period: The time required for the completion of one cycle.

Permanent Magnet: Piece of steel or alloy in which molecules are so aligned that the piece continues to exhibit magnetism without application of external influence.

Permeability: A measure of the ease, or difficulty, with which materials can be penetrated by magnetic flux lines. Iron is more permeable than air.

Phase: That portion of a whole period which has elapsed since the activity in question passed through zero position in a positive direction.

Photoelectricity: Voltage caused by the energy of light as it strikes certain materials.

Phototransistor: Also called a photocell. A type of solid-state device that will generate a voltage when exposed to light.

Photovoltaic: Capable of producing electricity when exposed to radiant energy, especially visible light.

Piezoelectric: Voltage caused by physical pressure applied to the faces of certain crystals.

Piezoresistive: A sensor whose resistance varies in relation to pressure or force applied to it. A piezoresistive sensor receives a constant reference voltage and returns a variable signal in relation to its varying resistance.

Pilot: A short plug at the end of a shaft to align it with another shaft or rotating part.

Pilot-Operated: Referring to a smaller internal valve (the pilot valve) that regulates the movement of the larger valve into which it is placed.

Pinion Gear: A smaller gear that meshes with a larger gear or toothed rack.

Pintle Valve: A valve shaped much like a hinge pin. In an EGR valve, the pintle is attached to a normally closed diaphragm. When ported vacuum is applied, the pintle rises from its seat and allows exhaust gas to be drawn into the engine's intake system.

Piston: A cylindrical part that moves inside a cylinder.

Piston Displacement: The volume displaced by the piston as it moves from the one end of the cylinder to the other.

Piston Pin: The cylindrical or tubular metal pin that attaches the piston to the connecting rod (also called wrist pin).

Piston Ring: One of the rings fitted into grooves in the piston. There are two types, compression rings and oil-control rings.

Piston Ring Land: The portion if the piston that supports the rings.

Piston Rod: *See*: Connecting rod.

Pitman Arm: The part of some steering linkages that joins the linkage to the steering gear sector shaft and transmits movement from the steering gear to the linkage.

Planetary Gear Set: Set of gears that includes a central spur gear, called the sun gear, around which revolves one or more meshing planetary gears. An internal gear, meshed with the planetary gears, completes the set.

Planet Pinions: The pinion gears mounted on the planet carrier assembly in a planetary gear set. The planet pinions rotate on the carrier and revolve around the sun gear.

Planet Carrier Assembly: One of the members of a planetary gear set. The carrier, or bracket, on which the planet pinions are mounted.

Platform: The flat surface, usually of metal, that forms the floor, underbody, and lower side panels of a unit-body car. Frequently, manufacturers build several different car models on the same platforms.

Play: The amount that mechanical parts can move without encountering another part.

Plenum: A chamber that stabilizes air and allows it to rise to a pressure slightly above atmospheric pressure.

Plunging Joint: A CV joint that allows plunging, or in-and-out, movement of a shaft. A plunging joint is always used at the inboard end of a front axle shaft and can be used at the inboard end or the outboard end of a rear axle shaft.

Polar Moment of Inertia: The tendency of a vehicle to maintain the same speed and direction. A high polar moment of inertia provides straight-ahead stability; a low polar moment of inertia provides more control during cornering and other changes in direction.

Polarity: Having poles, such as the north and south poles of a magnet. The poles of a battery or an electrical circuit are its positive and negative terminals.

Pole: The areas of a magnetized body where the lines of magnetic force are concentrated. One end of a magnet.

Poppet Valve: A valve that plugs and unplugs its opening by axial motion.

Ported Vacuum: The low pressure area (vacuum) located just above the throttle butterfly valve in a carburetor or fuel injection throttle body.

Positive: A term designating the point of higher potential when the potential difference between two points is considered.

Positive Crankcase Ventilation (PCV): Crankcase ventilation systems that return blowby gases to the combustion chambers.

Positive-Displacement Pump: A pump that delivers the same volume of fluid with each revolution. The gear and rotor pumps used in automatic transmissions are positive-displacement pumps.

Positive Offset: A characteristic of a wheel in which the face of the wheel disc is in front of, or further outboard than, the rim centerline.

Positive Temperature Coefficient (PTC) Resistor: A thermistor whose resistance decreases as the temperature increases.

Potential: Possible, but not yet in use. The voltage between two points.

Potential Difference: The arithmetical difference between two electrical potentials; same as electromotive force, electrical pressure, or voltage.

Potentiometer: A variable resistor with three terminals. Return signal voltage is taken from a terminal attached to a movable contact that passes over the resistor.

Pour Point Depressants: Additives that lower a fluid's pour point. The result of a lower pour point is that the fluid stays liquid, instead of becoming stiff, at colder temperatures.

Power: The rate at which work is done or force is applied. In mechanics, power is measured as torque times speed and expressed in units such as horsepower or kilowatts.

Power Booster: A vacuum, hydraulic, or electro-hydraulic powered device that multiplies the mechanical pressure applied to the brake pedal by the driver and relays the increased force to the master cylinder.

Power Chamber: The main housing of a vacuum booster that is internally divided in half by a flexible diaphragm. Pressure differentials between the halves move the diaphragm and create application force.

Power Cylinder: The part of a linkage power steering system that provides the hydraulic power assist.

Power Piston: The hydraulically operated piston in a power steering system that helps move the output member of the steering gear when pressure is applied to one side of it.

Power Steering: Vehicle steering by use of hydraulic pressure to multiply the driver's steering effort so as to improve ease of steering.

Power Stroke: The piston stroke from top dead center to bottom dead center during which the fuel-air mixture burns and forces the piston down so the engine produces power.

Power-Take-Off (PTO): An attachment for connecting the engine to power driven auxiliary machinery when its use is required.

Preignition: Premature ignition of the fuel-air mixture being compressed in the cylinder on the compression stroke.

Preload: The resistance one mechanical part exerts against the movement of another part, or the force required to overcome that resistance. Preload is measured in inch-pounds, foot-pounds, or Newton-meters.

Pressure: A measurement of the load placed on an object based on the amount of force applied to a specific area, usually measured in pounds per square inch or kilo-pascal.

Pressure Control Valve: An evaporator control device located between the evaporator and compressor that controls refrigerant flow into the compressor in response to pressure in the evaporator.

Pressure Regulator Valve: The valve that regulates mainline pressure in an automatic transmission by creating a variable restriction.

Pressure Differential: The difference in pressure between two areas. Vacuum boosters use a pressure differential to create brake application force.

Pressure Drop: A reduction of pressure between two points.

Pressure Relief Valve: A valve in any hydraulic component that opens to bleed excess pressure when fluid pressure is excessively high. In a power steering system, a pressure relief valve may be used in the pump and/or the steering gear.

Pressure Switch: An electrical switch on a power steering pump that signals the engine computer when pump pressure is high enough to place an excessive load on the engine. In response, the computer increases the engine idle speed to prevent stalling.

Primary Wiring: The low-voltage wiring in an automobile electrical system.

Primary Windings: The coil winding made of a few turns of a heavy wire, which uses battery current to create a magnetic field.

Program: The instructions a computer uses to do its job. The program consists of mathematical instructions and may include fixed data and require variable data from vehicle sensors.

Programmable Read-Only Memory (PROM): An integrated circuit chip installed in the onboard computer which has been programmed with operating instructions and database information for a particular vehicle.

Propeller Shaft: The driving shaft in the power train that carries engine power from the transmission to the differential.

Proton: Basic particle of matter having a positive electrical charge, normally associated with the nucleus of the atom.

Psi: Pounds per square inch, a measure of force per unit area.

Pull: A driving condition in which the driver must actively steer toward one side in order to keep the vehicle moving straight.

Pull-In Winding: The coil of large-diameter wire in a solenoid that is used to create a magnetic field to pull the solenoid plunger into the coil.

Pulse Width Modulation (PWM): The continuous on/off cycling of a solenoid a fixed number of times per second.

Pump: A device that transfers gas or liquid from one place to another.

Purge Valve: A vacuum-operated valve used to draw fuel vapors from a vapor storage canister.

[Q]

Quick-Take-Up Master Cylinder: A type of dual master cylinder that supplies a large volume of fluid on initial brake application to take up the clearance designed into low-drag brake calipers.

Quick-Take-Up Valve: The part of a quick-take-up master cylinder that controls fluid flow between the reservoir and the primary low-pressure chamber.

[R]

Rack: A gear made of a straight bar with teeth cut into it.

Rack and Pinion Steering Gear: A type of steering gear that uses a pinion as input gear and a rack as output gear.

Radial: Pertaining to the radius of a circle. Radiating from a common center.

Radial Load: A load resting on the circumference of a circular component. Wheel bearings carry a radial load because the weight of the car body rests on them.

Radial Play: Movement at a right angle to the axis of rotation of a shaft, or along the radius of a circle or shaft. Also called side thrust or side play.

Radial Runout: A variation in true rotation of a part that results in an out-of-round condition.

Radiation: The transfer of heat as pure energy, without heating the medium through which it is transferred.

Radiator: A device in the cooling system that removes heat from the coolant passing through it, permitting coolant to remove heat from the engine.

Radiofrequency Interference (RFI): A form of electromagnetic interference created in the ignition secondary circuit which disrupts radio transmission.

Radius: Distance from the center of a circle or from center of rotation.

Radius Arm: A sturdy suspension link that braces a twin I-beam, or sometimes an axle housing, against the frame.

Ram Air Effect: Forced circulation of ventilating air by opening the HVAC system to a high-pressure area caused by the forward motion of the vehicle.

Random-Access Memory (RAM): Computer memory in which information can be written (stored) and read. Whatever is stored in RAM is lost whenever the ignition system is shut off.

Ratchet: A mechanism with interlocking teeth that allow movement in one direction but not the other.

Ravigneaux Gear Set: A compound planetary gear system consisting of two sun gears and two sets of planet pinions that share a common ring gear.

Reaction Member: The member of a planetary gear set that is held in order to produce an output motion. Other members react against the stationary, held member.

Read-Only Memory (ROM): The permanent part of a computer's memory storage function. ROM can be read but not changed and is retained when power to the computer is shut off.

Rear-Wheel Drive (RWD): An automotive drive layout in which the rear wheels provide the power to move the vehicle.

Rebound: Suspension extension, occurring when the compressing force is removed and the suspension springs release their stored energy.

Receiver-Drier: The component between the condenser and expansion valve in which liquid refrigerant may be stored, gaseous refrigerant may change into liquid, and moisture is removed with a desiccant.

Reciprocating Engine: Also called piston engine. An engine in which the pistons move up and down or back and forth, as a result of combustion of an air-fuel mixture in the top of the piston cylinder.

Recirculating Ball Steering Gear: A type of standard steering gear that uses a worm gear as input gear and a sector gear as output gear and links them indirectly with a ball nut and a series of steel balls.

Recombinant: A non-gassing battery design in which the oxygen released by the electrolyte recombines with the negative plates.

Rectifier: An electrical device that changes alternating current to direct current.

Reduction: A chemical process in which oxygen is removed from a compound.

Reference Voltage: The basic operating voltage in an electronic engine control system. The reference voltage is often modified by sensors to provide the computer with information on engine and vehicle operation.

Refrigerant: A chemical compound used as the medium of heat transfer in a refrigeration system. It picks up heat by evaporating and gives up heat by condensing.

Relative Motion: Movement of a conductor in relation to magnetic flux lines or movement of magnetic flux lines in relation to a conductor.

Relative Humidity: The ratio of how much moisture the air actually holds at a particular temperature compared to how much it could hold.

Relay: An electromagnetic switch. A relay uses a small amount of current flow to control the flow of a larger amount of current through a separate circuit.

Reluctance: An object's resistance to magnetic lines of force. Magnetic lines will concentrate in areas of low reluctance, and avoid areas of high reluctance.

Replenishing Port: The opening between the fluid reservoir and low-pressure chamber that keeps the chamber filled with fluid.

Reserve Capacity Rating: A battery rating based on the number of minutes a battery at 80°F can supply 25 amperes, with no battery cell falling below 1.75 volts.

Reservoir: A tank, pan, or other container that stores fluid for use in a hydraulic system.

Residual Pressure: A constant pressure held in a pressurized system when the system is not in use.

Residual Magnetism: The magnetism retained by a material after all magnetizing forces have been removed.

Resilience: The ability of an object to return quickly to its original shape after being twisted or compressed.

Resistance: The opposition offered by a substance or body to the passage through it of an electric current.

Resistor: An electric component that resists current flow, used to lower the voltage applied to another device such as a motor.

Resistor-Type Spark Plug: A plug that has a resistor in the center electrode to reduce the inductive portion of the spark discharge.

Resultant Force: The combined force and oil flow direction produced by rotary flow and vortex flow in a fluid coupling or torque converter.

Resurfacing: The process of using a rotating cutting bit or a abrasive stone to remove minor damage and contaminants from a machined surface.

Reverse Bias: The application of a voltage so that normally no current will flow across the junction of a semiconductor.

Rheostat: A resistor for regulating the current by means of variable resistance.

Rich Mixture: Fuel-air mixture with a high proportion of fuel.

Rim: That part of a vehicle wheel on which the tire is mounted.

Ring Gear: A gear in the form of a ring, such as the ring gear on a flywheel or differential.

Road Draft Tube: The earliest type of crankcase ventilation; it vented blowby gases to the atmosphere.

Rock Position: The piston and connecting rod position (top or bottom dead center) at which the crank can rock -or rotate a few degrees without appreciable movement of the piston.

Rod: *See*: Connecting rod.

Rod Cap: The lower detachable part of the connecting rod which can be taken off by removing bolts or nuts so that the rod can be detached from the crankshaft.

Roll: Sideways tilting of the car body, effectively rotating the body around the longitudinal axis, that occurs when G-force pushes the center of gravity outward.

Roll Axis: Another name for the longitudinal axis.

Roll Center: A point located along the longitudinal axis around which a section of the vehicle rotates during cornering.

Roller Bearing: A type of bearing with rollers positioned between two races.

Roller Pump: A pump that uses a rotor and rollers inside an elliptic cam ring to produce fluid flow. The action of the rollers creates fluid chambers of varying volumes.

Rotary Flow: The oil flow path, in a fluid coupling or torque converter, that is in the same circular direction as the rotation of the impeller.

Rotary Control Valve: A type of power steering control valve that operates by one part of it rotating within the other. Also called a torsion bar control valve.

Rotational Motion: Movement that occurs when a shaft turns (rotates) on its axis. A dynamic seal is required to contain fluids where rotational motion is present.

Rotor: A part that revolves in a stationary part.

Rotor Pump: *See*: Rotary pump

Rpm: Revolutions per minute, a measure of rotational speed.

Runners: The passages or branches of an intake manifold that connect the manifold's plenum chamber to the engine's inlet ports.

Runout: Side-to-side deviation in the movement of a spinning rotor.

Rzeppa Joint: A fixed, ball-and-cage CV joint.

[S]

SAE: Society of Automotive Engineers.

SAE Horsepower: A measurement of engine power based upon number of cylinders and cylinder diameter.

Saturated: A condition in which air holds as much water vapor as possible without forming water droplets, at a given temperature and pressure.

Schematic Diagram: A drawing of a circuit or any part of a circuit that shows how it works.

Scoring: Extreme wear on a bearing or friction surface. Scoring is often caused by metal-to-metal contact, or foreign materials between the two surfaces.

Scrub Radius: The distance between the centerline of the tire contact patch and the point where a line drawn through the steering axis intersects the road.

Sealed-Beam: A type of headlight in which the reflector and lens are sealed together to enclose and protect the filaments.

Sealing Beads: On a metal fitting, a ridge around the diameter of the fitting. This is inserted into flexible tubing to create a leak-tight connection.

Select-Low Principle: The controlling principle for rear-wheel anti-lock systems which states that pressure to both wheels shall be limited to the level required by the wheel with the least traction.

Sector Gear: A gear with teeth cut along only a section of its circumference.

Self-Energizing Action: A characteristic of drum brakes in which the rotation of the drum increases the application force of a brake shoe by wedging it tighter against the drum.

Self-Induced Voltage: Voltage created in a conductor by the magnetic lines of a current through that same conductor.

Semiconductor: A material that is neither a good conductor nor a good insulator. Semiconductors are the raw material used to make solid-state devices such as diodes and transistors. Silicon and germanium are common semiconductors.

Semi-Elliptical Leaf Spring: A leaf spring installed so that, viewed from the side, it looks like half an ellipse.

Semi-Floating Axle: A solid, drive axle in which the wheel bearings mount onto the axle shaft or fit inside the axle housing, the brake drum mounts onto the end of the axle shaft, and the wheel mounts onto the brake drum.

Semi-Independent Suspension: A suspension system in which a cross-beam and a pair of trailing arms indirectly link the wheels. Semi-independent suspensions are used at the rear of FWD cars.

Semi-Trailing Arm: A control arm that runs at an angle to the car centerline and extends back from a crossmember to the axle housing or a knuckle.

Sensible Heat: Heat that causes a temperature change to a material when absorbed or given off, that does not change the of state of the material.

Sensor: A device which provides input data in the form of voltage signals to a computer.

Separator: In the storage battery, the wood, rubber, or glass mat strip used as insulator to hold the battery plates apart.

Series: A method of connecting several parts in a row so that one feeds into the next.

Series Circuit: An electrical circuit in which electricity has one path that it can follow if the circuit is complete.

Series Contacts: The normally closed set of contacts in a double-contact regulator. When they open, field current must flow through a resistor.

Series Motor: A motor that has only one path for current flow through the field and armature windings. Commonly used for starter motors.

Series-Parallel Circuit: A circuit that has some parts in series with the voltage source and some parts in parallel with each other and with the voltage source.

Serpentine Belt: One drive belt that transmits power to all engine-driven accessories. Also called a "V-ribbed, or poly-V belt".

Service Brakes: The primary vehicle brake system that is controlled by the brake pedal, operates the friction assemblies at all four wheels, and slows or stops the car in normal driving.

Servo: A hydraulic piston and cylinder assembly that controls the application and release of a reaction member.

Servo Brake: A drum brake that uses the stopping power of one shoe (primary) to help increase the application force of the other shoe (secondary).

Servomotor: An electric motor that is part of a feedback system used for automatic control of a mechanical device, such as in a temperature control system.

Setback: A condition in which one wheel of an axle is located further back than the opposite wheel.

Shackle: A swinging support that permits a leaf spring to vary in length as it is deflected.

Shift Program: The set of instructions that the computer in an electronic shift control system uses to decide when to upshift and downshift the transmission. Many systems offer a choice of two or more shift programs that provide different performance characteristics.

Shift Valve: A spool valve acted on by throttle pressure and governor pressure to time transmission shifts. Also called a "snap" valve or a timing valve.

Shim: A strip of copper or similar material, used under a part to adjust clearance.

Shimmy: Abnormal sideways vibration, particularly of the front wheels.

Shock Absorber: A cushioning device that provides friction to damp the oscillation of the suspension spring.

Shock Absorber Ratio: The proportion of shock absorber resistance during extension to resistance during compression.

Short Circuit: In electrical circuits, an abnormal connection that permits current to take a short path or circuit, thus bypassing important parts of the normal circuit.

Shorting Contacts: The normally open set of contacts in a double-contact regulator. When closed, they short-circuit the field to ground.

Shroud: A hood placed around an assembly to improve efficiency and protect components.

Shunt: An electrical connection or branch circuit in parallel with another branch circuit or connection.

Simpson Gear Set: A compound planetary gear system consisting of two ring gears and two planet carrier assemblies that share a common sun gear.

Sine Wave Voltage: The constant change, first to a positive peak and then to a negative peak, of an induced alternating voltage in a conductor.

Single-Phase Current: Alternating current caused by a single-phase voltage.

Single-Phase Voltage: The sine wave voltage induced within one conductor by one revolution of an alternator rotor.

Sintered: Welded together without using heat to form a porous material, such as the metal disc used in some vacuum delay valves.

Siphoning: The flowing of a liquid as a result of a pressure differential, without the aid of a mechanical pump.

Sliding Caliper: A caliper whose body moves on the anchor plate and makes metal-to-metal contact with it. Sliding caliper bodies move on machined ways and are retained by special keys.

Slip Yoke: Two pieces of a shaft, splined together, that can slide axially to allow variation in shaft length.

Slip Angle: The angle between the direction the tire is pointed and the direction that it actually moves.

Slipper Pump: A pump that uses a rotor and spring-loaded slippers inside an elliptic cam ring to produce fluid flow. The action of the slippers creates fluid chambers of varying volumes.

Solenoid: An electromagnetic actuator consisting of a moveable iron core or shuttle that slides into a cylindrical coil when current is applied, and is forced back out by a spring when current is cut off. Typically, a solenoid is used to physically move a valve or door attached to the core.

Solenoid Ball Valve: An assembly consisting of a ball and seat check valve controlled by an electrical solenoid. When the solenoid is not energized, flow is allowed through the check valve. When the solenoid is energized, flow through the check valve is blocked.

Solid Axle: A physical link between two wheels that permits vertical movement of one wheel to affect the other. A solid axle in an automobile may be a beam or a differential and axle shafts.

Solid-State: A method of controlling electrical current flow, in which the parts are primarily made of semiconductor materials.

Solvent: A liquid capable of dissolving another substance.

South Pole: The pole of the magnet into which it is assumed the magnetic lines of force pass.

Spark Plug: The assembly that includes a pair of electrodes which has the purpose of providing a spark gap in the engine cylinder to ignite the fuel mixture.

Spark Voltage: The inductive portion of a spark that maintains the spark in the air gap between a spark plug's electrodes. Usually about one-quarter of the firing voltage level.

Specific Gravity: The ratio of the weight of a substance to weight of an equal volume of chemically pure water at 39.2\ F.

Specific Heat: The number of calories needed to raise the temperature of one gram of a substance by one degree Celsius.

Speed: Rate of motion.

Speed Differential: The difference in speed between two objects.

Speedometer: An indicating device, usually connected to the transmission, that indicates the speed of motion of the vehicle.

Spider: In planetary gear sets, the frame, or part, on which the planetary gears are mounted.

Spiral Bevel Gear: A bevel gear having curved teeth.

Spline: Slots or grooves cut in a shaft or bore; a splined shaft onto which a hub, wheel, etc., with matching splines in its bore is assembled so the two must engage and turn together.

Spool Valve: A sliding valve that uses lands and valleys machined on its surface to control the flow of hydraulic pressure through ports in its bore.

Sprag Unit: A form of overrunning clutch; power can be transmitted through it in one direction but not in the other.

Spring: A cushioning device that compresses to absorb the force of movement between two parts and then returns to its original shape. The four common suspension spring types are: leaf springs, coil springs, torsion bars, and air springs.

Spring Frequency: The rate at which a spring oscillates after it is released from compression or extension.

Spring Rate: The strength or stiffness of a spring, in terms of how much weight it takes to compress the spring a certain amount. Also called "deflection rate".

Sprung Weight: Out of the total weight of an automobile, the weight that the suspension springs bear.

Spur Gear: A gear with radial teeth parallel to the axis.

Squat: Rearward tilting of the car body caused by acceleration forces pushing down on the rear of the car.

Stall Speed: The maximum possible engine and torque converter impeller speed, measured in rpm, with the turbine held stationary and the engine throttle wide open.

Starter: In the electrical system, the motor that cranks the engine to get it started.

Starting Bypass: A parallel circuit branch that bypasses the ballast resistor during engine cranking.

Starting Safety Switch: A neutral start switch. It keeps the starting system from operating when a car's transmission is in gear.

Static Electricity: Accumulated electrical charges, usually considered to be those produced by friction.

Static Friction: The amount of friction that exists between two surfaces at rest.

Static Load: The load that is continually applied to a spring installed in a suspension.

Static Seal: A seal that prevents fluid passage between two parts that are in fixed positions relative to one another.

Static Weight Distribution: The proportion of total vehicle weight resting on each tire when the vehicle is at rest.

Steering Arm: An arm, extending forward or back from the steering knuckle, that links the wheel to the steering linkage.

Steering Axis: The axis on which the steering knuckle pivots. The steering axis runs through the kingpin, through the centers of the upper and lower ball joints, or through the top pivoting point of the strut and the center of the lower ball joint.

Steering Axis Inclination (SAI): The angle between the steering axis and a line perpendicular to a level surface, viewed from the front. More simply, steering axis inclination is the inward or outward tilt of the steering axis.

Steering Column: The part of the steering system that links the steering wheel to the steering gear, consisting of the steering shaft, column jacket, and column cover, and which houses some other parts. U.S. Federal law requires that the steering column be collapsible.

Steering Damper: A shock absorber that damps steering linkage movement to reduce kickback and shimmy.

Steering Gear: That part of the steering system, located at the lower end of the steering shaft, which carries the rotary motion of the steering wheel to the vehicle wheels for steering.

Steering Geometry: A method of measuring wheel alignment using angles measured in degrees of a circle.

Steering Knuckle: A knuckle that includes a steering arm to link the wheel to the steering linkage.

Steering Limit Valve: A type of valve, used in some power steering gears, that drains some pressure away from the power piston at the extremes of piston movement to reduce power assist as the steering wheel approaches complete stop.

Steering Linkage: Linkage between steering gear and vehicle wheels.

Steering Ratio: The number of degrees of rotation a steering wheel must move in order to move the wheels one degree. High ratios are slower ratios, and low ratios are faster.

Stepper Motor: A direct current motor that moves in incremental steps from deenergized to fully energized.

Stoichiometric Ratio: The air-fuel ratio of approximately 14.7 that provides the most complete combustion and combination of oxygen and hydrocarbon molecules.

Storage Battery: A lead-acid electrochemical device that changes chemical energy into electric energy. The action is reversible; electric energy supplied to the battery stores chemical energy.

Stratified Charge Engine: An engine that uses 2-stage combustion: first is combustion of a rich air-fuel mixture in a precombustion chamber, then combustion of a lean air-fuel mixture occurs in the main combustion chamber.

Stress Raiser: A flaw in the metal of a part that creates extra stress on the metal, causing it to bend or distort more easily at that point.

Stroke: One complete top-to-bottom or bottom-to-top movement of an engine piston.

Strut Rod: A suspension link that braces a straight lower control arm against the frame.

Strut Suspension: A suspension system that uses at each wheel: a strut whose base rigidly mounts to the knuckle, a lower control arm or arms, and either a coil spring integral to the strut or a separate spring.

Stub Axle: A wheel spindle extending from a knuckle or suspension arm to support one wheel. A stub axle is used at each wheel of a non-drive axle with independent or semi-independent suspension.

Sub-Frame: A small frame, built separately from the platform, that is installed into a unit-body car to support the engine or the rear differential.

Substrate: The layer, or honeycomb, of aluminum oxide upon which the catalyst (platinum or palladium) in a catalytic converter is deposited.

Sulfation: The crystallization of lead sulfate on the plates of a constantly discharged battery.

Sulfur Oxides: Chemical compounds given off by processing and burning gasoline and other fossil fuels. As they decompose, they combine with water to form sulfuric acid.

Sump: The oil pan, or reservoir, that contains a supply of fluid for the transmission hydraulic system.

Sun Gear: The central gear of a planetary gear set around which the other gears rotate.

Supercharger: A pump used in connection with engine fuel-air system to supply more air at greater pressure to the-engine, thereby increasing volumetric efficiency.

Suppression: In the electrical system, the elimination of stray electromagnetic waves so that they cannot be detected by the radio and cause interference.

Suspension: The automotive system that supports the body and powertrain, and transfers vehicle weight to the wheels and tires.

Swaging: A method of locking a part in place by permanently deforming a portion of it or the surrounding material.

Swashplate: Axial plate; an offset plate attached to the drive shaft of a piston compressor to drive the pistons.

Swaybar: A connecting bar placed between wheel supports, parallel to the axles, which prevents excessive vehicle roll or sway on turns, also called anti-roll bar.

Swept Area: The area of a brake drum or rotor that contacts the brake linings.

Switch: A device within an electrical circuit that can stop current flow by moving a pair of contacts away from each other, or provide a path for current flow by placing the contacts so they touch each other. When the contacts do not touch, the switch is said to be "open"; when they do touch, the switch is said to be "closed".

Symmetrical: The same on both sides of center. In a symmetrical high-beam headlamp, the light beam is spread the same distance to both sides of center.

Synchromesh: A name designating a certain type of transmission which has the virtue of permitting gear-ratio shifts without gear clashing.

Synchronize: To make two or more events or operations occur at the same time or speed.

[T]

Tachometer: A device for measuring revolutions per minute.

Tandem Axles: Two axles, one placed directly in front of the other.

Tandem Booster: A vacuum power booster that uses two diaphragms to increase brake application force. Tandem boosters are smaller in diameter than single-diaphragm boosters.

Tangential Spring End: The end of a coil spring that is cut off mid-coil and left in the coil shape.

Taper: To make gradually smaller toward one end; a gradual reduction in size in a given direction.

Television-Radio-Suppression (TVRS) Cables: High-resistance, carbon-conductor ignition cables that suppress RFI.

Temperature: Heat intensity, measured by a thermometer.

Temperature Gauge: An indicating device in the cooling system that indicates the temperature of the coolant and gives warning if excessive engine temperatures develop.

Temperature Gradient: A situation in which an area of high temperature is connected to an area of low temperature, causing heat to flow from the hot to the cold area.

Tension: A stress caused by a pulling force.

Tension Rod: A strut rod that runs back from the frame to the lower control arm. Also called a "trailing strut rod".

Tension-Loaded Ball Joint: A load-carrying suspension ball joint in which the force exerted by the arm and the knuckle pulling away from each other seats the ball in the socket.

Tetraethyl Lead: A gasoline additive used to help prevent detonation.

Thermal Efficiency: Ratio between the power output and the energy in the fuel burned to produce the output.

Thermal Limiter: A special circuit breaker in a resistor block that opens the circuit if the resistor block fails and excessive current begins to flow through it.

Thermistor (Thermal Resistor): A resistor specially constructed so that its resistance decreases as its temperature increases.

Thermodynamics: The area of the physical sciences that deals with the interactions of heat energy and mechanical energy.

Thermoelectricity: Voltage resulting from an unequal transfer of electrons from one metal to another, when one of the metals is heated.

Thermostatic Expansion Valve: An air conditioning expansion device that removes pressure from the refrigerant as it flows into the evaporator and controls the flow rate in relation to evaporator temperature.

Thermostatic: Referring to a device that automatically responds to temperature changes in order to activate a switch.

Three-Phase Current: Three overlapping, evenly spaced, single-phase currents that make up the total a.c. output of an alternator.

Throttle: A mechanism in the fuel system that permits the driver to vary the amount of fuel-air mixture entering the engine and thus control the engine speed.

Throttle Body Injection (TBI): A fuel injection system in which one or two injectors are installed in a carburetor-like throttle body mounted on a conventional intake manifold. Fuel is sprayed at a constant pressure above the throttle plate to mix with the incoming air charge.

Throttle Pressure: The automatic transmission hydraulic pressure that is directly related to engine load. Throttle pressure increases with throttle opening and engine torque output, and is one of the principle pressures used to control shift points.

Throttle Valve: The valve that regulates throttle pressure based on throttle butterfly opening or intake manifold vacuum.

Thrust: A force tending to push a body out of alignment. A force exerted endwise through a member upon another member.

Thrust Alignment: A wheel alignment procedure, performed on vehicles in which a thrust angle cannot be eliminated, in which the front wheels are aligned to the thrust line instead of the vehicle centerline.

Thrust Angle: The angle between the thrust line and the geometric centerline of a vehicle.

Thrust Line: An imaginary line, running forward from the center of the rear axle, that bisects rear toe.

Thrust Load: A load transferred along the length of a shaft. Wheel bearings carry a radial load during cornering, as centrifugal force applies an outward load along the axle shaft or spindle.

Thyristor: A silicon-controlled rectifier (SCR) that normally blocks all current flow. A slight voltage applied to one layer of its semiconductor structure will allow current flow in one direction while blocking current flow in the other direction.

Tie Rods: The parts of a steering linkage that transmit movement to the steering arms. Most tie rods consist of an inner tie rod end and an outer tie rod end, and sometimes an adjusting sleeve or rod.

Timing: Refers to ignition or valve timing and pertains to the relation between the actions of the ignition or valve mechanism and piston position in the cylinder.

Tire: The rubber and fabric part that is assembled on the wheel rim and filled with compressed air (pneumatic-type).

Tire Contact Patch: The area of tire rubber that actually touches the road at any one time. Also called the tire footprint.

Tire Slip: The difference between vehicle speed and the speed at which the tire tread moves along the pavement. Tire slip is commonly expressed as a percentage.

Toe: The angle between the direction a wheel is aimed and a line parallel to the centerline of the car. When measured linearly, toe is the distance between the leading edges of the tires subtracted from the distance between the trailing edges.

Toe Change: A change in the direction a tire is aimed during suspension compression or extension. Tie rod height and length affect toe change, which is essentially the same condition as bump steer.

Toe-in: The amount in inches that the front of the front wheels point inward.

Toe-Out: A description of the toe angle when the leading edges of the tires point away from each other. Also called "negative toe".

Toe-Out on Turns: The tendency during turns for the outside wheel to travel in a larger arc than the inside wheel. Toe-out on turns is a result of the Ackermann angle.

Tolerance: The acceptable clearance between any two mechanical parts.

Top Dead Center (TDC): The exact top of a piston's stroke. Also a specification used when tuning an engine.

Torque: A twisting or turning effort. Torque is the product of force times the distance from the center of rotation at which it is exerted.

Torque Arm: A large suspension arm, used with a RWD powertrain, that runs alongside the driveshaft and bolts to the differential at one end and the transmission at the other. A torque arm distributes the force of axle windup along its length.

Torque Converter: A type of fluid coupling used to connect the engine crankshaft to the automatic transmission input shaft. Torque converters multiply the available engine torque under certain operating conditions.

Torque Curve: A graphic depiction of the amount of torque available at different engine speeds.

Torque Rod: Arm or rod used to insure accurate alignment of an axle with the frame and to relieve springs of driving and braking stresses.

Torque Steer: A driving condition in which the car steers to one side during hard acceleration from high speed and in the opposite direction during sudden deceleration. Front-wheel-drive vehicles with unequal-length axle shafts are prone to torque steer.

Torque-Tube Drive: The type of rear-end arrangement which includes a hollow tube that encloses the propeller shaft and also takes up stresses produced by braking and driving.

Torque Wrench: A special wrench that indicates the amount of torque in being applied to a bolt or nut.

Torsion: Twisting action, particularly as applied to turning one end of a rod while the other end is kept from turning.

Torsional Vibration: Vibration in a rotary direction; a portion of a rotating shaft that repeatedly moves ahead, or lags behind; the remainder of the shaft is exhibiting torsional vibration.

Torus: Rotating member of fluid coupling.

Total Ignition Advance: The sum of centrifugal advance, vacuum advance, and initial timing; expressed in crankshaft degrees.

Track Rod: Another name for a Panhard rod.

Track Width: The distance between the centers of the contact patches of same-axle tires.

Traction: The amount of grip between the tire tread and the road surface. Higher traction allows greater braking and cornering force to be generated.

Tractive Effort: The pushing effort the driving wheels can make against the ground, which is the same as the forward thrust or push of the axles against the vehicle.

Trailing Arm: A control arm that runs parallel to the vehicle centerline and extends back from a crossmember to the axle housing or a knuckle.

Transducer: A device to convert (transduce) one form of energy to another. A sensor is such a device, converting light or other energy into a voltage signal.

Transfer Case: The auxiliary assembly for applying power to both forward and rear propeller shafts, and to front wheels as well as rear wheels.

Transistor: An electronic device, made of semiconductor material, that controls electrical current flow.

Transmission: The device in the power train that provides different gear ratios between the engine and driving wheels, as well as reverse.

Transmission Band: A flexible steel band lined with friction material that is clamped around a circular drum to hold it from turning.

Tread: The design on the road-contacting surface of a tire which provides improved frictional contact.

Trunnion: Either of two opposite pivots or cylindrical projections from the sides of a part assembly, supported by bearings, to provide a means of swiveling or turning the part or assembly.

Turbine: A mechanism containing a rotor with curved blades; the rotor is driven by the impact of a liquid or gas against the curved blades.

Turbo Lag: The time interval required for a turbocharger to overcome inertia and spin up to speed.

Turbocharger: A supercharging device that uses exhaust gases to turn a turbine that forces extra air-fuel mixture into the cylinders.

Turning Radius: The distance from the turning center to the outside wheels during cornering. Sometimes this term is used to refer to toe-out on turns, since that angle determines the turning radius.

Turning Center: The imaginary point around which a vehicle turns during cornering.

Two-Way Check Valve: A type of switching valve that controls fluid flow in two separate hydraulic circuits, and allows them to share a single fluid passage.

[U]

Uncompressed Length: The length or height of a spring with no load applied to it. Also called "free length".

Understeer: A driving condition, resulting from greater slip angles at the front tires than the rear, in which the vehicle turns less sharply than steering system input demands.

Unit-Body Construction: A method of building a car frame and body so that the frame is integral to the body and consists of reinforced body panels.

Universal Joint (U-Joint): A shaft coupling, consisting of two yokes with a steel crosspiece joining them together, that allows changes in the angle between two rotating shafts. Also called a "Cardan joint".

Unsprung Weight: The weight of any suspension and brake components not supported by the vehicle's springs. High unsprung weight makes suspension movement more difficult to control.

Upper Control Arm: In an A-arm suspension, the higher and shorter of the control arms linking the knuckle to the frame.

[V]

V-belt: A drive belt with a V-shaped cross section that transmits power to one or more engine-driven accessories.

Vacuum: A pressure less than atmospheric pressure.

Vacuum Advance: The use of engine vacuum to advance ignition spark timing by moving the distributor breaker plate.

Vacuum Modulator: A housing divided into two chambers by a flexible diaphragm. One chamber is open to atmospheric pressure, the other is connected to intake manifold vacuum and contains a spring. Changes in manifold vacuum cause movement of the diaphragm against spring tension. In automatic transmissions, this movement is often used to control a throttle valve.

Vacuum Pump: A mechanically or electrically driven pump that provides a source of vacuum. Vacuum pumps are commonly used on diesel engines which have limited manifold vacuum.

Vacuum Servo: A flexible diaphragm with a linkage attached to it installed in a sealed housing. When vacuum is applied to one side of the diaphragm, atmospheric pressure on the other side moves the diaphragm and linkage to perform work.

Vacuum Motor: An actuator that provides mechanical control of a component by using vacuum to create movement of a rod, lever, or crank.

Vacuum Switch: In the starting system, an electric switch that is actuated by vacuum to open the starting system control circuit as the engine starts, producing a vacuum in the intake manifold.

Valve: A mechanism that can be opened or closed to allow or stop the flow of a liquid, gas, or vapor from one place to another.

Valve Body: The casting that contains most of the valves in a transmission hydraulic system. The valve body also has passages for the flow of hydraulic fluid.

Valve Seat: The surface, normally curved, against which the valve operating face comes to rest, to provide a seal against leakage of liquid, gas, or vapor.

Valve Seat Insert: Metal ring inserted into valve seat; made of special metal that can withstand operating temperature satisfactorily.

Valve Spring: The compression-type spring that closes the valve when the valve-operating cam assumes a closed-valve position.

Valve Lifter: The component that rides on the valve-operating cam and transmits motion from the cam to the valve stem or push rod.

Valve Timing: A method of coordinating camshaft rotation and crankshaft rotation so that the valves open and close at the right times during each of the piston strokes.

Valve Train: All of the moving parts that work in conjunction with each other to operate the valves of an engine.

Vane Pump: A pump that uses a slotted rotor and sliding vanes to produce oil flow.

Vapor Lock: A condition in which gasoline has vaporized in the fuel line, so that fuel delivery to the carburetor is blocked or retarded.

Variable-Displacement Pump: A pump whose output volume per revolution can be varied to increase or decrease fluid delivery. The vane pumps used in automatic transmissions are variable-displacement pumps.

Variable-Rate Spring: A spring that compresses more slowly as more weight is applied to it.

Variable Steering Ratio: A steering ratio that is higher, or slower, during the first degrees of steering wheel movement and decreases, or becomes faster, the further the steering wheel is turned.

Varnish: An undesirable deposit, usually on the engine pistons, formed by oxidation of fuel and of motor oil.

Velocity: The rate of motion or speed at any instant, usually measured in miles-per-hour or feet-per-second or minute.

Venturi: A restriction in an airflow, such as in a carburetor, that increases the airflow speed and creates a reduction in pressure.

Vertical Axis: An imaginary line, running from top-to-bottom of a vehicle and intersecting the center of gravity, around which the car body rotates (yaws) after the car changes direction.

Vibration: An unceasing back and forth movement over the same path; often with reference to the rapid succession of motions of parts of an elastic body.

Viscosity: The tendency of a liquid such as oil to resist flowing.

Volatility: The ease with which a liquid turns to a gas or vapor.

Volt: The unit for measuring the amount of electrical force.

Voltage: The electromotive force that causes current flow. The potential difference in electrical force between two points when one is negatively charged and the other is positively charged.

Voltage Decay: The rapid oscillation and dissipation of secondary voltage after the spark in a spark plug air gap has stopped.

Voltage Reserve: The amount of coil voltage available in excess of the voltage required to fire the spark plugs.

Voltage Regulator: A device used in connection with the generator to keep the voltage constant and to prevent it from exceeding a predetermined maximum.

Voltmeter: A meter used to measure electromotive force in volts.

Volumetric Efficiency: Ratio between the amount of fuel-air mixture that actually enters an engine cylinder and the amount that could enter under ideal conditions.

Volute Springs: Helical coil springs made from flat steel tapered both in width and thickness.

Vortex Flow: The oil flow path, in a fluid coupling or torque converter, that is at a right angle to the rotation of the impeller and to rotary flow.

[W]

Wander: To ramble or move without control from a fixed course, as the front wheels of a vehicle.

Wastegate: A diaphragm-actuated bypass valve used to limit turbocharger boost pressure by limiting the speed of the exhaust turbine.

Water Jacket: The passages in the engine cylinder head and block that allow coolant to circulate throughout the engine.

Water Injection: A method of lowering the air-fuel mixture temperature by injecting a fine spray of water which evaporates as it cools the intake charge.

Water Pump: In the cooling system, the pump that circulates coolant between the engine water jackets and the radiator.

Watt: The unit of measurement for electric power. One way to measure the rate of doing work. Watts equals volts times amperes.

Ways: Special sliding surfaces machined into the anchor plate and caliper body where these parts of a sliding caliper make contact and move against one another.

Weight Bias: An element of vehicle design that results in either the front or rear suspension having to support more than half of the vehicle's weight. Most cars have a forward weight bias.

Weight Transfer: The shift of weight toward the front of a vehicle that occurs when the brakes are applied while driving forward.

Wheel Alignment: The positioning of a vehicle's wheels in relation to each other and to the vehicle structure.

Wheelbase: The distance from the center of the front wheels to the center of the rear wheels.

Wheel Cylinder: The device in a drum brake that converts hydraulic pressure back into the mechanical force used to apply the brake shoes against the drum.

Wheel Offset: The distance between the rim centerline and the mounting plane of the wheel.

Wiring Harness: A bundle of wires enclosed in a plastic cover and routed to various areas of the vehicle. Most harnesses end in plug-in connectors. Harnesses are also called looms.

Wobble Plate: A variable-angle swashplate used in a variable-displacement compressor.

Wobble: A ride problem, resulting from lateral runout, that occurs when the top of a rolling tire constantly moves in and out.

Work: The transfer of energy from one system to another, particularly through the application of force.

Worm Gear: A gear that is shaped like a shaft with gear teeth cut as a continuous spiral around its outer surface. A worm gear changes the axis of rotation when it turns another gear.

[X,Y,Z]

Y-Type: An alternator stator design in which one end of each of the three windings in a 3-phase alternator is connected at a neutral junction. This design is used in alternators that require high voltage at low alternator speed.

Yaw: Swaying movement of the car body, effectively rotating the body around the vertical axis, that occurs when road forces push the front or the rear of the car to one side.

Zener Diode: A junction of semiconductor materials that has been heavily doped so that the junction will allow reverse current flow without damage at any voltage above a specific value.